Praise for *Live Life i̶* T0267807

"There's another habit of highly effective people: they envision the future in an upward trajectory. This wonderful last gift from Stephen Covey, made with his daughter Cynthia, will inspire you to dream bigger and bolder."

—Adam Grant, #1 *New York Times* bestselling author of *Think Again* and host of the TED podcast *WorkLife*

"Stephen Covey lived his life in crescendo and constantly inspired others to do the same. He helped change the trajectory of my football career and my life, when by happenstance we sat together on a plane. On that flight, I was inspired and rejuvenated. I had been in the presence of greatness as he masterfully shared principles in this book, which revealed the tremendous opportunities before me. His legacy shines on through this book and the lives of his family."

—Steve Young, NFL Hall of Fame quarterback and Chairman & cofounder, HGGC

"The dictum that I promote is 'Making money may be happiness but making other people happy is super happiness.' Simply put, happiness comes from many sources, not just from financial success. It is when we share with and serve those in need that we experience our truest joy at a much deeper and fulfilling level. *Live Life in Crescendo* teaches us how to achieve a life of purpose, meaning, and contribution, by giving much, with full purpose of heart, for the greater good. Thank you, Stephen and Cynthia, for living life in crescendo and for this beautiful, inspiring, and important work."

—Professor Muhammad Yunus, Nobel Peace Prize Laureate 2006 and founder of Grameen Bank

"Stephen Covey, in his final leadership book, *Live Life in Crescendo*, completed by his daughter Cynthia, proposes a paradigm shift around retirement, suggesting that although we may retire from a job or career, we don't ever have to retire from making meaningful contributions to those around us. With new insights and inspiring personal stories, the book helps us focus on leading a life of service with the same passion we brought to building successful careers."

—Arianna Huffington, founder & CEO of Thrive

"Retiring is not an end, but truly a beginning. We have more time to build even stronger relationships and to contribute and give back to our greater community. This inspiring, beautiful book provides us with examples, stories, and the wisdom needed to create lasting legacies that will live on far beyond our years. Thank you, Stephen and Cynthia, for *Live Life in Crescendo*, this wonderful book, which is a tribute to Stephen R. Covey and his legacy."

—Indra Nooyi, former CEO and Chairman of the Board of Pepsi-Co and author of the *New York Times* bestseller *My Life in Full*

"I love *Live Life in Crescendo*. It will help all those looking to improve their lives and is filled with fun, wise, and great stories. It was like having Dr. Covey with me once again. *The 7 Habits of Highly Effective People* was important to me as a young physician, but I found his new book, written with his daughter Cynthia, even more important, guiding us, no matter what our age, to go further than we ever thought possible."

—Daniel G. Amen, MD, CEO and founder of Amen Clinics and author of *You, Happier* and *The End of Mental Illness*

"Whether you've enjoyed success, encountered adversity, or feel stagnation, our best times can still lie ahead. With Stephen Covey's signature wisdom and warmth, this delightfully hopeful book shows how life can truly keep getting better and better."

—Daniel H. Pink, #1 *New York Times* bestselling author of *The Power of Regret*, *When*, and *Drive*

"It's such a temptation to believe that we have done our best work. That we have peaked. That we are in decline. That our glory days are behind us. So this book from Stephen Covey and Cynthia Covey Haller is a breath of fresh air. It inverts the situation entirely and invites us to believe that our greatest contribution is always ahead of us. Indeed, this book being published at all, ten years after Stephen's passing, illustrates its very premise. Cynthia has captured the spirit of her father's work so faithfully and added her essential voice, too. Reading this has been a huge blessing to me, and it will be to you as well. You'll never think of your life the same way again."

—Greg McKeown, *New York Times* bestselling author of *Essentialism* and *Effortless*

"Like most everyone in our generation, we have made the lovely transition from parenting to grandparenting, and our writing has shifted accordingly. Just when we were trying to come up with a book about the joy of the fourth quarter of life, we found that our old, dear friend Stephen had already written it, or most of it, before he died. His remarkable eldest daughter, Cynthia, who had worked on it with him from the start, picked up the baton and finished it. The result is *Live Life in Crescendo*, and it is fabulous!"

—Richard and Linda Eyre, *New York Times* #1 bestselling authors of *Teaching Your Children Values*, *Grandmothering*, and *Being a Proactive Grandfather*

"Stephen R. Covey's books have shaped my life and leadership. This book, *Live Life in Crescendo: Your Most Important Work Is Always Ahead of You*, based on his own mission statement, is an invitation to live life fully and engage at every intersection. For everyone who sees life as an opportunity for advancing growth and impact, this is a must-read from one of the best. In it you will find proof that every person can make an incredible contribution with their life."

—Celeste Mergens, founder of the award-winning global nonprofit Days for Girls

"Cynthia Covey Haller builds on the work of the late, great Stephen Covey in this inspirational book. *Live Life in Crescendo* will give everyone who reads it inspiration and hope to live a life that is productive and meaningful, from beginning to end.

—Arthur C. Brooks, professor, Harvard Kennedy School and Harvard Business School, and #1 *New York Times* bestselling author of *From Strength to Strength*

"*Live Life in Crescendo* is a great reminder that every single one of us has a story, experiences heartache and trauma, but ultimately, we have the power inside us to rise up and move forward and not only survive what often feels the impossible but go on to be happy again. It is encouraging and lovingly written. I am honored to have my story included."

—Elizabeth Smart, author of the *New York Times* bestselling *My Story* and of *Where There's Hope*

"Cynthia Covey Haller, as her father's faithful translator, has so beautifully captured what it truly means to *Live Life in Crescendo*. I hear Dr. Covey's voice as I turn each page. This book inspires us all to seize every moment by living a life of purpose, service, love, and contribution, while knowing that our most important work is always ahead of us."

—Muriel Summers, former principal of A.B. Combs Leadership Magnet Elementary, the first Leader in Me School in the world and the only magnet school to have been twice honored as the #1 Magnet School in America

Also by Stephen R. Covey

The Leader in Me

The 3rd Alternative

The 8th Habit

Living the 7 Habits

The 7 Habits of Highly Effective Families

First Things First

Principle-Centered Leadership

The 7 Habits of Highly Effective People Personal Workbook

Primary Greatness

Live Life in Crescendo

Also from FranklinCovey Co.

The 7 Habits of Highly Effective Teens

The 7 Habits of Highly Effective Teens Workbook

The 7 Habits of Happy Kids

The 7 Habits of Highly Effective College Students
(College Textbook)

*The 6 Most Important Decisions You'll Ever Make:
A Guide for Teens*

The 4 Disciplines of Execution

The 5 Choices: The Path to Extraordinary Productivity

Project Management for the Unofficial Project Manager

*Everyone Deserves a Great Manager: The 6 Critical
Practices for Leading a Team*

Leading Loyalty: Cracking the Code to Customer Devotion

The Leader's Guide to Unconscious Bias

Live Life in
Crescendo

Your Most Important Work
Is *Always* Ahead of You

Stephen R. Covey

and

Cynthia Covey Haller

Simon & Schuster Paperbacks

NEW YORK   LONDON   TORONTO
SYDNEY   NEW DELHI

Simon & Schuster Paperbacks
An Imprint of Simon & Schuster, Inc.
1230 Avenue of the Americas
New York, NY 10020

Copyright © 2022 by Cynthia Covey Haller

All rights reserved, including the right to reproduce this book
or portions thereof in any form whatsoever. For information,
address Simon & Schuster Paperbacks Subsidiary Rights Department,
1230 Avenue of the Americas, New York, NY 10020.

First Simon & Schuster trade paperback edition September 2023

SIMON & SCHUSTER PAPERBACKS and colophon are registered
trademarks of Simon & Schuster, Inc.

For information about special discounts for bulk purchases,
please contact Simon & Schuster Special Sales at 1-866-506-1949
or business@simonandschuster.com.

The Simon & Schuster Speakers Bureau can bring authors to your
live event. For more information or to book an event, contact the
Simon & Schuster Speakers Bureau at 1-866-248-3049
or visit our website at www.simonspeakers.com.

Manufactured in the United States of America

10 9 8 7 6 5 4 3 2 1

Library of Congress Cataloging-in-Publication Data is available.

ISBN 978-1-9821-9547-2
ISBN 978-1-9821-9548-9 (pbk)
ISBN 978-1-9821-9549-6 (ebook)

To my magnificent parents, Stephen and Sandra Covey,
who modeled "living in crescendo" throughout their lives.

And to my wonderful husband and best friend, Kameron—
the love of my life—for his good humor, continual steadiness,
and unconditional love.

Contents

Preface:
Creating Your Best Future

by Cynthia Covey Haller

"What we leave behind is not what is engraved on stone monuments, but what is woven into the lives of others."
—Pericles

My dad taught me the best way to predict your future is to create it. He always planned to work and contribute as long as he lived, and he planned to live forever. He made it very clear to his children and those who knew him well that the "R" word—retirement—was not in his vocabulary. He lied without conscience about his age and cringed when someone referred to the stage of life he was in as his "golden years."

Dad lived with a carpe diem—or "seize the day"—attitude and taught all nine of his children to do the same. He loved to quote Thoreau's admonition to "suck the marrow out of life" whenever we had a great opportunity ahead of us. This outlook kept him young and constantly learning. We understood he wasn't going to miss any opportunity to enjoy his life and make a difference in the lives of others.

After my dad graduated from the Harvard Business School at the age of twenty-five, his brother asked him what he was going to do with his life. He answered simply, "I want to unleash human potential." For the next fifty-five years, he carried out that goal across the globe through his inspiring books and dynamic teaching, generally around what he called "principle-centered

1

leadership." The symbol of his company was the compass, signifying the importance of aligning one's life with what he called "True North"—a symbol for bedrock principles that don't change over time. Dad believed that teaching these timeless, universal principles, common to all people, could dramatically change and impact individuals and organizations for good. He was a visionary man of great ideas and ideals.

He loved to learn by asking everyone he met about their lives, their work, families, beliefs, what they felt passionate about—just to learn from them. He would often pick people's brains to get a different perspective. He listened intently to their opinions and asked questions as if they were experts in their fields. He listened to teachers, cabdrivers, doctors, CEOs, waitresses, politicians, entrepreneurs, parents, neighbors, blue-collar workers, professionals, even heads of state—and treated them all with equal interest and curiosity. It used to annoy my mom, who would roll her eyes and sometimes say, "Stephen, why do you always act like you don't know anything when you talk to people?" And he would say as if it were so obvious, "Sandra, I already know what I know, but I want to know what they know!"

As the oldest of nine children, I grew up listening to my father discuss principle-centered ideas at home and in his various presentations to many audiences worldwide. One of my favorite principles was First Things First, also the title of one of his books and one of the 7 Habits. Dad tried hard to live what he taught, and family relationships were a top priority for him. Though there were nine children, each of us felt we were an important member of the family and had good relationships with both of our parents.

One of my favorite childhood memories is when I turned twelve and Dad invited me to accompany him on a business trip to San Francisco for a few days. I was so excited, and we carefully planned every minute we had together after his presentations.

Preface: Creating Your Best Future

We decided that the first night we would ride around the city on the famous trolley cars I'd heard about and then shop in some of the fancy stores for some school clothes. We both loved Chinese food, so we planned to go to Chinatown and then head back to the hotel for a quick swim before the pool closed. Our evening would be topped off with room service—a hot fudge sundae—before calling it a night.

When our big night finally came, I anxiously waited for him at the back of his presentation. Just before he reached me, I saw one of his old college friends greet him excitedly. As they embraced, I remembered Dad's stories of all the great adventures and fun times they'd had together in the years before. "Stephen," I heard him say, "it's probably been at least ten years since we've seen each other. Lois and I would love to take you out to dinner tonight—let's catch up and talk about old times." I heard Dad explain that I had accompanied him on the trip, and he glanced my way and said, "Oh, of course we'd love your daughter to join us as well. We could eat down on the wharf together."

All our grandiose plans for our special night with just the two of us were falling apart. I could see my trolley car rolling down the tracks without us and our plans to eat Chinese replaced with seafood, which I hated. I felt betrayed. But I realized Dad would probably rather be with his good friend than a twelve-year-old all night anyway.

Dad put his arm around his friend affectionately. "Wow, Bob. It's so great to see you again too. Dinner sounds fun . . . but not tonight. Cynthia and I have a special night planned, don't we, honey?" He winked at me, and to my astonishment the trolley car came back into view. I couldn't stop smiling.

I couldn't believe it, and I don't think his friend could either. We didn't wait around to find out; we were out the door and on our way.

3

"Gosh, Dad," I finally got out. "But are you sure . . . ?"

"Hey, I wouldn't miss this special night with you for anything. You'd much rather have Chinese food anyway, wouldn't you? Now, let's go catch a trolley car!"

As I look back on my childhood, this one seemingly insignificant experience remains representative of my Dad's character and built a level of trust in our relationship that I carried from that day on. He taught and always modeled that "in relationships, the small things are the big things," and each of my siblings could relate similar "San Francisco" experiences of feeling important and valued. This deposit of love and trust was central to our self-worth and made all the difference to us while we were growing up.

Dad believed we should develop what he called the "four-square person": one who is physically, mentally, socially, and spiritually balanced, as each of those areas is fundamental to human fulfillment. Each day of Dad's life, he tried to make a conscientious effort to live a balanced life by developing himself in each area, and he taught others to do the same. He wrote: "Our first energies should go to our own character development, which is often invisible to others, like the roots that sustain great trees. As we cultivate the roots, we will begin to see the fruits."

Though he struggled with his own imperfections like all of us, he consistently tried to improve himself and overcome his flaws more than anyone I've ever known. We knew his professional life was admirable, but we felt it paled in comparison to the private life we knew as a family. For decades, along with our mother, he was actively engaged in creating a rich family culture in our home, and he tried to unleash our greatest potential as well as the potential he unleashed in others through his professional work. Our family never imagined the day would actually come when he would be unable to approach life in the same proactive way he always had.

4

Then in April of 2012, at age seventy-nine, Dad had a bicycle accident, and although he was wearing a helmet, it was on too loose, and he hit his head and suffered bleeding on the brain. He was in the hospital for several weeks, and was really never the same after returning home. Eventually, the bleeding began again and ultimately took his life.

Though we grieved his passing deeply, we knew our father to be a very spiritual man who had taught us that God always has a purpose behind what happens in our lives—even in our Dad leaving us much earlier than we'd imagined. As a family, we'd been blessed to have had such an amazing father for so many years, and we felt grateful for the unconditional love and insightful guidance we received. We are equally grateful for our loving mother, the matriarch of the entire Covey family, who also recently left us.

Several years before my Dad passed away, he asked if I would help him on a new book built around what we now realize was the last "big idea." He was viscerally charged about it. He often worked on several books and projects simultaneously, but I was intrigued and enthusiastic about this particular new idea and wanted to be involved.

Like the master plan for his life, he had clearly envisioned the book's full title, years before it was completed: *Live Life in Crescendo: Your Most Important Work Is Always Ahead of You*. He believed that by adopting what will be known as the "Crescendo Mentality," one could keep looking ahead and progressing through all the various ages and stages of life. He spoke passionately about it often, and encouraged those who were unhappy concerning where they were in life, or discouraged due to past challenges or failures, to think and act proactively about their future, and what they could still accomplish and contribute in the years ahead of them. For him, the best End in Mind (one of the habits from his book, *The 7 Habits of Highly Effective People*) was to continually make meaningful contributions to bless the lives of others, and that, ultimately, this mentality holds the key to true, long-lasting happiness.

He believed in the Crescendo Mentality as much as anything he had ever taught in his professional work. Before writing about it, he began introducing it in some of his presentations, as was his pattern, and in his later years, it became his personal mission statement. Dad felt so passionate about the concept of Living in Crescendo, and he truly believed that if implemented, it could have a tremendous impact for good throughout the world.

We actively worked on the book together for three years, and I met with him regularly to record his thoughts and ideas. He always encouraged, and even pushed, me to finish my part, which was holding the book up, yet he understood my time limitations with young children at home and other pressing responsibilities. While I deeply shared his passion on the subject and collected material and wrote when I could, regrettably my part of the book was still mostly unfinished when he unexpectedly left us.

Over the last several years, I finished writing the stories, examples, and commentary that were my part of the project, as he had requested. You will notice that some portions will sound as if he's still living—this was purposely written that way. Much of the material, relayed to me years ago, reflects his thoughts, experiences, and insights at the time. Other material was taken from his writings, presentations, and personal conversations. I consciously made the decision to write this book in *his* voice because the idea of Living in Crescendo is uniquely his, not mine. I also included true stories and experiences from his own life, as well as observations and interactions he had with various people throughout his career regarding this material, and those experiences are set off to indicate that they are specifically from my perspective and in my voice.

He envisioned *Live Life in Crescendo* to be the introduction of this new idea to people worldwide. This book represents what we as a family consider his final contribution—his "last lecture"—his concluding opus. Victor Hugo wrote, "Nothing is more powerful than an idea whose time has come." Though our father wrote many other principle-centered books, we believe the idea behind this one is unique and greatly needed today. He envisioned that the Crescendo Mentality would promote looking to the future with hope and optimism, believing that we can always grow and learn, serve and contribute—through every stage of our lives—and believing that our greatest and most important achievements may still lie ahead.

Live Life in Crescendo is built around this singular central idea, illustrated through four parts that represent different stages and ages to support and bolster your understanding of this principle, offering practical ways to implement this mentality at every period of life. Dad and I wanted to include a wide variety of stories and inspiring examples from both well-known and "ordinary" people to highlight this idea. We hoped the experiences of others would inspire many to believe that they too can make positive ongoing contributions to impact the lives of others within their own Circle of Influence.

Several days after our father passed away, my sister Jenny and I were talking about how different our lives would now be without him. Suddenly, the truth came very powerfully to us both when Jenny said, "Even though he's not here, he isn't really gone; he lives on through us—his kids, his grandkids, and everyone who tries to live the principles he taught. *This* is his legacy."

Ralph Waldo Emerson wrote: "Our death is not an end if we live on in our children and the younger generation. For they are us."

Perhaps Jim Collins captured it best in his foreword to the

twenty-fifth anniversary edition of *The 7 Habits of Highly Effective People*:

> No person lasts forever, but books and ideas can endure. When you engage with these pages, you will be engaging with Stephen Covey at the peak of his powers. You can feel him reaching out from the text to say, "Here, I really believe this, let me help you—I want you to get this, to learn from it, I want you to grow, to be better, to contribute more, to make a life that matters. His life is done, but his work is not."

I only hope to be a faithful translator of my dad's vision for this book. And perhaps it will lead people, as he liked to say, "to communicate to another person their worth and potential so clearly they are inspired to see it in themselves."

My father, Stephen Covey, deeply believed that *Live Life in Crescendo* could powerfully affect and inspire those who strive to create their best future, which ultimately will become their own unique legacy. My hope is that this book will be a lasting and living part of his great legacy and serve to unleash *your* greatest potential. And although he is gone from our sight for a time, his legacy truly does continue on, in crescendo.

Introduction

The Crescendo Mentality

"I went to the woods because I wished to live deliberately, to front only the essential facts of life, and see if I could not learn what it had to teach, and not, when I came to die, discover that I had not lived. I did not wish to live what was not life, living is so dear. . . . I wanted to live deep and suck out all the marrow of life."

—Henry David Thoreau

How do you see the many ages and stages of your life as you progress through them? How will you respond to your own unique journey through life? I believe it is crucial to make a life plan for how you will handle the highs and lows of living: the doldrums, the successes, the unexpected challenges, and the vast changes you most likely will face. It is most important to create your best future before you actually live it.

This book will introduce the Crescendo Mentality of thinking in any stage of life. Living in Crescendo is a mindset and a principle of action. It's a unique perspective of approaching life through making contributions to others and always looking at what's ahead for you to accomplish. It redefines success from how society usually measures it. If you adopt the Crescendo Mentality, I believe it can make an enormous difference in your life, to those around you, and even throughout the world.

In music, *crescendo* means to continually swell and grow

in grandeur, and to increase energy, volume, and vigor. The sign of a crescendo $<$ shows that if you keep extending the lines, the music continues increasing in volume and enlarging indefinitely. Diminuendo means exactly the opposite: the music is lessening in volume and power, lowering in energy, backing away; and as the sign $>$ shows, it eventually fades out, dies down, and comes to an end. Living a life in diminuendo means that you don't seek to stretch, grow, and learn anymore; you are content to rely on what you've already accomplished, and eventually you stop producing and contributing.

When a piece of music reaches a crescendo, it does not just get louder. The sense of growing, intensifying, and expanding in a composition or performance results from an expressive mix of rhythm, harmony, and melody. These in turn are grounded in the fundamental elements of pitch and rhythm as well as the dynamics of volume, combined with the passage of time in a composition or performance.

In the same way, it will be shown that living your Life in Crescendo expresses our passions, interests, relationships, beliefs, and values—which in turn rest on the fundamental principles that guide us through all the stages of our lives.

Living your Life in Crescendo means continually growing in learning, influence, and contribution. The mindset that *"your most important work is always ahead of you"* is an optimistic, forward-thinking mentality that teaches you can always contribute regardless of what's happened to you or what stage you are in. Imagine how life would change if you adopted the perspective that your greatest contributions, achievements, and even happiness, are not only behind you, but are always *ahead* of you! In the same way that music builds on previous notes but leave us anticipating the next note or chord, your life builds on your past but unfolds in the future.

10

This mentality is not a "one and you're done" event, but over a lifetime becomes a rich and proactive part of who you are. The Crescendo Mentality promotes using whatever you have—your time, talents, skills, resources, gifts, passion, money, influence— to enrich the lives of people around you, whether they be part of your family, neighborhood, community, or the world.

> *"The meaning of life is to find your gift. The purpose of life is to give it away."*
>
> —attributed to Pablo Picasso

Picasso's words could be the mission statement for this book. You can choose a forward-thinking mindset that focuses on always learning and growing through life's ebbs and flows, while you continually look for ways to contribute to those around you.

The Greek version of this philosophy was first to "know thyself," then "control thyself," and then "give thyself." The Greeks emphasized the importance and power of that sequence. When you live with a sense of the purpose of your unique mission, and take control of your life through good choices, then you are able to serve others and help them find their purpose and mission as well. This leads to a sense of fulfillment and joy in others and in you.

Live Life in Crescendo is divided into four main parts, each based on pivotal stages in life when, depending on your response, you could choose to Live in Crescendo and continue to do your best work, or Live in Diminuendo, and eventually fade away and have no influence. And just as composers and performers express themselves through music that, no matter how complex, is always grounded in fundamentals, all of us live our lives in ways that embody fundamental principles of human behavior and interaction.

Part 1: The Midlife Struggle

This stage concerns where you are compared to where you want to be. During your midlife years, you may feel discouraged and believe you have accomplished little of value. Perhaps you've already given up trying to achieve much at all, believing the opportunity has passed? But in reality, you may have accomplished more than you realize concerning what matters most. And if your life does need improvement, you can choose to change and re-create your life to one of contribution and true success.

Part 2: The Pinnacle of Success

If you have experienced great success in some part of your life, the tendency may be to sit back, enjoy your spoils, and coast. You may have a "been there, done that" attitude and feel like you've given all you're capable of. However, Living a Life in Crescendo means you don't look in the rearview mirror, focusing on past successes (or failures); instead, you *look ahead* to what your next worthy goal or great contribution will be. It could be that during this exciting stage of life your greatest work is still to come.

Part 3: Life-Changing Setbacks

An accident happens, you have a serious health problem, you get laid off or fired from your job, you're diagnosed with a terminal illness, someone close to you dies—there are so many moments in life when you experience a major setback. At such moments, it's natural to reevaluate your life, goals, and priorities. Do you drop out and withdraw? Do you let this experience define you? Or is it time to face the challenge, consciously choose how to respond, reorient your life, keep moving forward, and continue to make significant contributions?

Part 4: The Second Half of Life

When you reach the traditional retirement age, or what society has erroneously labeled the "winding-down years," you face a significant choice of what to do with your remaining time. This period of life can be a vastly self-serving, even monotonous and unfulfilling phase you pass through or simply endure. Or you can choose to be extremely productive and make tremendous contributions to those within and beyond your Circle of Influence. Your potential can be used or wasted depending on whether you believe your most important contributions could still be ahead of you.

The Crescendo Mentality uses key principles to guide you through each of these four stages of life:

- **Life is a mission, not a career**
- **Love to serve**
- **People are more important than things**
- **Leadership is communicating worth and potential**
- **Work to expand your Circle of Influence**
- **Choose to Live in Crescendo, not Diminuendo**
- **Transition from work to contribution**
- **Create meaningful memories**
- **Detect your purpose**

Though there may be things that separate us from one another—cultural differences; misunderstandings; disparities in opportunities, background, and experience—as part of the human family we share far more important commonalities than we may fully understand. If you have ever traveled and been exposed to people around the world, you will have discovered that we are all basically the same—rich and poor, famous and unknown—all striving for happiness and value and sharing the same hopes, fears, and dreams. Most people feel strongly about their families, and have the same needs to be understood, loved, accepted.

I agree with the quote attributed to George Bernard Shaw: "Two things define you. Your patience when you have nothing and your attitude when you have everything."[1] How you respond to these opposites in life is both a challenge and an opportunity and will be illustrated throughout the book.

I am optimistic about people. I do not buy into a cynical view of our world, and though our problems are great and increasing, I believe that at the core of most people is goodness, decency, generosity, a commitment to family and community, resourcefulness, ingenuity, and extraordinary spirit, grit, and determination. Even more, I see great hope and potential in the rising generation. You have tremendous potential, far beyond anything you could ever imagine.

PART 1

THE MIDLIFE STRUGGLE

fermata (fer-ma-ta) noun: symbol used to indicate a pause; a pause of unspecified length

"Three grand essentials to happiness in this
life are something to do, something to love,
and something to hope for."

—George Washington Burnap

Many people sell themselves short on what they are capable of accomplishing, mostly because they don't have a correct vision of themselves. They get stuck doing the same things in the same way, and they never really "break out" by pushing past their own labels and how others see them. Believing they are just ordinary people who can't make a difference, they have expectations of what they can do and accomplish that are so low they fulfill their own prophecy and produce little. Though they may have known a life rich in significance through contribution, they relegate themselves to mediocrity by shortchanging their worth and happiness.

But their yearnings to do and be more are still there. So if you have these feelings, be grateful! Deep within each of us is an inner longing to live a life of greatness and contribution—to matter, to really make a difference. We can consciously decide to leave behind the life of mediocrity we think we have, for a life of greatness—at home, at work, and in the community.

Chapter 1

Life Is a Mission, Not a Career

"There is no greater gift you can give or receive than to honor your calling. It's why you were born. And how you become most truly alive."

—Oprah Winfrey

The Christmas film classic *It's a Wonderful Life* tells an important story to all of us who have ever wondered if our life truly matters. As you likely recall, George Bailey is a stand-up guy who gave up bigger dreams to stay in his small hometown of Bedford Falls and manage his father's savings and loan. He seems to be doomed to life in a low-paying job, and when faced with financial ruin due to no fault of his own, George despairs. Believing there is no hope left, he considers jumping off a bridge.

Like George Bailey, have you ever felt that life has totally passed you by, that your dreams and aspirations have been sidelined? Are you where you wanted to be, or did you see yourself doing something different? Is your résumé thin and your track record relegated to the slow lane? Is your passion for life waning because you feel disillusioned, more cynical and less confident about the reality of what you can really accomplish? Are you, like George Bailey, looking for a bridge to jump from, wondering if what you do makes a difference to anyone at all?

Society has a name for this affliction—it's called a "midlife crisis." It can be quite overwhelming for those in the throes of it, men and women ages forty to sixty who find they're not where they thought they'd be, or who they thought they'd be. Often they feel they don't measure up to those around them whose lives appear to be more on track and "successful."

There are many challenges people face during this crucial stage of life:

- Your employer doesn't recognize or reward your skills and talents
- You feel overworked and underappreciated and wonder if your job is even worth it
- Your career path is boring and unfulfilling and you feel trapped with few options
- You struggle in your marriage or other important relationships
- You can't seem to find personal fulfillment and real happiness, and you wonder if you should totally start over
- You can't believe you are in the situation you find yourself in; you thought you'd be further down the road of success than you actually are

Signs of people suffering from a midlife crisis are:

- Depression, apathy, burnout
- Lack of real purpose or ambition
- Loss of long-range vision
- Self-centered blindness to the needs of those closest to them
- Searching for artificial or external stimulation

During this midlife stage, people sometimes panic and do things they normally wouldn't do—like buy an expensive, flashy car (so they *look* successful), quit their stable job and start a risky new career, start dressing and acting like a teenager, or even engage in daring or dangerous activities.

Worst of all, sometimes they bail out and leave their spouse and their family behind, hoping that different surroundings and a new start or a new relationship will make them feel younger and improve their stagnating image of themselves.

When the father of a friend of mine was in his forties, he experienced a classic midlife crisis. When I talked to him, he shared his story, which I offer here in his own words:

When my father was forty-three, he was transferred to another city a few hours away, uprooting my mom, my younger siblings, and me from the schools we loved and right before my senior year. We tried to make the best of it, but a few months later we moved again because my dad had quit his job at the bank he'd worked at for years, to chase a new opportunity. It was only a few months after that when my father came to my mom, sat her down, and said he was leaving her and the family to run off with his secretary, who happened to be seventeen years younger.

A few months later we discovered that my father and his new wife (old secretary) had relocated a state away, to Southern California, leaving my devastated mom to continue picking up the pieces of her own crisis. The pain was indescribable, though "horrific" does an adequate job. A twenty-two-year marriage was over, three teenage children faced uncertainty, lack of understanding, abandonment, no father in the home, and little if any explanation. The disruption to everyone's emotional stability was immeasurable—all while "Dad" was flitting about San Diego golfing with his new trophy wife.

The trickle down from my father's midlife crisis is still felt today, even some thirty-eight years later. A mother who was emotionally rocked for the rest of her life, living single for thirty years and dying young. While my siblings and I were left doubting ourselves, lacking confidence, operating below potentials, not trusting love, experiencing general family dysfunction, and even divorce ourselves. On it goes. Sure, "get over it" has been the dominant counsel for decades, but it's not that simple. [2]

But if you don't like the life you're leading right now, the answer usually lies in facing your problems head on, not running away from them. Leaving your family rarely solves your problems and devastates those left behind. The grass is rarely greener; maybe you just need to water your side instead. It's wise to look for reasons to fix where you are and preserve those relationships with loved ones in whom you've already invested so much.

At this point, it's worth remembering what happened to George Bailey. In the movie, Clarence Odbody (an angel who hasn't yet earned his wings) is assigned to stop him from jumping off the bridge. When George says he wishes he'd never been born, Clarence fulfills his wish and shows him how different life in Bedford Falls would have been without him.

Without his presence and influence, Bedford Falls became the dark and sickly Pottersville. The wonderful little town George wanted to escape turned, in his absence, into a contentious nest of bitter people at the mercy of a banker, Henry Potter, driven by greed and the lust for power.

Appalled, George prays fervently for one more chance to live and enjoy the life he never fully appreciated. His prayer granted, he runs home to all the people important to him, even though he still faces arrest for bank fraud. But his family and friends have gathered to rescue him from ruin, repaying the many sacrifices George has made for them over the years.

"Strange, isn't it?" Clarence says to George. "Each man's life touches so many other lives. When he isn't around he leaves an awful hole, doesn't he? You see, George, you've really had a wonderful life."[3]

Like George Bailey, you may be very successful in many areas of your life without recognizing it. True success is not always what it appears to be, or what others celebrate. You may not measure up to other people's expectations, but if you succeed in the most important roles in your own life, you are successful in the things that truly matter most.

While work is essential to support ourselves and our families, it is not our life's mission. A crucial part of the Crescendo Mentality is not to worry about being a success in the eyes of the world. Instead, we should redefine what success means and work toward being a significant influence for good in the world.

Create Your Own Future

"You cannot predict the future, but you can create it."
—Peter Drucker

Often in my presentations, I ask people to write their own obituary. Though that may sound strange, the process enables them to think about what they want to be remembered for—and then they can work to bring it about. Create your own best future. If you carefully consider what you want to be said of you at your funeral, you will find your very own definition of success.

To help you get started with your own obituary, take a moment and ask yourself these questions:

- What do you want said about you at your funeral?
- What will you be known for?
- What will your greatest accomplishments be?
- What will give you the most joy and satisfaction as you look back on your life?
- What legacy do you want to leave?

Now compare the obituary you hope will be written about you with what you are currently doing in your midlife to bring it about. Does your life align with how you want to end up? Are you on track to be remembered for what you truly care about? With these important questions in mind, you can start to create your future life—plan, set goals, make adjustments, and then go to work to bring it about.

As you examine yourself and where you're at during this critical midlife stage, keep in mind these two principles of the Crescendo Mentality:

First, see true success for what it is without comparison to others—work diligently to succeed in your most important roles.

Second, identify what needs improvement in your life and courageously and proactively bring about positive change—use your initiative and work to make it happen!

Choose the Right Yardstick

Despite how you might feel or what you believe, you do have the power to choose your own response to the circumstances of your life. Ineffective people transfer responsibility by blaming others or their environment—something or somebody "out there" is why they can't succeed. This type of inner dialogue does nothing to improve your condition.

Proactive people say: I know the scripts that are in me, but I am *not* those scripts. I can rewrite my scripts. I need not be the victim of conditions or conditioning. I can choose my response to any situation. My behavior is a function of my decisions.

My friend whose story I told is an example of bringing about positive change by intentionally improving your life. He couldn't do anything about his father's poor choice to desert his family; however, he could learn from what had happened to him and make different choices with his own family. He could choose to act and not react to what had happened to him. And this is what he eventually chose to do, some thirty years later.

The cycle of devastation and destructive behavior stopped with him. He learned that his behavior was a function of his decisions, not his conditions, and he worked to become a "transition figure" (more on this later). He determined not to repeat the same horrific scenario in his family, but instead chose to pass on love, loyalty, and responsibility. Though it was understandable he might carry some baggage from the consequences of his painful background, through self-control and conscious effort he has chosen not to let it define his present. As a result, he and his wife have created a new, beautiful, and successful family culture.

My friend feels that his career has not been as successful as he had hoped. But from my vantage point, his is an incredible success story. He has overcome a difficult past and has built a loving marriage and strong family culture with his six children, leaving them with a different legacy from the one he was left. And what could be more successful than that?

If you feel like you're stuck in a midlife crisis or you're experiencing "fermata"—a pause of unspecified length—don't panic by running away or running off. Rather, use your gift of self-awareness to stand apart from yourself and observe your situation. Recognize that you can consciously choose the course that you'll be happy you chose in the future.

> *"The only person you are destined to become is the person you decide to be."*
>
> —attributed to Ralph Waldo Emerson

Within the freedom to choose your response lies the power to achieve growth and happiness and to create your own path.

I remember hearing of a man who became somewhat embarrassed when he was asked to talk about himself to a prominent leader. He said:

Well, I haven't been what you'd call very successful, though we have had a happy home life. I have always had a decent job but haven't really distinguished myself in my career or made a lot of money. We have lived a modest lifestyle in an average home, and I certainly am not well known to many outside my immediate circle.

However, my greatest joy is that I do have a wonderful wife of nearly fifty years and children that I'm very proud of. My youngest of five was just recently married, and we feel blessed that all our children have grown up to be responsible, independent, caring adults. They love their own children and are teaching them good values; we are grateful to have such a wonderful family. But . . . in relation to my career and anything that would stand out at all, I've never really been successful and sometimes wonder if I've made much of a difference at all.

Life Is a Mission, Not a Career

In response, the leader answered, quite astonished: *"Why, that's one of the greatest success stories I've ever heard! I've rarely known such success!"* This man was like "a fish who discovers water last," being so immersed in his element that he was totally unaware of it. He'd actually had "true success," and the things that mattered most, all along, yet he didn't see it. Success in our society usually refers to wealth, position, prominence in a career, and by that measure this didn't have success. However the success being defined here is measured very differently.

A song by Phil Vassar, "Don't Miss Your Life," speaks to where we spend our time and what really matters most. Here are a few verses:

> *On a plane to the West Coast, laptop on my tray*
> *Papers spread across my seat, a big deadline to make.*
> *An older man sitting next to me said, "Sorry to intrude,*
> *Thirty years ago my busy friend, I was you.*
> *I made a ton of money and I climbed the ladder,*
> *Yeah, I was superman, now what does it matter?*
>
> *I missed the first steps my daughter took*
> *The time my son played Captain Hook in "Peter Pan"*
> *I was in New York, said "Sorry son, Dad has to work"*
> *I missed the father daughter dance*
> *The first home run, no second chance*
> *To be there when he crossed the plate,*
> *The moment's gone now it's too late*
> *Fame and fortune come with a heavy price*
> *Son, don't miss your life.* [4]

What a poignant reminder of one of our most important roles in life—in this case, that of a parent. Don't miss your *real life*—the one that brings lasting joy through time spent with those you love.

This isn't to say that your profession isn't essential in providing security and opportunities for your family. It's simply important to recognize that living a Life in Crescendo means not sacrificing important relationships and valuable experiences with those you love most in exchange for temporal things that ultimately matter little in the end.

When someone is faced with a serious life-threatening health crisis, what they regret more than anything else is not being able to spend more time with those they love. Just as an experiment, try this: start talking with someone about their family, and see how tender they become almost immediately. I have found this reaction to be universal.

Clayton Christensen, an esteemed Harvard professor of business and a friend, wrote a book the title of which asks the reflective question, *How Will You Measure Your Life?* After he graduated from the Harvard Business School in 1979, Clayton relates, all his classmates went their separate ways with big dreams of being successful in all aspects of their lives. When Clayton went to his five-year reunion, he found that most of his friends were married, having children, beginning business ventures, and just starting to make money. By the ten- and fifteen-year reunions, many of his classmates were very successful in their careers and were extremely wealthy.

But Clayton was shocked to find that many of them were also already divorced and unhappy with their personal lives. As time went on, many of his friends didn't live with their children anymore and had limited relationships with them because they were scattered across the country. It was eye-opening for him to see that their success in the business world didn't necessarily translate into living happily with the families who had been with them at the start of their journey:

> I can guarantee you that not a single one of them graduated with the deliberate strategy of getting divorced and raising children who would become estranged from them. And yet a shocking number of them implemented that strategy. The reason? They didn't keep the purpose of their lives front and center as they decided how they would spend their time, talents, and energy.

Clayton believes it's about "choosing the right yardstick" to determine how to measure your life. He said:

> It's actually really important that you succeed at what you're succeeding at, but that isn't going to be the measure of your life. . . . Too often we measure success in life against the progress we make in our careers. But how can we ensure we're not straying from our values as humans along the way?[5]

My grandfather Stephen L. Richards was as successful in his private life as he was in his public life. Perhaps nothing he taught has had more of an impact on me than this powerful principle: *"Life is a mission, not a career."*

As we work to uncover and utilize our skills, beliefs, talents, passion, abilities, time, resources—all we are—we will ultimately discover our own unique mission. When we listen closely and follow our conscience more regularly, the ability to discern whom to help and what to do grows stronger. The answer will come.

This means you don't allow social media, the entertainment industry, your neighbor, friend, butcher, baker, candlestick maker, or even your beautician to define success for you. Success is different for different people. You must align your definition of success with your values. Show integrity by being true to who you are.

There are certain universal principles that are generally known and accepted among most people and that transcend culture and geography: honesty, fairness, decency, loyalty, respect, consideration, integrity, and so forth. Like the true north that a compass points to, they are objective and external, reflecting natural laws, not values that are subjective and internal.

A compass provides direction, purpose, vision, perspective, and balance. The more closely our values are aligned with correct principles, the more accurate and useful they will be. And if we know how to read maps, we won't get lost, confused, or fooled by conflicting voices and values.

It's important to discover your purpose and mission in regard to your family, your occupation, your community, and in whatever other roles you may play. Then you must live by that purpose. As we go through the ups and downs of life, especially in the midlife phase, we need to use our moral compass to guide and direct us.

Living the Crescendo Mentality means you can take control and respond to what's happening to you by improving or changing your situation—believing you can make positive choices and change your paradigm from a challenging and even stagnant midlife to an expanding and fulfilling life.

> *"Life isn't about finding yourself—life is about creating yourself."*
>
> —attributed to George Bernard Shaw

Truly believing *"your most important work is always ahead of you"* will give you the motivation to keep trying, learning, changing, and adapting to new challenges and temporary setbacks. Believing and responding proactively will put the helm of your life back into your own hands and empower you to chart your own exciting course . . . at any age, midlife or otherwise.

If you are experiencing midlife issues, adopting this paradigm is key. I have learned that if you want to make small changes in your life, work on your attitude. *But if you want to make big and primary changes, work on your paradigm.* Like a pair of glasses, a paradigm is the lens through which we see life. Your choice of this lens will affect the way you view everything.

Keep First Things First

I have often taught that you don't want to get to the end of your life and realize the ladder to success you've been climbing is leaning against the wrong wall! You must take the responsibility and initiative to decide what you value and prioritize around the most important things—that is, those things that truly matter in the long run. First Things First is the third habit in *The 7 Habits of Highly Effective People*; this principle is often the most crucial to apply during the midlife battle of life. It is a principle of action and power.

The Crescendo Mentality promotes the idea that it's never too late to begin, regardless of your age or stage, even if you've never succeeded before. Though you may be struggling and feel you're losing the midlife battle, it is entirely within your power to change. It's never too late to repair broken relationships within your family, to start spending more time with those you love, to realign your priorities.

It's entirely your choice and decision to begin to restore important relationships, even if you have to do some damage control and apologize for past behavior or neglect before you start. Muster the courage and vision to make it happen. It will be one of the best decisions you will ever make, and one that you'll never regret. To achieve success in the most important roles and relationships in your life is to find true success and happiness.

As United Nations Secretary-General Dag Hammarskjöld observed, "It is more noble to give yourself completely to one individual than to labor diligently for the salvation of the masses." An executive might be very involved and dedicated to work, and to church and community projects, and yet not have a deep, meaningful relationship with his or her own spouse. It takes more nobility of character, more humility, more patience to develop such a relationship with a spouse than it would take to give continued dedicated service to many people.

We often justify neglecting the one, partly because we receive many expressions of esteem and gratitude from the "masses." Yet it is crucial to set aside time and give yourself completely to individuals. Children in particular are more open when you are alone with them and when they feel genuinely understood and cared about.

I remember hearing a story about a father who took his family on a series of vacations one summer, including going to some significant historical sights. At the end of the summer he asked his teenage son what he enjoyed the most. Rather than choosing one of the important places they visited, his son simply said, "The thing I liked best this summer was the night you and I lay on the lawn and looked at the stars and talked!"

What a paradigm shift this father experienced when he realized it doesn't really matter what you do, but what you feel while you're doing it. He always had the ability to give his son something of great value, without even leaving his backyard. And it didn't cost him a penny!

> *"Things which matter most must never be at the mercy of things which matter least."*
> —attributed to Johann Wolfgang von Goethe

So what does all this have to do with Living a Life in Crescendo, particularly during the midlife stage that is often such a struggle, and sometimes even a battle? Many people feel pulled in too many different directions during this period of life and must fight to stay in line with priorities they value. There is so much pressure to excel in a career, to achieve "success" as the world views it, to do it all by a certain age or stage, that it pulls at (and distorts) those things that truly matter most in life. It is an ongoing battle to fight the tendency to give in to the social norms of trying to "keep up with the Joneses" and to obtain more and more for "me and mine."

Though there are many important things an individual or

a family needs—a comfortable home, educational opportunities, transportation, and recreation—the thing they need most is time, love, and attention.

Work to Succeed in Your Most Important Roles

All family situations are unique, and you may play many different roles within yours. You may not be a parent yourself, but as a son or daughter, you can be a blessing to your aging parents, who may have health issues. I know of a single daughter who lives with her mother, who suffers from diabetes and a heart condition. This woman takes her role as daughter and caregiver seriously, making personal sacrifices and rarely going out with friends. A couple times a year, a sister who lives out of town will relieve her for a couple days. But knowing she has very little time left with her mother, this woman is content to love and care for her in her own home, where she's happiest.[6]

You may be a brother or sister to a sibling who has gone down the wrong path and could use encouragement, advice, or some service. Maybe you don't have children of your own, but if you're an aunt or uncle you can have great influence on a niece or nephew simply by showing interest in them, by going to their soccer games, plays, or volunteering to take them to music lessons or help with a special school project.

I know someone who is diligent in his role as a supportive brother to his older, single sister Jenny, who lives alone. Because their aging parents live four hours away and have many health issues, they aren't as involved in their daughter's life as they'd like to be. Jenny is estranged from her other siblings, often saying insensitive things to them without thinking and sometimes taking advantage of them financially.

However, her brother Blake takes the initiative to stay in touch with Jenny weekly with phone calls or texts, helping her find employment, providing support during health challenges, or just checking in on her. Blake's wife is equally supportive and makes sure to include Jenny in many of their family's activities, especially during holidays and special events. Consequently, Jenny is comfortable at family gatherings and has a good relationship with their children.

Recently, Blake invited her to a birthday dinner at her favorite restaurant with family, and Jenny confessed that she would have stayed home alone on her birthday if he hadn't planned a celebration in her honor. What a different life she would experience if Blake didn't value his important role as a sibling and make the effort to be involved in her life, blessed by a valuable family connection.[7]

I have always believed and taught that the most important work you will ever do in life will be within your own family circle and ultimately it is where you will find the most lasting happiness and fulfillment.

> *"As important as your obligations as a doctor, lawyer, or business leader will be, you are a human being first. And those human connections with spouse, with children, and with friends are the most important investments you will ever make. At the end of your life, you will never regret not having passed one more test, not winning one more verdict, or not closing one more deal. You will regret time not spent with a husband, a friend, a child or a parent. . . . Our success as a society depends not on what happens at the White House but what happens inside YOUR house."*
>
> —Barbara Bush, to graduating students
> at Wellesley College[8]

Whatever specific roles are important and meaningful to you—your role within your family, as a mentor, as a reliable friend, in your job and career, as a contributing community member, giving service to worthy causes—these roles are all a good measure of success. Success then is determined by what you value and how you respond—instead of how society defines it or how you compare and measure up to others. As you work to succeed in your most important roles in life, it will enable you to align your definition of success with your values.

You show integrity when you live true to *your* own values.

At his clinic in Ethiopia, "Dr. Rick" doesn't have a light box to view X-rays, so he improvises by holding them up to the blazing sun. It does the trick, and he is able to diagnose the many people he sees every day at no cost to them. In Ethiopia, it's a hard reality that there is only one doctor for every forty thousand people. Many of his patients travel hundreds of miles from remote villages, sometimes in the back of trucks, to be seen in his one-room clinic at Mother Teresa's Mission in Addis Ababa. Dr. Rick examines them, makes a diagnosis, and then works creatively to obtain the medicine, surgery, or special care they need, relying on the generosity of others to solicit funds and on doctors to perform surgeries pro bono. He does all he can to help his patients, as he knows he may be their only hope for survival.

A native of Long Beach, Dr. Rick Hodes first went to Ethiopia as a relief worker during the 1984 famine. He was immediately drawn to the great need for humanitarian work he saw firsthand, and when he discovered Mother Teresa's Mission, he kept returning to help and eventually stayed. In 2001, as a single, middle-aged man, Dr. Hodes made the decision to adopt two orphans so they could have surgery under his insurance plan. As he thought and prayed about it, "the answer that came to me," he recalls, was "God is offering you an opportunity to help these boys. Don't say no!"

Dr. Hodes is a specialist in cancer, heart disease, and spinal conditions. He arranges for American doctors to provide free surgeries for many with cleft palates and other facial deformities, as well as other medical conditions. He happily shares his modest home with up to twenty kids who live with him in Addis Ababa at any given time. He has adopted five children, the maximum number allowed in Ethiopia. "Whenever half a mattress is free, I take in someone new," he says simply.

When Dr. Irving Fish, then the director of Pediatric Neurology at New York University Medical School, visited the mission where Dr. Hodes worked, he was struck by his total unselfishness and his uncanny ability to solve tough medical problems. "Rick could have done very well for himself practicing in the United States, but he chose to do something so much harder," says Dr. Fish. "I've never met anyone like him. He's a keen diagnostician. It's just him, his stethoscope, his brain, and his heart."

While most Americans take hot water and reliable electricity for granted, Dr. Hodes lives without these comforts. He has made enormous contributions to the health of the entire region where he lives and serves, and his work has inspired filmmakers, authors, and news media alike. His personal mantra, taken from his favorite passage in the Talmud, gives insight to where his priorities lie: "Saving one life is like saving an entire world."[9]

During his midlife stage, Dr. Rick Hodes is true to what he values—service to an underprivileged community—and is enormously successful in this most important role. To him, life *is* definitely a mission and not only a career.

Take Control and Act!

Many years ago, I inadvertently came across a powerful idea that was literally life-changing to me and has influenced my thinking ever since. Though I've never been able to track down the source or the author, the idea is essentially this:

Between stimulus and response there is a space. Within that space lies our freedom and power to choose our response. In those choices lie our growth and happiness.

The second perspective of the Crescendo Mentality in the midlife stage is clear. If you're fighting a midlife battle—stuck in a rut, needing to change a destructive behavior and improve or reinvent yourself, your relationships, or your career—own it, take control and act to bring about positive change.

At 397 pounds, principal Ernie Nix could barely walk through the halls of his middle school without feeling exhausted. His cholesterol level was at 440, his blood pressure was 220 over 110, and his doctor told him he was headed toward a very painful death, likely within five or six years.[10]

"If I was going to be any good to anybody . . . if I was going to lead the school where I know it should go . . . the leader needed to change," Nix admitted. "There was no way to continue at 400 pounds."

Ernie determined to take responsibility and control of his health and ultimately his future by making enormous changes in his life. He woke at 4:30 each morning and walked around the track from 5 to 6 a.m., the only time he could make this significant lifestyle change with his busy schedule. Besides adding regular exercise, he joined Weight Watchers for education and support, and completely changed his eating habits. His wife was not in good shape either, so she joined him in this new healthy lifestyle quest.

Though it was a very slow process and took a lot of discipline, it eventually paid off. Ernie lost 173 pounds the first year, and this inspired the assistant principal, secretary, custodian, some teachers, and a counselor to follow his example, and they all lost significant weight as well. Ernie wanted to be a good example, so he offered his students healthier lunch options, and made their PE more competitive and fun. One of his greatest payoffs was when a student who hadn't seen him in a long time stopped dead in his tracks and enthusiastically called out with a huge smile, "Mr. Nix—dude!"

After losing 150 pounds, Ernie started running, and eventually he ran marathons, even being featured in *Runner's World* magazine. After two years, Nix had lost a total of 220 pounds (his wife dropped 100 pounds), and had much more energy and enthusiasm to offer his students and administration. He felt healthy and happy for the first time in years.

Ernie used that "space" between stimulus and response to pause and change his habits, and it ultimately saved his life and elevated those around him. In Ernie Nix's words, "I choose not to be miserable—it *is* a *choice*."[11]

If you feel stagnant in your midlife stage, the good news is there is much you can do; you can pivot, you can change and make improvements. As Ernie Nix learned, your behavior is a function of your decisions, not your conditions. You have the power to reinvent yourself so that your best days can still be ahead of you.

Occasionally in the middle of a successful career, something unexpected happens and you're forced to completely change directions.

Steve, a business owner, suddenly found himself forced out

by his partners of a company he had started twenty years earlier. At forty-six, he was discouraged, unemployed, and with a family of four he was in fear for his future. After careful deliberation, he determined to change careers and began law school at age forty-seven, by far the oldest student in his class.

After a few months of law school, Steve remembers pulling into his school's empty parking lot at 5 a.m. one bleak winter morning. It was pitch-dark, cold and icy, and the terrifying thought of "what have I done?" swept over him like a cloud of gloom. Years of school lay ahead, and at his age, he couldn't help but feel doubt and anxiety. Near paralyzed with thoughts of failure, he fought his fears and reaffirmed his resolve that he was going to see it through regardless of the rough road ahead. He determined to only focus on looking ahead at a new future, and he moved forward with courage and optimism.

Steve studied hard year-round and ended up graduating in two and a half years, and at forty-nine he set up his own law firm. Within a few years, his practice was thriving and he had more work than he could handle, in a new, satisfying career.[12]

Keep Moving Forward!

Though an unexpected "fermata" (pause) may occur during the midlife stage, don't get discouraged, give up, or bail out. With your newfound Crescendo Mentality paradigm, you know there are many more symphonies to write and perform. Though you cannot always choose what course your life will take, you can always focus on what you can control, look with optimism to the future, work hard and persevere, and believe your situation will eventually improve. Use that space between stimulus and response to step back, examine, reset, and choose wisely.

Many times people feel discontent with their work in the

middle of a career because they have not kept up with new practices, methods, training, or technology. Boredom or lack of fulfillment are not the only reasons people stagnate or want to change careers. Often, it is because they haven't made much effort to stay current and competent in their chosen field.

You may need to reinvent yourself by going back to school, researching what you are passionate about or have a natural inclination toward, and network with people who could help you undertake a significant career change. We need to constantly develop in order to avoid becoming obsolete.

Remember that today isn't forever! Once you're past the crisis, you may come to see that what you learned along the way was the most valuable part of the journey.

> *"I know of no more encouraging fact than the unquestionable ability of man to elevate his life by conscious endeavor."*
>
> —attributed to Henry David Thoreau

Although I didn't think of it as a "midlife crisis," at the time, I went through my own personal struggle during this stage in my life. After earning an MBA, I felt my passion and skills were in teaching, so instead of going into the family hotel business, which I had no interest in, I accepted a teaching position at a private university. I loved teaching students new concepts and ideas they could apply personally to their lives as well as to a future career. I taught a variety of business and organizational behavior classes for over twenty years. After about a decade, I worked to complete my doctorate degree—something that really broadened my vision in the area of human development.

During the 1970s and early 1980s, I began doing some private business consulting to various leaders and organizations throughout the United States. I loved taking principles I had developed in the classroom and applying them directly to the many businesses that I was hired to work with. About this time, I was very honored and excited when my colleagues in the Organizational Behavior Department nominated me to become a full professor. However, the head of my department cast a dissenting vote and influenced the committee to not grant me full professorship yet because I had not done enough research or published enough to justify the promotion.

This was a huge disappointment, as I felt that my true passion and mission was in teaching, not research. Though I was constantly reading and writing in my field and had begun exploring what would eventually become *The 7 Habits of Highly Effective People*, I had little interest in publishing within my department's journals. I had also consistently carried a heavy teaching load of twelve to fifteen hours a semester when most professors were teaching six to nine hours. I knew, however, that research and publishing were crucial for success at a university, so I had to seriously reconsider my options.

I had begun more business consulting, and it became difficult to juggle teaching and traveling while helping my wife, Sandra, raise a young family. But teaching what I called "principle-centered leadership" to business executives who could apply my leadership ideas directly to their employees and organizations was exhilarating. After twenty years of teaching and lately feeling somewhat stagnant in my job, it was time for a change.

Sandra and I wrestled with the decision for a time, but we eventually decided to take a giant leap of faith and step into the business world on our own. It was a risky move to walk away from a regular and stable salary at the age of fifty-one, but I knew I wanted to start my own consulting firm. We decided to mortgage both our home and cabin and begin a new company:

Stephen R. Covey & Associates. Sandra was a joint partner in this decision and had total confidence that I could make it a success, offering all the support I needed to undertake this enormous change in our lives. With several children living at home and a few in college, we knew we had to tighten our belts and make a lot of sacrifices. But we both felt the timing was right.

The decision proved to be a good one. Working as a business consultant full-time stretched and enlarged my skills and capacities in different ways from what I'd ever experienced before.

After I had spent ten years developing the material for a book, Simon & Schuster took a chance on an unknown author and in 1989 published *The 7 Habits of Highly Effective People*. From there, things really took off. It was the fulfillment of a dream to speak worldwide on core principles that I believed were innate in every culture and people.

I have always considered myself a teacher at heart, though I would never have had the opportunity to reach as many people had I not left the university when I did. I am so grateful for my years of teaching that provided the foundation for my own movement out of midlife and into a consulting and writing career (Living Life in Crescendo).

I share my own personal experience here because it's not always easy to find where your passions, talents, or mission in life lie, and it may take some time and considerable effort to discover what you're good at and want to do.

But it's important to take control of what's stagnant in your life and proactively and courageously *act* to bring about positive change. Like the Crescendo sign ⟨, during this midlife stage you should be continually progressing and increasing, broadening your scope and opportunities, and anticipating new things to learn and accomplish—preparing you for the next exciting opportunity in life.

Chapter 2

Love to Serve

"Don't look for big things, just do small things with great love."

—Mother Teresa

The love of serving others is a core characteristic of Living in Crescendo. Whatever stage of life they're in, people who serve look outside themselves and see needs they can meet. Though ordinary, and seemingly unimportant, our small, good deeds can spring into something worthwhile for someone else.

Doing small acts of service is much like planting a mustard seed. A mustard seed is so tiny, you can hardly see it, yet when planted and grown, it becomes the greatest herb of all. A mustard seed eventually grows into an enormous tree, so large that birds come to lodge in its branches. So it is with opportunities to serve. They're all around you if you just look for them, and many small acts of service yield enormous results.

Show Gratitude

"Cultivate the habit of being grateful for every good thing that comes to you, and give thanks continuously. And because all things have contributed to your advancement, you should include all things in your gratitude."

—Ralph Waldo Emerson

When you start to feel that life has passed you by, ironically the best thing you can do is to recognize and be grateful for all you have. Living Life in Crescendo includes showing consistent gratitude—even when you don't feel there is much to be grateful for. There is something about switching your mindset from one of self-pity to one of outwardness and gratitude that is healing and even transforming.

The love of service begins by looking outside of ourselves. Once we do, even in the midst of a midlife setback, we can see things that we can be grateful for. And our gratitude can give us perspective on whatever struggles we are undergoing.

At age fifty-three, John Kralik found his life at a terrible, frightening low. His small law firm was failing. He was struggling through a painful second divorce. He had grown distant from his two older children and was afraid he might lose contact with his young daughter. He was living in a tiny apartment where he froze in the winter and baked in the summer. He was forty pounds overweight. His girlfriend had just broken up with him. Overall, his life dreams seemed to have forever slipped beyond his reach.

Inspired by a beautiful, simple note his ex-girlfriend had sent to thank him for his Christmas gift, John imagined that he might find a way to feel gratitude by writing thank-you notes. To keep himself going, he set a goal—come what may—of writing 365 thank-you notes in the coming year.

One by one, day after day, he began to handwrite thank-you notes for gifts or kindnesses he'd received from loved ones and coworkers, from past business associates and even opposing attorneys, from college friends and doctors and store clerks and handymen and neighbors—anyone, absolutely anyone, who'd done him a good turn, however large or small.

Not long after he'd sent his very first notes, significant and surprising benefits began to come John's way—from financial gain to true friendship, from weight loss to inner peace. While John wrote his notes, the economy collapsed, the bank across the street from his office failed, but thank-you note by thank-you note, John's whole life turned around. Ironically, he discovered as he looked outward and expressed sincere gratitude to those who'd blessed his life, he healed inwardly and could once again look to the future with optimism.

After practicing law for thirty years in California, John Kralik achieved his dream and was appointed a judge in the Los Angeles Superior Court. Just two years after his life was at an all-time low, John published his story of overcoming his apparent "midlife crisis" in a book titled *A Simple Act of Gratitude: How Learning to Say Thank You Changed My Life*. His simple message of actively looking for reasons to show gratitude for others in your life through a sincere handwritten note has inspired countless others who became beneficiaries of his actions. Though saying thank you is something we learn when young, actually handwriting a note is an uncommon and surprisingly valued practice in this digital age.[13] This is the Crescendo Mentality way of thinking; as your focus shifts from yourself to others, your life and influence expands, and as John discovered, your best years can still be ahead of you.

Mother Teresa, who lived a life of service, knew the importance of gratitude and the rewards to the giver:

> A beggar one day came up to me and said, "Mother Teresa, everybody gives you things for the poor. I also want to give you something. But today, I am only able to get ten pence. I want to give that to you."
>
> I said to myself, "If I take it, he might have to go to bed without eating. If I don't take it, I will hurt him." So I took

it. And I've never seen so much joy on anybody's face who has given his money or food, as I saw on that man's face. He was happy that he too could give something.[14]

This seemingly small offering from such a poor man probably blessed him more than anyone who received it—but his attitude of gratitude was evident. He experienced true joy in being able to give to someone even less fortunate than himself. He was filled with an attitude of gratitude. Likewise, if you find ways to show gratitude for what you do have, even in the midst of a midlife crisis, I promise you will discover an abundance of joy you never thought possible and will gain insights into how to improve your own situation as well.

Give Back

"The best portion of a good man's life is his little, name-less, unremembered acts of kindness and love."
—William Wordsworth

If you're struggling in the midlife stage and waiting for something good to happen, forget yourself and your problems for a while and go out and serve someone. As you help someone or encourage them, if even in a small way, it can lighten their load and lift their spirits in ways that will lift your own.

One couple organized a small group to clean the house and yard of one of their neighbors who was overwhelmed and needed a little injection of hope. They worked hard for several hours when she was away and made her home and yard look cleaner and brighter. When the neighbor returned home, she was very surprised and grateful, and posted this touching message on Facebook:

A huge heartfelt thank you to the "cleaning fairies" who decided to visit my house today, whoever you are. There had to be more than one of you to move my fridge! Words cannot express how grateful and blessed I am to have friends like you in my life. I cried when I walked through my door tonight. I am overwhelmed by the love I feel. You truly know the meaning of service and I could never convey how much I appreciate you!! You've eased a burden—so from the bottom of my heart, THANK YOU![15]

Besides the positive impact in this person's life, imagine the effects on those who initiated the effort. Sometimes if we look around, we find someone in a more difficult situation than our own. Though we don't know what personal challenges this young couple faced themselves, the end result of lightening a struggling neighbor's burden was bound to bring joy into their own lives. That's something money can't buy and you can't get enough of. The act of giving to others without any expectation of receiving back is its own reward.

When you're struggling with difficult challenges, imagine the feeling when you offer a helping hand to someone who is in a similar situation. Part of the Crescendo way of thinking is actually believing *"your most important work is ahead of you,"* so you actively offer assistance to others during their time of need, especially if you've received help yourself.

Jorge Fierro grew up in Chihuahua, Mexico, and always dreamed of coming to America and starting a business. When he finally did cross the border years later, he was alone with very little money and didn't speak a word of English. His first job was in El Paso, Texas, digging ditches for a dollar an hour. Next he worked as a sheepherder in Wyoming. But he knew he wouldn't achieve the high goals he set for himself unless he learned English, and he was very committed to working hard and doing whatever it would take to one day live the American dream.

Jorge heard from other immigrants that if he could get to Salt Lake City, he could learn English from various programs that were already in place. So on his own, he made his way to Utah. When he first arrived, he didn't know anyone and immediately became part of the homeless population. But he soon discovered he was in a community of people who were good at heart. Somehow, there was always someone who would feed him. Jorge stayed at the Rescue Mission for a couple of months, began learning English, and worked at a minimum wage job washing dishes to support himself.

One day, he was really missing home and craved a classic Mexican dish of beans and rice, but he was less than impressed with what was available. He remembered with fondness his mother's delicious recipe for pinto beans and decided to make some to sell at a downtown farmer's market. He was encouraged when people tried the authentic beans that he called "De La Olla" and kept making more for several returning customers. He soon became a regular seller at the market. Jorge began to make his own authentic burritos too and sold those and other favorite Mexican dishes.

Jorge had a great desire to share the diverse and colorful flavors of his native cuisine, becoming a sort of ambassador for his culture and food. Little by little, he expanded his business from pinto beans and burritos, to tortillas, rice, salsa, guacamole, and eventually more than seventy-five products.

Today these products, under the Rico Brand, are delivered weekly to nearly one hundred supermarkets, coffee shops, and restaurants in his community. Over the years, Rico Brand has thrived and become a multimillion-dollar corporation.

Some friends approached Jorge with the idea of participating in "The Burrito Project," a nationwide movement, with no political or religious affiliations, with a mission to feed the hungry and homeless in cities around the world. Jorge, now in his midlife stage, immediately wanted to be a part of it since he valued service as one of his most important roles. As someone who had experienced homelessness himself, he had made a personal commitment that one day he would give back to others. "Pay it forward" became Jorge's mantra, and he was so committed to this inspiring idea that he had it prominently tattooed on his arm. With the perfect opportunity to help the homeless population, Jorge founded Burrito Project SLC.

Operating out of the Rico Brand distribution warehouse, the Burrito Project's volunteers made and distributed between six hundred and one thousand rice-and-bean burritos per week between April and December of 2012. Under Jorge's direction, fresh tortillas, rice, and beans were also prepared at the site. Then groups of volunteers gathered to roll burritos in foil and put them in coolers or bags to retain the heat. Other volunteers delivered them by car, walking, or bike messenger, in quantities of up to five hundred per day.

Since 2012, hundreds of volunteers have donated their time and services to making this unique humanitarian project a huge success, and true to their mission the Burrito Project is "committed to ending hunger one burrito at a time." Since 2017, Burrito Project SLC has made and delivered between nine hundred and fourteen hundred warm, nutritious burritos in Salt Lake City four days a week (Monday through Thursday), more often than any of the other thirty cities who run Burrito Projects throughout North America.

Jorge explains his motivation by saying, "Often we don't realize how blessed we are. I was eager to be a successful American and thankful for those who came along and helped me succeed."

The Burrito Project is a unique humanitarian effort because anyone can participate and make a difference—you don't need to be rich to help, just donating time is what is needed. Jorge believes this program has impacted the homeless population because "more than anything else . . . besides feeding them, we're just letting them know we care."[16]

This service blesses Jorge and those who are involved as much as the recipients because they focus on others in need rather than their own problems. Living Life in Crescendo can translate into seeing a need, paying it forward, and giving back regardless of how things are going for you. These are key components in helping you conquer your midlife battles. As you look outward to bless others, you will also find ways to overcome your own struggles.

> *"We can never pay in gratitude; one can only pay 'in kind' somewhere else in life."*
>
> —Anne Morrow Lindbergh, *North to the Orient*

Brian LeStarge went into the teaching profession because he wanted to light a fire in his students for a subject he was passionate about—science. He loved thinking of as many hands-on experiments as he could to engage his eighth-grade classes. He knew if they could get past the theory and rules of how things work, his students would have fun turning science into action.

He explained his philosophy in this way: "As a junior high teacher, I feel like my job is to 'romance' students into my discipline. I need to win them over to my subject to make it more interesting. . . . I'm always monitoring whether the kids are enjoying the class, and I try to teach with enthusiasm."

Every year, he "romanced" them by having students make their own rockets, shoot them off on the school's back lawn, measure how far they went, and discuss why some had more propulsion than others. This was the highlight of the year, and students became very competitive building just the right rocket to win the prized award for going farthest. They would also blow things up in class using certain chemicals (under supervised circumstances), and the kids loved finding the right combinations to make something explode. Mr. LeStarge was a popular teacher because he showed genuine interest in his students, knew their names, and shared his passion for science in a fun and interesting way.[17]

However, after many years of teaching and during his midlife stage, he started to question if he really was successful at making a difference in how they felt about science and if it was affecting them in their future. He found it difficult to see real results of the goals he set, and without much positive feedback, he became discouraged and began to lose sight of why he had gone into teaching in the first place.

Fortunately, about this same time, he was unexpectedly nominated for a prestigious teaching award in his school district by a group of parents who, unbeknownst to him, knew the impact he was having on his students. Many former students wrote about the direct influence he'd had on them going into a science-related field in college.

After he won, LeStarge's wife wrote this note thanking those involved:

I can't thank you enough for nominating my husband for this teaching award. It means so much to know someone would take the time and make the effort to do this. He has tried so hard for many years, but frankly it's a burnout job that doesn't get much credit or respect. This comes at just the right time because he recently became discouraged in his job, and even considered going into something else after all these years. But winning this award has shown him that his teaching efforts have actually made a difference in the lives of so many of his former students and he feels renewed again! His hope was always for others to be inspired because of his dedication and passion in teaching science, and now he sees this is actually happening. Please relay our deep gratitude to all those who helped with this nomination.[18]

In the years to come, former students would randomly show up in LeStarge's classroom unannounced and thank him for his influence, and it always motivated him to keep at it.

A decade after taking his class, one student, who graduated from college in mechanical engineering and got a job in that field, returned to tell him of the impact his teaching had on her life. "I want you to know," she said, "that you were the spark of what I ended up doing in college and beyond. . . . The seed you planted grew . . . it sparked a fire. You did a great job and it affected me."[19] And after twenty-seven years of teaching, it was still good to hear.

As discussed, during the midlife stage, many simply don't realize how successful they actually are in the lives of others because they may not see their direct impact right away. Or they may not get the necessary feedback that reflects their positive influence. Many people tend to compare themselves to others to gauge their success, but true success isn't always what it appears to be. A feeling of true success may take someone acknowledging another's positive impact and giving back in return. One success usually promotes another, and this continues on and on, doing good all along the way.

Service comes in such a variety of ways. Remember the first principle of Living in Crescendo during the midlife stage is to work to succeed in your most important roles. Often people who serve don't realize the positive impact they make in others' lives that eventually reflects "true success" in their own. The following examples are of ordinary people doing extraordinary things that bless others in their midlife stage of life.

One woman related this story: "My mother was stopped in a grocery store by an older gentleman who knew her mother, Cleo Smith, and wanted to share her impact on his life. He related that he and his brother were raised by an alcoholic father while they were growing up, and had a very hard, unhappy childhood. Their mother had left when he was little, and he had no memory of her. They lived far outside of town in a run-down house, and rarely had any visitors. But every year on his birthday, he would hear a knock at the door and when he opened it, there was Mrs. Smith standing there with a birthday cake! She was the only person who had ever made him a birthday cake while growing up, and the only one in his life who had made him feel special and loved. She was a light in his difficult world. Years later, this man recalled that of all the things in his childhood, this event stood out and made a significant difference in how he felt about himself, and ultimately he was able to re-create a better and happier life for himself and his own family."[20]

Robyn, a caring and proactive PTA president whose children attended a high school with more than a hundred refugees from thirty different countries, saw that many of these students couldn't focus during after school tutoring because they were so hungry. She got permission to clean out an old storage room in the cafeteria, asked parents to donate some ready-to-go foods, and soon students could pick up nutritious snacks that were available to them after school. She was caught off guard when one young man asked if he could bring something home for his siblings to eat, which prompted Robyn to expand the limited snacks to a full food pantry. The community responded to her requests for canned food and supplies, and soon volunteers and donors began showing up to help stock the pantry and distribute food to students in need.

It has since grown to a large and efficient pantry that weekly distributes hundreds of canned goods, hygiene items, surplus bread and bakery items from grocery stores, and often fresh fruit and vegetables, which always are in high demand. Robyn's small snack room is now an efficiently run community food pantry, and they are currently serving more than one hundred refugee families once or twice a week. Like the mustard seed, this project began small and has grown into a large and much needed service.[21]

> "Services rendered for love's sake have in them a poetry that is immortal."
>
> —Harriet Beecher Stowe

There are a myriad of ways to give much needed service to others. One woman volunteers to deliver food for Meals on Wheels and brings her older children along. She wants them to serve so they can meet wonderful yet sometimes forgotten older people who need assistance and long for friendship in their later years. A busy lawyer volunteers his time on weekends, helping the homeless to resolve their legal problems free of charge so they can have access to the resources they need, find adequate employment, and better their future. Someone else runs a mobile shower and haircut truck, providing free services to anyone in need of improving their hygiene and, consequently, their confidence and ability to secure a job.[22]

One mother was told by her son Mike that his new friend TJ never brought a lunch to school, or sometimes just bought a bag of chips. She discovered that TJ didn't have a mother in the home, and his father was doing his best, trying to juggle raising three young boys and working two jobs. TJ played on the basketball team with Mike, so she knew when they had practice right after school, he would be running on empty. So from then on, every day when she made lunch for her kids, she'd make an extra one for Mike to take to TJ. She never felt it was an inconvenience to make just one more when she knew TJ would benefit from a nutritious lunch just like Mike did.

She continued this small service for TJ all through junior high and high school, and the boys remained good friends while playing on teams together. Once when someone was asking TJ about his family, he said with pride, "Oh, I have a mother who looks out for me." Her service, though small, built a strong bond of love between them, and that brought her a lot of joy as she watched him progress through the years.[23]

> *"If you can't feed a hundred people then feed just one."*
> —Mother Teresa

Our service to another may not always be easy, convenient, or pleasant, but it is greatly needed. During the midlife stage, having the service mentality builds self-esteem, gratitude, and enriches your life as well as the people you serve. Marian Wright Edelman, the founder and chairman of the Children's Defense Fund, made this insightful observation: "Service is the rent you pay for being. It is the very purpose of life and not something you do in your spare time."[24]

What a powerful idea—service is the very purpose of life. Like the examples of those who "do small things with great love," you too have the power and the ability to love to serve, and you will bless others as well as yourself in the process.

Love to Serve

"I slept and dreamt that life was joy.
I awoke and saw that life was service.
I acted and behold, service was joy."

—Rabindranath Tagore[25]

I've asked many people through the years who their most influential role model or mentor is, and almost everyone can immediately name someone—a teacher, relative, friend, leader—who had a significant impact on their life. Working to succeed in an important role as a mentor is a powerful way to impact another person, particularly in your midlife years. And while you're seeking to lift someone else and help them realize their potential, you may inadvertently realize yours. Let's look at another example of "true success" as we have defined it during the midlife years.

Only his family and close friends know this, but Michael Clapier has mentored nearly two thousand young men along the way while raising his own family. For years, Mike spent extra time without pay with boys needing to improve their wrestling skills and build their confidence so they could compete at the junior high, high school, and club level. He encouraged their progress, gave them a positive vision of themselves in the future, and celebrated even small successes as if they were his own kids.

He and his wife, Linda, also brought some of these athletes into their home and gave them the love and attention many of them lacked from their own families. Some of these boys came from homes where they were not really appreciated, and a few were even neglected by their parents. They craved the love and attention they received from the Clapiers, who were raising six children of their own. Linda always made them feel welcome and often invited them to enjoy a homemade meal, or to share a holiday or special occasion with their family.

Though Michael and Linda weren't wealthy, they shared what they had and were very generous when they saw a need, regardless of their own financial situation. Without any recognition or even being asked, they bought clothes and sports equipment when needed, and fed several boys for years on a regular basis. The Clapiers became "second parents" to many and earned the love and gratitude of vulnerable boys who lacked direction and confidence.

One of the fathers, whose son Michael had worked with in wrestling, regretfully told him, "You've spent more time helping my son in wrestling than I have as his dad." As a direct result of Michael and Linda's efforts, these "adopted sons" have grown into outstanding young men, better equipped to go out in the world and live productive lives. Years later, they have earned college degrees, married, and started their own families, and are now employed in successful careers, which is very satisfying to the Clapiers, who greatly contributed to their formative years.

Years ago, at one of his son's wrestling matches, Michael met Lewis, a brilliant retired professor who had taught engineering at MIT. While they visited together, Michael discovered that Lewis was seventy-two years old, divorced, and lonely, with no family living nearby. The Clapier family immediately adopted him, spending many Sundays, holidays, and birthday celebrations together. Lewis was loved and appreciated by the Clapiers' grown children, their spouses, and the grandkids, who enjoyed his company and looked to him as an adopted "grandfather." In turn, he tutored the younger Clapier boys in math and science and mentored them from his life's experiences.

Lewis passed away at ninety-two years of age, after enjoying a full twenty years of being an important part of the Clapier family, where he felt loved and valued. What a different life of joy

Lewis experienced that he never would have known had he not been included in the family he'd never before had.[26]

True success? Without a doubt! The Crescendo perspective reminds us that true success may not be what it appears and or how others perceive it. The Clapiers enjoy the kind of rich family culture that all the money in the world cannot buy. Besides the six outstanding children of their own they've raised, many other lives have been enriched because Michael and Linda also cared about succeeding in their role as inspiring mentors. And most likely, some who appear to be "successful" would jump at the chance to trade places with this kind of success if they could.

Your Most Important Work Is Still Ahead of You

At the height of his career, country music star Garth Brooks shocked the music world when he unexpectedly announced his retirement in October of 2000. By that time he had won Entertainer of the Year at the Country Music Awards four times. He had performed before an estimated 1 million people in New York's Central Park in 1997 for a live HBO concert special. He had sold an astounding 100 million albums.[27]

But despite these professional successes, he was facing personal challenges. His mother, Colleen, who was his greatest support, had recently died of cancer, and his marriage to his wife, Sandy, was coming to an end. His biggest heartache, however, was that he felt he'd lost touch with his three young daughters. "Someone else was raising them," he said with regret. He recognized that he still had "important work ahead of him"— raising his young daughters—and he needed to focus on his most important role, being a parent. "Everything was telling me

I need to be there for my children. . . . People asked me, 'How could you walk away from music?' But being a dad—there's nothing that can touch that."[28]

So at age thirty-eight—just entering the prime of his middle age—he courageously followed his heart and paternal instincts and stepped away from a booming music career to start another one—raising his children . . . for the next fourteen years!

He never regretted it. He and his ex-wife worked together so their three young daughters could be with both their parents every day. He became a very hands-on father, organizing summer-long projects such as building a fifty-foot bridge spanning their property. After they completed this monumental task together, his daughters were so proud of their work, they believed they were capable of doing anything, and he felt great satisfaction knowing *he* was involved in raising them.

In 2005, he married music star Trisha Yearwood, whom he called "the love of my life." And when his youngest daughter finally left for college, Brooks decided he would give music another go. It was quite a leap of faith to attempt to jump back into the mainstream of country music and tour again. "I was scared nobody would show up, scared to death. Because you don't want to disappoint people. . . . I wanted them to say, 'That's better than I remember it.'"

Despite his fears, the "Garth Brooks World Tour with Trisha Yearwood" kicked off in Chicago with 140,000 sold tickets in three hours. Fans thronged to his concerts as if he had never left, and the world tour successfully ran from 2014 to 2017. After his "retirement," he won the Entertainer of the Year award in 2016, 2017, and then in 2019, for an unprecedented seven times.[29]

Exemplifying the Crescendo symbol $<$ as the years pass, Brooks continues to broaden and expand his talents and opportunities, instead of having them lessen and diminish. Always conscious of the needs around them, Garth and Trisha sponsored a prime-time music special performed from their home recording studio in March 2020, giving fans a much-needed escape from coronavirus quarantine stress and sending an important message that we can get through this together. "We're seeing how big things can be when we all do them as one. In addition to the special, we and CBS will donate $1 million to charities . . . combating the COVID-19 virus," they said in a joint statement.[30]

While rehearsing for his 2019 tour, in the Biography special *Garth Brooks—The Road I'm On*, Garth spoke to his musical staff about the Crescendo mentality of looking ahead and not behind them:

> "I love having the history that we have, but history is in the
> past. This is going to be the roughest tour we've been on.
> Do not ever think that what we've done is good enough. . . .
> If you think the hardest time in your life to challenge your-
> self in music is behind you, then think again."[31]

Just as believing *"your most important work is always ahead of you,"* working to succeed at your most important roles and changing what needs to be improved in your life will give you the motivation to keep trying, learning, and adapting to new challenges and setbacks. Believing and responding positively will put the helm of your life back into your own hands and empower you to chart your own exciting course . . . at any age, midlife or otherwise.

PART 2

THE PINNACLE OF SUCCESS

forte: (for-tay) adjective or adverb: loud, strong,
lively; a thing at which someone excels

*"Success . . . is to leave the world a bit better, to know
even one life has breathed easier because you lived."*
—Ralph Waldo Emerson

Imagine driving in a car and instead of looking ahead at what's coming, you constantly glance in your rearview mirror and over your shoulder to see what you left behind. It wouldn't take long before you ended up in a ditch. We must avoid the temptation to keep looking in the rearview mirror at what we've accomplished in our career and in life, and instead look ahead with optimism at what's coming next.

As we have seen so far, the Crescendo Mentality carries such power that it can propel one from a midlife crisis back on course toward success and fulfillment. But it isn't just for people who struggle and need to readjust. Living Life in Crescendo can also pour joy into the lives of those who believe they have already reached some Pinnacle of Success.

Just as we navigated through the midlife stage, with its ups and downs, the Pinnacle of Success has its own challenges. It's easy to relax and not feel much responsibility or obligation to reach out when you've experienced a comfortable degree of success for you and your family. But the best is yet to come!

The powerful *key* to Living in Crescendo is truly believing that *"your most important work is always ahead of you."* Whatever you are presently working on *is* your most important work. That's the work you must give yourself to now because what you've accomplished in the past is past. Forward-thinking people look ahead to what they can accomplish tomorrow.

Why is this so vital? What motivation and desire would there be to get out of bed in the morning if you thought you had nothing else to offer—if all your most important contributions were already finished? What would be your purpose? When you rise each morning, you should have purpose, vision, and goals that need to be accomplished. These may be completely different from before, but your greatest contributions may be yet to come.

To personalize this point, one of my daughters once asked me if I would ever again write anything like *The 7 Habits of Highly Effective People*. Her question, though not intended this way, insulted me! Were all my good ideas and teaching concepts contained in *7 Habits*? Did I have nothing else to contribute? Was I "one and done"? If I had nothing of value left to produce, then what was I doing every day? I told her that my best stuff was yet to come and that I had several books still in my head.

Now, I didn't say that to inflate or overvalue myself, but why shouldn't I feel that way? Why shouldn't you? I have always believed that regardless of my stage of life, my best work is still ahead of me, waiting for me to discover and teach it. Maintaining that attitude—the Crescendo Mentality—is the key to lifelong passion, dreaming, excitement, and mission. It is why you and I should be getting up every day.

Peter Jackson worked for fourteen years to bring J.R.R. Tolkien's *Lord of the Rings* series to life on screen. After his incredible success and numerous Academy Awards, he was asked if this was his greatest work and life legacy. His answer reflects exactly what we should all feel: "If I say yes, that's assuming I'm not going to make anything better. That may be the case, but I'm not going to concede that now—I still have more to produce."[1]

He certainly did. Jackson went on to direct the *Hobbit* trilogy, *King Kong*, *The Lovely Bones*, and *They Shall Not Grow Old*, in addition to many others still on his production slate. Imagine if he had believed that *Lord of the Rings* was all that was in him? Yet after experiencing great financial success in his career, Jackson has also given back in a big way. He and his wife, Fran, have contributed $500,000 to stem cell research in the hope that others will benefit.[2] They also saved a historic and much loved church from demolition in their community, donating more than 1 million dollars to renovate St. Christopher's in Wellington, New Zealand.[3] Clearly, after great success in his profession, Peter Jackson continued to make significant contributions in other areas of life through his charitable giving.

The idea of Living Life in Crescendo is a very empowering one and, as said, something I have adopted as my own personal mission statement. When I have shared this principle in my professional work, I have had as strong a positive reaction and connection to it as anything I have previously taught. I have seen it ignite and empower people who believed they had nothing else to offer and were done with their life's work. I have seen fire in the eyes of those who found new life and passion in their profession, or in some great social cause they felt drawn to promote due to this motivational mindset. To many, it gave hope and inspiration to believe that their most important and greatest work might still be ahead of them, regardless of past achievements and success.

"Be the change you want to see in the world."
—attributed to Mahatma Gandhi

In each of the four life stages identified in this book, my goal is to provide practical and useful takeaways that can be directly applied to your personal life in regard to Living in Crescendo, at any age or stage you're in. At the end of this section is a personal inventory that hopefully will help you in setting your own goals related to the Pinnacle of Success.

Chapter 3

People Are More Important Than Things

*"It's not what we have in our life, but who
we have in our life that counts."*

—J. M. Laurence

In the winter of 1999, Chip Smith, a contractor, was hired to build a cabin in Montana for our family. Chip shares his story:

While I was in the middle of building Stephen and Sandra's cabin, I was going through an unwanted divorce and my life had really turned upside down. There were a few time-sensitive and critical questions that needed to be answered about the project, and they had agreed to drive over 350 miles to meet with me for two hours over dinner, rest at the hotel, and drive back home at 5 a.m. the next morning, as Stephen had to fly out immediately for business when they returned. I knew our time together would be short but important, so I had prepared an agenda and had all the plans and materials ready for an efficient meeting. We greeted one another and sat down for business.

We ordered dinner and Sandra spoke. "Chip, Stephen and I understand that you are going through some difficult times in your personal life right now." I thanked Sandra for her concern and tried to change the subject in order to get on with the details concerning their cabin. Sandra interrupted again and asked if there was anything that she and Stephen could do for me. I thanked her and said that I was really doing fine, and just needed to continue working through the troubles.

Sandra reached for my hand and said, "Chip, we are here for you. Please know what you're going through now is so much more important to us than worrying about decisions for the cabin."

Well, needless to say, I broke down in tears, and we spent the next three hours talking about my problems and concerns. I was so embarrassed that they had traveled such a distance on icy roads, and we had not addressed any of their needs before they returned. It was such a bonding moment for me, as I realized they truly cared, and that I was more important to them than building their family cabin.

Sometime after, Chip put the pieces of his life back together, and resumed building a beautiful cabin for our family. Several years later, when Dad passed away, our family returned to the cabin and found it had a severe bat problem. Still full of emotion from the funeral, and not knowing what to do since Dad had always taken care of such things, I called Chip and explained the situation. Without hesitation, Chip came immediately, brought a big crew with him, worked throughout the day to fix the problem, even swept out the garage without being asked, and refused any compensation for the work. He insisted it was his chance to repay my parents for being there for him during the darkest time of his life.[4]

—*Cynthia Covey Haller*

In relationships, people are infinitely more important than things. It's vital to continually renew your basic commitment to that principle, which will unite you with those most important in your life. Differences are not ignored; they are subordinated. The issue or one's point is never as important as the relationship. You will always be grateful you chose to take the time to build and maintain your relationships with your family and friends over devoting that time to material things.

> *"One who knows how to show and accept kindness will be a friend better than any possession."*
>
> —Sophocles

Life Is About Contribution, Not Accumulation

> *"I don't know what your destiny will be, but one thing I know: the only ones among you who will be really happy are those who will have sought and found how to serve."*
>
> —Albert Schweitzer

The story is told of two friends at the funeral of a wealthy man. One turned to the other and whispered, "Do you have any idea how much he left?" The other replied matter-of-factly, "Of course I do. He left it all!"

In my presentations over many years, I have often related that no one on their deathbed wished they had spent more time at the office. But they do regret alienation from a child, useless grudges held, opportunities missed serving, unfulfilled dreams, or time not spent with family and loved ones. When I go to the funeral of a close friend or family member and approach the coffin, it is a reminder and sometimes even a surprise that the deceased person's body is all that's in there. All that remains is the good that was done while they were alive, their precious relationships with family and friends—those they loved and who loved them back. This is their legacy.

Through the years, I have gained the perspective that it is *contribution* that brings light to the eye and meaning to the soul. There are a myriad of ways you can contribute to the lives of others throughout your lifetime, and by so doing, you will experience fulfillment and happiness, something that money simply can't buy. And for those of you who have achieved some level of financial success or influence in your life, the opportunities to give and contribute are even greater. I deeply believe that the great secret to happiness is contribution, not accumulation.

Aleksandr Solzhenitsyn was an outspoken critic of the Soviet Union after World War II and became a prisoner of the Russian forced labor camps for many years. These difficult experiences gave him a unique perspective about wealth and contribution. He wrote: "The endless accumulation of possessions will not bring fulfillment. Possessions must be subordinated to other, higher principles so that they must have spiritual justification, a mission."[5] Clearly if we don't have an accurate perspective concerning possessions, they can possess each of us. This section teaches that living the Crescendo Mentality and looking outward—living a life of contribution—gives you a sense of inner peace and security that possessions can't match.

Mother Teresa, who spoke to people in more than a hundred countries, taught that the *purpose* of wealth was to bless others with it:

I think that a person who is attached to riches, who lives with the worry of riches, is actually very poor. If this person puts his money at the service of others, then he is rich, very rich. . . . Many people think, especially in the West, that having money makes you happy. . . . If God has given you this gift of wealth, then use it for his purpose—help others, help the poor, create jobs, give work to others. Don't waste your wealth."[6]

Clearly Mother Teresa believed wealth wasn't the problem in itself. In fact, it could be part of the solution to alleviating many of the world's most difficult problems. But I have found that focusing on accumulating wealth will not provide lasting happiness and fulfillment in your life if you don't also use your wealth to bless others. These contributions will be what you will cherish more than the money itself.

Consider the story of Karl Rabeder, an interior furnishings entrepreneur from Austria, who from humble beginnings became extraordinarily successful by worldly standards. "I came from a very poor family where the rules were to work more to achieve more material things, and I applied this for many years," said Mr. Rabeder. "But wealth doesn't create happiness. I know this because for 25 years I lived this life, growing richer and feeling worse."

Karl was a passionate glider and went on numerous trips to South America and Africa, witnessing firsthand the immense poverty in these countries. This had a powerful impact on his life. After living a luxurious lifestyle, he finally admitted that deep down he was miserable, working like a slave for things that he didn't even want or need. After years of living what he described as a "horrible, soulless, and without feeling five-star lifestyle," he finally listened to the voice inside him that said: "Stop what you are doing now—all this luxury and consumerism—and start living your real life!"

For many years he was not gutsy enough to give up the trappings of his comfortable existence, but after a three-week holiday with his wife to the Hawaiian Islands, he realized that "if I don't do it now, I won't do it for the rest of my life." He bravely acted on his inner prompting and sold his luxurious £1.4 million villa overlooking the Alps, his beautiful stone farmhouse valued at £613,000, and his six gliders, which sold for £350,000, as well as his Audi, worth around £44,000. He moved out of his beautiful Alpine retreat into a small wooden hut in the mountains and began to live simply and happily, he claims, for the first time in a very long time.

After selling his possessions, he invested £3 million into a microcredit charity, offering tiny business loans to self-employed people in Central and Latin America who struggled to keep their small businesses alive from day to day. He offered them microloans at little or no interest so they could buy supplies to sell and grow their business. He realized how remarkable it was that they could be successful with very little capital. They then began to earn a decent living for their families while retaining their dignity, and eventually repaid their loan.[7]

Karl discovered that the key to lasting happiness is not accumulation of possessions but contribution to others. While traveling around the world Karl met so many people, and in his own words, "I began to realize I didn't need my house, nice cars, gliders, or overpriced dinners. The next step was to connect with people. . . . For 25 years, I worked like a slave for things I didn't want or need. Now," he exclaimed gleefully, "my dream is to have nothing!"[8]

Isn't that ironic? *Nothing* in terms of material wealth, but *everything* in terms of real contribution and value. Imagine the impact his microcredit loans had on struggling entrepreneurs who could now provide for their families, help their children get an education, and even hope for a better future. Karl found true happiness not in accumulating wealth, but helping others build theirs.

"What do we live for if it is not to make life less difficult for each other?"

—Mary Ann Evans, pen name—George Eliot

Now obviously I'm not suggesting we need to give up all our money, sell our possessions, and live a simple life in a wooden hut like Karl Rabeder—but there is a great lesson to be learned from his story. Karl found meaning in his life when he was focused on serving other people more than on his material wealth.

The author Jeff Brumbeau wrote a most insightful children's book titled *The Quiltmaker's Gift*—a message also beneficial for adults. The story he tells is of a greedy king who has every material thing he could ever want, yet his possessions do not make him happy.

The king hears of an old woman who makes the most beautiful quilts in the world and who gives them away for free to people who can't afford them. She works all day on her quilts, and although she has few material possessions, she is very happy with her simple life. So the king decides he wants one of her quilts more than anything else, and is stunned when she won't sell him one for any amount of money. She explains that they are only for those who can't afford them. He is livid, but the old woman won't bend, no matter what he does to threaten or punish her . . . and he certainly tries!

Finally she makes a deal with the king, since she knows how selfish he is and how he doesn't like to share any of his beautiful things. She tells him for each possession he gives away, she will make a square for his quilt. He reluctantly agrees because, though he loves all of his treasures, her beautiful quilt is the one thing he can't have. At first, he can't find anything in all his treasures he can part with, but finally he decides to give away a single marble. To his surprise, the boy who receives it is so happy that the king decides to find other things to give away, and each time when he sees the joy on the face of the receiver, he can't resist smiling.

"How can this be?" the king cries. "How can I feel so happy about giving my things away?" Though he doesn't understand why, he orders his servants to "bring everything out! Bring it all out at once!"

And so each time he gives a gift away, the quiltmaker adds another piece to his quilt. After everyone in his kingdom has received a gift from him, he begins giving away his things to people all around the world, trading his treasures for smiles.

Soon the king has nothing left to give, and the old woman finishes his beautiful quilt and wraps it around him, since his royal clothes are now in tatters. "As I promised you long ago," the old woman says, "when the day came that you, yourself, were poor, only then would I give you a quilt."

"But I'm not poor," protests the king. "I may look poor, but in truth my heart is full to bursting, filled with memories of all the happiness I've given and received. I'm the richest man I know."

And so from then on, the quiltmaker sews her beautiful quilts by day, and at night the king takes them down to the town, searching out the poor and downhearted, never happier than when he is giving something away.[9]

> "You give but little when you give of your possessions.
> It is when you give of yourself that you truly give."
> —Kahlil Gibran

Live Outside Yourself

"Life's most urgent question—what are you doing for others?"

—Martin Luther King Jr.

This piercing question, frequently asked by Dr. King, should strike at every heart and motivate all to action.

In 2014, Adam Grant was the youngest tenured and highest rated professor at the University of Pennsylvania's Wharton School of Business. He wrote a book called *Give and Take*, which explains why we should include giving when formulating our personal goals.

Grant wrote: "When I think about people who are givers, I would just define them as being the kinds of people who enjoy helping others and often do it with no strings attached." Grant believes most people think they need to achieve success first and then you can give charitable service—but his research actually suggests just the opposite. "There are some people like Bill Gates who succeed first and then start giving back, but the majority of successful people out there began giving long before they achieved greatness." Grant says, "I would love to redefine success to say it's not just what you achieve, it's also what you help other people achieve."[10]

Now imagine the impact you could make if your money, influence, and efforts literally saved countless lives, illustrated in the following inspiring example.

For many years, Bill Gates made a successful name for himself in the technology industry with Microsoft, which he cofounded and turned into a multibillion-dollar enterprise that revolutionized technology by making computing accessible to consumers worldwide. He has even been at the very top of the Forbes list of the wealthiest people in the world. However, history may one day honor him as the greatest philanthropist of our time. His lasting legacy may be not only one of innovation, but of inspiration to millions of people whose lives have been impacted for good because of his worldwide health and education initiatives. Perhaps most important, he is inspiring others who also have great wealth and influence to do the same. Like a rock thrown into a lake, his influence for giving, and consequently the good it does, spreads wider and wider, and the ripples affect all they touch.

In the movie *Spider-Man*, Uncle Ben gives his nephew Peter a key to using his gift for good when he shares the now familiar axiom: "With great power comes great responsibility." Bill Gates was raised by parents who had a high interest in community service and giving back to those around them. This upbringing was complemented by the influence of his wife, Melinda, who had a similar background and is also very service-minded. Additionally, Bill's study of the lives of philanthropists such as Rockefeller and Carnegie instilled in him a sense of duty to give his resources to charity—especially while he was still living, so he could manage it himself. Though he never met Rockefeller, he admired the strategic way in which before he died he gave most of his fortune away to causes he believed in.

> *"Money has no utility to me beyond a certain point. Its utility is entirely in building an organization and getting the resources out to the poorest in the world."*
>
> —Bill Gates[11]

In 2000, Bill Gates stepped down as CEO of Microsoft and began devoting more time to the Bill and Melinda Gates Foundation with the goal of changing the world through the paradigm of giving.[12] Their friend and co-trustee Warren Buffett once gave them some great advice about philanthropy: "Don't just go for safe projects; take on the really tough problems." They've taken his advice to heart and gone to work taking decisive action.[13]

With the belief and vision that "all lives have equal value," the Gates have created the nation's largest philanthropic trust and donate their time and money to some of the world's most urgent issues, among them being adequate health care, preventing premature births, combating infectious diseases (particularly malaria), working on extreme poverty, sanitation issues, education inequity (particularly girls' and women's), and equal access to information and technology worldwide.[14]

Bill and Melinda were stunned to learn that a half million children in poor countries around the world—but not in the United States—were dying every year from diarrheal diseases. Low-cost oral rehydration salts could save their lives, but no one felt any responsibility to intervene on their behalf.

The Gates realized *they* needed to seize the opportunity right in front of them to literally save these children's lives. They learned they could have a big impact through their foundation by looking for problems governments and markets weren't addressing and seeking solutions they weren't trying. Saving children's lives was the goal that launched their global work, with their first big investment in vaccines that hadn't yet reached poorer countries.

One vaccination initiative focused on children five and under, and helped cut the number of childhood deaths in half, from 12 million a year to 6 million.[15]

> *"We believe all lives had equal value, but we saw that the world didn't act that way, that poverty and disease afflicted some places far more than others. We wanted to create a foundation to fight those inequities."*
>
> —Melinda Gates[16]

Before their vaccination campaign, polio—which had been eradicated almost everywhere in the world—still raged and destroyed lives in Afghanistan, India, Nigeria, and Pakistan. In 2012, more than half of all polio cases worldwide were found in Nigeria. The World Health Assembly launched the Global Polio Eradication Initiative largely through a massive immunization campaign which the Bill and Melinda Gates Foundation and Rotary International joined. Two years later, the Gates Foundation committed to pay $76 million of Nigeria's polio debt (over the course of twenty years), and due to their successful efforts, no new cases of polio were reported in Nigeria in 2017.[17]

As of 2017, the Gates Foundation has contributed nearly $3 billion to the Global Polio Eradication Initiative, ultimately reducing the number of polio cases by 99.9 percent and saving more than 13 million children from paralysis. What had been 350,000 cases of polio each year fell to below 20, found in just two remaining countries, Afghanistan and Pakistan.[18]

Bill Gates discovered that working full-time at the Gates Foundation was as demanding and consuming as being the CEO of Microsoft was, and it continues to be interesting and challenging.[19] And as a wealthy American woman who excels in technology herself, Melinda Gates could have taken a much easier path and not become intimately involved in the many complicated and critical issues of worldwide extreme poverty, but she willingly made a different choice.

Melinda has particularly influenced the direction and priorities of their work for their foundation. She hasn't just studied data and analyzed theories from the comfort of her home; she has gone to the communities the foundation works with. She has visited low-income countries in Africa and South Asia multiple times with her team and spoken with mothers, midwives, nurses, and community leaders, to learn about their lives and challenges. Not willing to ignore difficult problems, Melinda has worked hard to study and understand various cultures in order to promote change and progress for women in several important areas. Many of the cultural breakthroughs her team has achieved through education and empowerment have resulted in not only enriching but also saving lives.[20]

Melinda soon discovered that "in societies of deep poverty, women are pushed to the margins. Women are outsiders. . . . Overcoming our need to create outsiders is our greatest challenge as human beings. It is the key to ending deep inequality. . . . This is why there are so many old and weak and sick and poor people on the margins of society. . . . Saving lives starts with bringing everyone in. Our societies will be healthiest when they have no outsiders. We have to keep working to reduce poverty and disease. . . . It's not enough to help outsiders fight their way in—the real triumph will come when we no longer push anyone out."[21]

After years of firsthand observing, learning, and actively working to find answers to very difficult problems, Melinda wrote an enlightening account of her experiences and insights into the lives of those living in extreme poverty: *The Moment of Lift: How Empowering Women Changes the World*.

After reaching the Pinnacle of Success, Bill and Melinda have chosen to live outside themselves and have expanded their Circle of Influence around the world. Though the Gates divorced in 2021, both remain committed to the work of the foundation as cochairs and trustees, dedicated to continuing the work they've been doing since 2000. How easy it would have been to sit back and rest on their fortune. What more was there to prove or conquer? Yet, *life is about contribution, not just accumulation,* and their worldwide contributions are immeasurable.

In 2010, Bill and Melinda, along with Warren Buffett, established the Giving Pledge, whose mission is to "invite wealthy individuals and families to commit to give the majority of their wealth to philanthropic causes and charitable organizations of their choice, either during their lifetime or after their death." The Giving Pledge "takes its inspiration from the example set by givers of all financial means and backgrounds. We are inspired by the example set by millions of Americans who give generously (and often at personal sacrifice) to make the world a better place."[22]

> *"Someone is sitting in the shade today because someone planted a tree a long time ago."*
> —Warren Buffett

Since the creation of the Giving Pledge, and as of December 2021, the group's membership has risen to 231 signatories from twenty-eight countries around the world, and ranges in age from people in their thirties to those in their nineties, pledging their fortunes to a wide range of causes (givingpledge .org).[23] This group of entrepreneurs and business leaders also represents diverse industries such as technology, medicine, biotech, real estate, and dairy farming.[24] From health care to education to poverty alleviation, this far-reaching initiative is a new global and multigenerational approach to working on some of society's biggest problems.

Bill Gates has committed to give 95 percent of his wealth away, mostly during his lifetime. In 2006, Warren Buffett pledged that 99 percent of his wealth would go to philanthropy during his lifetime or after his death. He explained, "The reaction of my family and me to our extraordinary good fortune is not guilt, but rather gratitude. Were we to use more than 1% of my claim checks on ourselves, neither our happiness nor our well-being would be enhanced. In contrast, that remaining 99% can have a huge effect on the health and welfare of others."[25]

Al Ueltschi, the father of modern flight training, donated most of his fortune to fight blindness. Cataract disease is the cause of 51 percent of all blindness, and yet a five-minute $50 surgery can reverse it. Ueltschi gave $5.1 million to HelpMeSee, which performs these life-changing operations. When he signed the pledge, he encouraged others to not wait until it's too late: "I have never seen a hearse pulling a U-Haul trailer. You can't take it with you!" He died a month later, in 2012, at the age of ninety-five, having given $260 million dollars away.[26]

What an incredible difference it would make to various philanthropic causes and charitable organizations if those who had reached the Pinnacle of Success took the challenge and signed the Giving Pledge. Imagine how their billions of dollars would change the lives of countless people. Their Circle of Influence (which includes the causes they value and choose to support) would be felt worldwide; the impact would not just life-altering but life-saving.

For most of us, our Circle of Influence may be smaller, affecting individuals or a group closer to us. But these contributions are still very valuable. Large- and small-scale contributions are both needed to promote positive change and lasting good in our society.

Instead of focusing on all the things they can't do anything about, like past successes or failures, proactive people in the Pinnacle of Success stage focus their time and energy on things they can do to build a bright future, on needs they see around them, and respond; they build on the connections and resources they have that can influence others for good.

"Giving frees us from the familiar territory of our own needs to the unexplained worlds occupied by the needs of others."

—Barbara Bush

Take Kerry and Kevin, for example. After years of hard work establishing themselves in a small town in northern Texas where they are raising their six children, Kerry and Kevin have experienced a type of Pinnacle of Success in their community. Instead of coasting and just focusing on their family alone, they have chosen to give of themselves generously through service and community involvement, as their town has many needs.

Kevin works as a dentist and has served as president of the Rotary Club and coached most of the youth sports teams for both boys and girls for many years. One year the city didn't pay for the local baseball field to be prepared and grass to be watered, so Kevin did the work and paid for the water himself, ensuring the kids wouldn't have to miss out on the baseball season that spring. Every year, Kevin and the other dentist in town provide local children with sealants on their teeth to prevent cavities, free of charge.

Besides helping run the Sealant Clinic, Kerry has been active in organizing a Christmas open house tour, raising money for other local charities, including food drives through the years, and volunteering to read with students weekly at her children's Title 1 elementary school.

One day a second-grade girl named Maria came into class crying, so Kerry spontaneously gave her a big hug, which quickly calmed her down. For the next few weeks, Kerry kept her eye on Maria and noticed she had a very strong personality and was generally disliked, and even bullied, by some of the kids in her class. Besides struggling socially, Maria's reading and math skills were far below her grade level, yet this was not being addressed by the teacher at all.

Kerry determined to befriend Maria and asked the principal for her parents' contact information so she could invite her to play with her own children after school. She was shocked with the principal's blunt response: "Oh, no. Believe me, you don't want to have anything to do with either her or her father. Their mother is in prison and has been for a long time! Their whole family has real honesty problems—they lie and steal. You'd be better to just stay away from them."

To Kerry, this explained a lot of the emotional and behavioral problems Maria exhibited. Despite the principal's warning, Kerry determined she needed to be involved with Maria and her younger sister, Angie, and eventually got hold of their father.

Kerry discovered that their family lived on the outskirts of town. The father didn't own a car and was very disengaged from his daughters' education since he was illiterate himself. With his approval, Kerry arranged to have his girls come home with her kids after school one day. The first time they came over, they were so happy to be there, they just cried. She soon discovered the girls' favorite thing was just to sit close to Kerry as she read them book after book, most of them on a toddler level. They craved her attention and loved when she would show them any sort of motherly affection. Once when they were reading, Angie leaned close into Kerry and timidly asked, "Can you just pretend to be my mom?" Their need for a normal family life with loving parents was heartbreaking, and Kerry soon found that although they liked to play with her kids, they mostly just wanted attention and love from her.

Both Maria and Angie loved coming home after school with Kerry, and she made it a weekly event, getting into a routine of helping them with their homework before they'd play, and typically inviting them to stay for dinner. Though their father was a decent man, he didn't have many of the skills a single parent needs, and he struggled making a living. Kerry began giving him a ride to school programs and activities, and eventually he saw how important it was to his girls that he was there, and realized if he didn't come, they would be the only ones without a parent to support them.

Maria and Angie began to blossom. It didn't take long before the behavior problems stopped, and their reading and math skills increased drastically through Kerry's tutoring after school. By playing with her kids they learned to be more socially aware, which greatly improved their likeability with other kids at school. As their skills improved, their confidence soared.

When the annual Living Wax Museum activity came around in Angie's class, Kerry made sure she had a character costume from history, just like the other students, as well as an informative poster and video so she could represent herself well in this important project. By the end of her presentation, Kerry could see that for the first time, Angie knew she could succeed.[27]

What an infusion of hope this surrogate mother injected into the lives of these two neglected girls who lacked a mother to love and nurture them. After creating a beautiful home life for her own family and becoming a person of influence in her community, Kerry helped create a new life for these girls where they too could succeed and feel loved and valued.

The key to happiness is to live outside yourself—to work together with others—driven by a common vision or mission to contribute. One young mother remembers her grandmother always saying, "It's been a challenging day. Let's go find someone to serve." What a remarkable and wise perspective! Reacting to needs and giving to others in ways that only *you* can do is an essential part of living the Crescendo Mentality.

> *"But if you want to be a true professional, you will do something outside yourself, something to repair tears in our community, something to make life better for people less fortunate than you. That's what I think a meaningful life is. One lives not just for one's self but for one's community."*
> —Ruth Bader Ginsburg[28]

Chapter 4

Leadership Is Communicating Worth and Potential

My dad had many abilities, but being mechanically minded was not one of them. According to a family story, in our parents' early years of marriage, Dad once hired an electrician to see what was wrong with a light and was told he just needed a new bulb. My mom claims Dad then asked what the electrician would charge to install one! He never lived that one down.

After my father died, I was reminded of this because of a good man named John Nuness, whom he relied on over the years to help with the equipment in our family's favorite vacation spot in Montana. He cheerfully provided top-notch service and attention and took pride in our machines as though they were his own. Dad absolutely depended on him, and John would often go to the lake at night after work so our Jet Skis and other equipment would be working the next day. This was so valuable to us, since vacation time for some of our family was limited.

After my dad passed away, John continued to help us, which we really appreciated. One day when I thanked him, he surprised me with his response.

"I have to tell you something. Stephen was the only person who has ever truly appreciated what I do for a living. I have loved working with him through the years mostly because he made me feel so good about myself, and he sincerely valued my skills and service to your family. I'm happy to keep helping you because your father made me feel appreciated as a person and in my profession—and it means the world to me."[29]

> I had no idea. Such a simple thing to say, "I really appreciate what you do, thank you." How often do we sincerely thank someone who blesses our lives?
>
> —Cynthia Covey Haller

Many years ago, Kenneth Blanchard wrote a powerful little book called *The One Minute Manager*. One of the great ideas from Blanchard's book was this blunt but true statement: "Unexpressed good thoughts aren't worth squat!" Blanchard further writes:

> Of all the concepts that I have taught over the years, the most important is about "catching people doing things right." There is little doubt in my mind that the key to developing people is to catch them doing something right and praising them for their performance. You will notice when you do . . . that person's attention perks up.[30]

Make a commitment now that when you have a good thought about another person, you will take the time to express it in that very moment. If you delay, sometimes that opportunity is gone—maybe forever. By developing this good habit—something that takes just seconds—you can make someone's entire day, reinforce good behavior, instill confidence, show appreciation, and maybe help someone with an unseen need or issue. Expressing good thoughts about people motivates them to keep doing their best. An old Japanese proverb says: *"One kind word can warm three winter months."*

Don't let the moment pass, because as a once popular song laments, "we may never pass this way again." No decent person ever said or thought, "I wish I hadn't been so good to my children while they were growing up!"

> *I have wept in the night*
> *At my shortness of sight,*
> *That to others' needs made me blind.*
> *But I never have yet had a twinge of regret,*
> *For being a little too kind.*
>
> —Unknown

Every parent knows that getting young children to behave while out to dinner is no easy feat, especially if you're on your own. A young single mother took her children to a Pizza Hut one weekend in Raleigh, North Carolina. She was going through a messy divorce, and two of her young children had special needs. She approached a man seated nearby and apologized in advance for the noise and commotion they were about to make. He assured her that he was a father himself and understood the situation.

It wasn't until the mother went up to pay for their meal that the man's kindness was revealed. He had already paid for her family's dinner, bought them a gift card so they could return another time, and wrote a note on the back of her receipt that brought her to tears:

I do not know your back story, but I have had the privilege of watching you parent your children for the past thirty minutes. I have to say thank you for parenting your children in such a loving manner. I have watched you teach your children about the importance of respect, education, proper manners, communication, self-control, and kindness all while being patient. I will never cross your path again, but I am positive your children will have amazing futures. Keep up the good work and when it starts to get tough, do not forget that others may be watching and will need the encouragement of seeing a good family being raised. God bless. Jake.[31]

She was so grateful for what had happened that she contacted a local TV station in an attempt to thank Jake for giving her an enormous boost at a particularly low time of her life. "You just don't know what people go through," the mother told ABC 11. "Here I've had the worst few years of my life and I never get recognition like this! I just do what I can to get by. I want him and his family to know that he's awesome! You never know who's watching you."[32]

Jake's effort to acknowledge this struggling single mother for her patience and fortitude in raising some challenging kids was of immeasurable value. More than paying for the meal and the gift card, Jake acknowledged the worth and importance of raising a young family.

> *"Too often we underestimate the power of a touch, a smile, a kind word, a listening ear, or the smallest act of caring— all of which have the potential to turn a life around."*
>
> —Leo Buscaglia

The Dulcinea Principle: The Power of Positive Affirmations

I love the story of the classic musical *Man of La Mancha*, taken from Cervantes's *Don Quixote*, which teaches the inspiring message of believing in the potential of another person. Don

Quixote is a medieval knight who falls in love with Aldonza, a simple peasant girl and a prostitute. Everyone else around her treats her as she is, but the valiant knight ignores this reality—he alone responds to her according to what he believes she can become, her potential as a virtuous woman.

At first, she doesn't believe he is sincere. But Don Quixote affirms his vision of her, again and again, and calls her by a new name, Dulcinea—providing a new identity through which she can see herself. He patiently persists until his affirmations gradually begin to penetrate Aldonza's tough overlay. Little by little she makes changes in her life and embraces his perception of her, much to the disappointment of those who can only see the prostitute. With this new paradigm, she eventually *becomes* Dulcinea, a woman of beauty and virtue, who with a new image has a completely different life of opportunity ahead of her.

Finally, when Don Quixote is dying, she comes to his deathbed, where he again affirms her worth and sings that inspiring song, "The Impossible Dream." His message to her is clear: Never give up on your potential. Or your dreams! Always believe in the best that is inside you. He looks into her eyes and affirms her new identity once more and essentially pleads, *"Never forget that you are Dulcinea."*[33]

> *"It is only with the heart that one can see rightly; what is essential is invisible to the eye."*
>
> —Antoine de Saint-Exupéry, *The Little Prince*

Don Quixote saw in Aldonza something more than what she was, something that even she couldn't see. With unconditional love, he revealed it to her. We can learn much from Don Quixote. The "self-fulfilling prophecy" of the Dulcinea Principle is that people will live up to and become what you truly believe of them.

Leadership Is Communicating Worth and Potential

Each of us has the power to do that for someone else—especially if you've reached the Pinnacle of Success in some area of life, when your potential influence holds more power to affect another for good than you realize. I've often advised those who are in influential positions to take this opportunity and focus on someone other than themselves: in other words, "seek to bless—not to impress."

Look around and see who needs someone to believe in them. Believe in and reinforce their greatness of character, even if it hasn't shown fruit yet. As you do, the potential of that person becomes their reality. You can love and inspire someone to become the person they are meant to become, regardless of their past and the reality of the present.

> *"Treat a man as he is and he will remain as he is. Treat a man as he can and should be, and he will become as he can and should be."*
>
> —Johann Wolfgang von Goethe

Engaging the power of positive affirmations is the role of a true mentor, a true teacher, and true leadership. There is nothing more fulfilling than helping another human soul see their potential and inspiring them to greatness.

- Be open to inspiration—from your own conscience and from outside sources. Recognize that and you will soon have greater influence with other people.

- Acknowledge that people must first *feel* you understand them and genuinely care; only then will they be open to your influence.

- After building a relationship with someone you would like to mentor, look for natural "teaching moment" opportunities, where you can convey what you know and believe is important.

- Use real-life examples of what is happening to them to teach them how to respond—even role-playing.
- Give them a new, inspired vision of themselves.
- Help instill confidence that they can meet the challenges they face and make good choices.
- Teach them to live out of their imagination, not their history.

A powerful source of internal security is another person who loves and believes in us, even when we don't believe in ourselves. The value and power of affirmations you offer can be vital to someone else's growth and to them achieving their potential, offering great internal peace and security and enabling them to break from confining comfort zones with less fear of failure.

An affirmation is personal, positive, present tense, visual, and emotional. It should be simple, sincere, and applicable to their abilities:

- "I know these finance classes are really tough and competitive, but you've always been such a conscientious student that I really think your hard work will pay off. Hang in there, Angie—even if you have to repeat a class. In this major it usually takes a while to understand the concepts, but I know your work ethic—you'll eventually succeed."
- "You're a natural artist, John. You're creative and paint with such emotion that your paintings give a different perspective than most do. You're gutsy to try working with oil now; what a range of new skills you will learn."
- "You're a better father than you give yourself credit for. Don't

beat yourself up over the typical teenage antics you see! You spend so much time at the baseball field pitching to Sam that he knows you care. Building relationships has always been your strong suit."

- "I liked how you interacted with your team members today when different opinions were expressed. That could have been explosive, but you led the discussion in such an open and accepting way, everyone felt they could share their ideas. That isn't easy to do—you've got some natural leadership abilities that can really help our team."

- "Thanks for always listening when others just want to be heard. I depend on your advice with your siblings because you really let them express themselves first, and then they're more open to your influence. You have a good head on you to make tough decisions. I sure depend on you."

Of course, all affirmations are subjective to the person you're trying to affirm, but given thoughtfully and sincerely, they could have enormous effect, since most people reflect what others think and believe of them. At the Pinnacle of Success, you are in the ideal position to affirm others effectively by following a couple of simple but important practices. Make these your habit, and your influence will be powerful:

Change the name or old script or label of the person you are affirming.

- Old names, labels, titles, nicknames, and identities block progress. In almost every society, rites of passage include conferring a new title or name, as these greatly facilitate changes in behavior. You don't literally need to give someone a new name—like Dulcinea—but you must get past your own perception of them and help them do the same.

- Help them see themselves differently from how they have been seen before. It's important to teach those you care for to live out of their imagination, not their history.

- Recognize that often we are our own worst enemies. We defeat ourselves believing old scripts about us instead of re-creating ourselves.

Affirm them in their new identity.

- Helping someone re-script their lives and mission requires courage, but it is within our power. Old scripts can be changed and rewritten, especially if someone loves and believes in you.

- There is great strength and power that comes when this happens, especially when people don't totally believe in themselves yet. When someone believes in another person, it helps that person escape victimization and forces them to take responsibility for their actions.

- It also compels them to become active agents of change rather than accepting a negative mentality of self-pity.

> *"By making him aware of what he can be and of what he should become, he makes these potentialities come true."*
> —Viktor Frankl, *Man's Search for Meaning*[34]

The foundation of affirmation is faith—a bone-deep belief in the unseen potential of a person, product, or project. That belief usually comes from the wellspring of vision. The fruits of innovation and creativity naturally result from a challenging vision, childlike faith, and patient, diligent work:

Faith + Work = Fruit

Believing in the unseen potential of another person is analogous to planting a bamboo tree. In China, those who plant such trees see absolutely nothing for four years—nothing above the ground except a tiny bulb and shoot. All growth during the first four years goes into building the root structure. But incredibly, in the fifth year the plant grows eighty feet!

Without the roots, we don't get the fruits. The fruits of affirming another person and believing in their unseen potential follow from enabling the roots to grow deep into the ground and form a solid foundation. Only then—and this may take years like the bamboo tree—do the roots produce the fruits. And what a sweet fruit it is to the one who has finally blossomed, as well as to the trusted mentor who helped lay the foundation. It's essential that we never define a person by their weaknesses; always define them by their strengths.

Leadership Is a Conscious Choice

For years in my presentations, I would ask those in the audience this revealing question:

How many of you have achieved your present level of success largely because someone believed in you when you didn't believe in yourself?

Without fail, about two-thirds of those present would raise their hands. My next question was:

Who believed in you? How did they show it? What impact did it have on you?

I would then walk around the room and ask some to share

their experiences. Many times people would get very emotional while relaying their personal stories. Lastly, I would ask the most important question of all:

Are you attempting to do the same thing with someone else?

My best definition of leadership is *communicating another's worth and potential so clearly that they are inspired to see it in themselves*. Most of us have been inspired, encouraged, and mentored by someone who truly believed in us, and that made all the difference. We may not realize what a powerful impact we can have on another person, and this impact can spread to the next generation and beyond.

> *"In everyone's life, at some time, our inner fire goes out. It is then burst into flame by an encounter with another human being. We should all be thankful for those people who rekindle the inner spirit."*
>
> —Albert Schweitzer

I was blessed to have many people in my life who believed in me and inspired me to rise to what they saw was my potential, beginning with my parents. I once woke up in the middle of the night and discovered my mother standing over me, whispering words of affirmation that I would do well on an important test the next morning. I'll admit at the time it did seem a little strange, but I also had no doubt that she believed in me and did all she could to affirm me in whatever I was involved in, as did my father. Their collective belief in me had a tremendous impact on my life.

When I was twenty, I had a volunteer service opportunity in England that profoundly shaped my life. A. Heimer Reiser was the adult leader there, and after several months, he asked me to train local leaders in some of the major cities throughout England, some of whom were two and three times my age. I could hardly believe what he was asking me to do as I had serious doubts about my abilities to do something so far outside my comfort zone. But he said to me, "I have great confidence in you. You can do this." He saw much more in me than I saw in myself.

To my surprise, I discovered that I had some natural abilities to convey ideas in a way that inspired others, and I developed a passion for teaching. Mr. Reiser became a trusted mentor who saw my potential to teach and train leaders, and because of my respect for him, I rose to his level of belief and expectation. I grew, I saw others grow, and I found my voice. This experience changed my whole paradigm—how I saw myself—and eventually directed my entire life's profession. Teaching ultimately led to writing, which became a vehicle to impact more people than I had ever imagined.

I believe that true leadership is a conscious choice. I have found three methods of influence that are the work of true mentors.

Model by Example: Those we mentor *see* what we do. We encourage obedience to the laws of life when we live the laws of love. People are extremely tender inside, particularly those who act as if they are tough and self-sufficient. We must listen to them with the "third ear," the heart. We can gain even greater influence with them by showing love, particularly unconditional love, which gives people a sense of intrinsic worth and security without enforcing behavior or comparisons with others. Our words are hollow unless we model what we would like other people to become. What we are communicates far more eloquently and persuasively than what we say or even what we do.

Build Caring Relationships: Those we mentor *feel* what we do. Our efforts to classify and categorize, judge and measure often emerge from our own insecurities and frustrations in dealing with complex, changing realities. There are many dimensions to every person. Sometimes a person's potential is readily evident, but for many it lies dormant. People tend to respond to how we treat them and what we believe about them.

Some may let us down, or take advantage of our trust, considering us naïve or gullible. But most will come through, simply because we believe in them. Don't bottleneck the many for fear of a few! Whenever we assume good faith, born of good motives and inner security, we appeal to the good in others. Assuming good faith produces good fruit.

Mentor by Instruction: Those we mentor *hear* what we say. It's always important to prepare your heart and mind before you prepare what you're going to say if you truly want to have influence. What we say may be less important than how we say it. You will have the opportunity to mentor those who admire and follow you, especially close family members.

Here's a practical example if you are a parent. Before your children return home from school full of their own needs, or when you return home from work, take time to prepare. In other words, before you are in a situation, stop and get control of yourself first and decide how you are going to respond to whatever they throw at you.

- Gather your resources
- Set your mind and heart
- Choose pleasantness and cheerfulness
- Choose to give full attention to their needs

- Prepare to listen to what they say (as well as what they're not saying), rather than preparing your speech while they are talking

- Choosing to be your best self will arrest fatigue and renew your best resolve

Train those you mentor in what has been known as the *Law of the Harvest*—you "reap what you sow." With most things that have value, there is no shortcut, no easy out, no quick fix. What you put into the ground and how you attend to it ultimately determine what you get out. There are no shortcuts on the farm—no cramming or procrastinating or possible way to trick Mother Nature into producing a bountiful harvest without paying the price beforehand.

Ultimately, it is the same with relationships. Teach those you mentor the timeless "agricultural principles" of preparing the soil, seeding, cultivating, watering, weeding, and harvesting to reap success in life. Remember we are teaching one thing or another all of the time, because we are constantly radiating what we are.

Building Bridges

There is an insightful old poem called "The Bridge Builder" by a woman poet named Will Allen Dromgoole. It's interesting to note that this poem was published in 1931, a time that was less "me centered" and more service-oriented than our day.

> *An old man going a lone highway,*
> *Came, at the evening cold and gray,*
> *To a chasm vast and deep and wide.*

Through which was flowing a sullen tide
The old man crossed in the twilight dim,
The sullen stream had no fear for him;
But he turned when safe on the other side
And built a bridge to span the tide.

"Old man," said a fellow pilgrim near,
"You are wasting your strength with building here;
Your journey will end with the ending day,
You never again will pass this way;
You've crossed the chasm, deep and wide,
Why build this bridge at evening tide?"

The builder lifted his old gray head;
"Good friend, in the path I have come," he said,
"There followed after me today
A youth whose feet must pass this way.
This chasm that has been as naught to me
To that fair-haired youth may a pitfall be;
He, too, must cross in the twilight dim;
Good friend, I am building this bridge for him!"[35]

Sometimes what we do doesn't necessarily benefit or impact us directly, but it blesses those who follow. How valuable it is to have someone wise and experienced standing at the crossroads to show the way. There are many good people who have significantly influenced and impacted the rising generation, setting profound examples and making the way ahead easier to follow.

"We are all shaped by people we've never met."
—David McCullough

Leadership Is Communicating Worth and Potential

While still in college, one young man had the good fortune to be hired as a personal assistant to Scott, the CEO of a large regional bank. Scott shocked this young hire by pulling him aside the first day on the job and saying, "You're not going to be an intern who files paperwork, but rather you are going to be an intern that learns how to run a multimillion-dollar business."

The CEO was good to his word. In the intern's own words:

Scott didn't just assign me something and back out. He really cared about the projects I was working on and supported me when I would give him input. He often told me how valuable it was to hear my opinion and a fresh perspective and would have me present my findings to his board executives during weekly Monday morning board meetings. I knew I had to be on my A-game, so this was a win-win for both of us; I had the amazing opportunity to present to top executives as a freshman intern, and Scott got a quality report I carefully prepared that benefited the firm. I naturally wanted to do my best work for him and achieve more than the week before.

To be honest, presenting was tough and intimidating and really challenged me to sharpen my skills. But it helped that Scott would always introduce me before and essentially say how important the project was that I was working on. When I finished, he emphasized my main takeaway points to make sure that his board valued what I said. He would always follow up, and doing so made me feel important and a part of the team.

Sometimes when top people would meet Scott in his office, he would let me sit in on the meetings so I could hear what they'd discuss and then we'd talk about it later. I learned so much from just listening. I was amazed that he actually seemed proud to introduce me to well-known people. He'd say with enthusiasm, "You've got to meet my new intern"—like I was a big deal or something!

I was invited to accompany him on some business trips, and while we traveled Scott used the time to teach me many practical skills he'd learned about running a large company as CEO. He would also give me advice on my own career path and connected me with people he thought would be helpful to me. Scott recommended good books to read, took such a personal interest in me, and not just with work, but in my school and social life too, that I came to value him as a trusted mentor. His belief in me steadily built my confidence and inspired me to want to imitate him and follow a similar career path. The summer I interned for him was a remarkable experience, and I set a future goal to one day positively influence someone else as he had me.[36]

Here is another example of a person of influence building a bridge for someone starting out to follow.

It must have been evident that I wasn't a natural hire when I got my first job in the high-tech industry. After hearing someone in the office refer to Code 3, I naïvely asked, "So do we have to speak in code here?" After everyone got a good laugh, I learned that Code 3 was the name of one of our clients! I'm sure it was then that my manager knew I needed someone who was good at teaching me the ropes since I was just starting out, and I was fortunate enough to be assigned to a woman who had been in the industry for fifteen years.

She took me under her wing and made sure I knew the jargon and the terminology of the computer industry so I wasn't embarrassed again. She invited me to accompany her on appointments and meetings, and trained me in strategy and sales effectiveness, and what I needed to do to be successful.

More importantly, she instilled a belief in me that I too could be successful. She was positive and affirming and got me off to a great start. I hate to think how I would have struggled in this, my first real job out of college, had I been assigned to someone who may have not bothered to teach me the ropes, or cared to ensure I would be successful.[37]

The Crescendo Mentality promotes the belief that some of the greatest contributions are unselfishly made by those who want to bless others by building bridges—with no concern for the accolades. Their influence is immeasurable in another's life and can inspire excellence and change.

> *"If you could only sense how important you are to the lives of those you meet; how important you can be to the people you may never even dream of. There is something of your-self that you leave at every meeting with another person."*
>
> —Mr. Rogers

Leadership as Character Building

In the last book John Wooden wrote (with Don Yaegar), *A Game Plan for Life: The Power of Mentoring*, the renowned basketball coach names seven great mentors who influenced his own life—mentors such as his father, a few of his coaches, his beloved wife Nellie, Mother Teresa, and Abraham Lincoln. The second half of the book focuses on several people whom he, in turn, mentored, giving back what he was given—Kareem Abdul-Jabbar, Bill Walton, and other less known people, like his granddaughter.

While teaching English and coaching basketball in his first year at Indiana's Dayton High School, Wooden had the first and only losing season of his career. Imagine if he had given up then, believing he didn't have the skills to be a successful coach! Instead, John Wooden went on to lead the UCLA Bruins to 665 victories and an unprecedented ten NCAA championships in twelve years—seven of them in a row—four perfect seasons, an 88-game win streak (most consecutive victories ever), and eight perfect conference seasons. He was the first person ever inducted into the Naismith Memorial Basketball Hall of Fame as a player and a coach. In 2009 he was named by *Sporting News* as the "greatest coach in American sports history."[38]

Without a doubt, Coach Wooden reached the Pinnacle of Success in the basketball arena, but the role that meant the most to him was that of teacher to others. He believed his highest calling was to teach his players not just to become great basketball players, but to be men of character. He wrote:

> I have always tried to make it clear that basketball is not the ultimate. It is of small importance in comparison to the total life we live. . . . I have lived my life to be a mentor—and to be mentored!—constantly. . . . Many people look at mentoring as some kind of assignment . . . mentoring can be any action that inspires another.[39]

Mentoring doesn't have to be a formal relationship, he says. It means treating people with kindness, encouraging or inspiring them, teaching them core values to believe in—a sacred trust.

"Leaders don't create followers, they create more leaders."
—Tom Peters, *In Search of Excellence*

When John Wooden and his brothers graduated from high school, their graduation gift from their father was a single paper that listed his seven-point creed. Through the years, John always kept it in his wallet as a reminder and a legacy passed from father to son. Since then, it's been passed on from John Wooden to thousands and thousands of others:

1. Be true to yourself.
2. Make each day your masterpiece!
3. Help others.
4. Drink deeply from good books, especially the Bible.
5. Make friendship a fine art.
6. Build a shelter against a rainy day.
7. Pray for guidance and give thanks for your blessings every day. [40]

Wooden's definition of success wasn't just about winning, which he believed was a by-product of attitude and preparation. Wooden believed success was "making your best effort of which you are capable" and being "more concerned with your character than your reputation, because your character is what you really are, while your reputation is merely what others think you are." [41]

Wooden spent more than a third of his life involved in meaningful work after his incredible coaching career ended (his own Pinnacle of Success). Unbelievably, until he was ninety-six, he was still going strong—Living Life in Crescendo, writing books, giving between twenty and thirty speeches a year, as well as making himself available to many of his players, friends, and admirers. He died in June 2010, at just a few months short of one hundred years of age. To honor his legacy, the UCLA Bruins basketball team wore black triangles symbolizing the character-building Pyramid of Success model he taught throughout his lifetime. Amid all the awards and accolades Coach Wooden received through the years, he only wanted to be remembered for enriching lives.[42]

> *"There is nothing you know that you haven't learned from someone else. Everything in the world has been passed down. . . . If you understand it as I do, mentoring becomes your true legacy. It is the greatest inheritance you can give to others. It is why you get up every day—to teach and be taught."*[43]
>
> —John Wooden, *A Game Plan for Life*

Chapter 5

Work to Expand Your Circle of Influence

"You can widen your circle of influence by widening your circle of service."

—Joseph Grenny, author of *Influencers*

Proactive people work on the things they can do something about—they focus their efforts within their Circle of Influence. With positive energy, they can enlarge and magnify their influence in an ever-widening circle.

Every person has unique gifts and talents to offer specific people within their Circle of Influence. There is always a reason to stretch, learn, contribute, and expand, and to help others do the same for themselves. That is what makes life exciting and worthwhile.

> *"No man is an island, entire of itself; every man is a piece of the continent. . . . And therefore never send to know for whom the bell tolls; it tolls for thee."*
>
> —John Donne

In 1782, William Wilberforce was a young and popular member of the British Parliament who felt driven to put forth a bill to abolish slavery in England. However, almost all the members of Parliament represented the interests of the slave trade. They resented Wilberforce for refusing to give up on his bill and easily defeated it again and again.

Wilberforce's commitment to the cause of abolition deepened when he reunited with his former mentor, John Newton, who earlier in his life had been a captain of a slave ship—a ruthless businessperson and unfeeling participant contributing to the misery of slavery. In an effort to make some sort of penance for the sinful life he had led, Newton gave up the slave trade completely and became a priest in the Anglican Church. He went on to write "Amazing Grace," one of the most enduring folk hymns of all time.

Wilberforce began to appeal to his fellow legislators' compassion and Christian roots, showing the evidence of slavery—handcuffs, shackles, and branding irons—so they could see for themselves the brutal reality. Another time, he tricked government and prominent citizens into going on an outing where they could see with their own eyes the horrors of a slave ship and smell the scent of death.

Over a period of twenty years, Wilberforce's efforts slowly began to impact the conscience of more members of Parliament, and his influence enlarged. More legislators began to reconsider their position. In 1806, the time was finally right, and Wilberforce's bill to abolish the slave trade in Great Britain overwhelmingly passed, 283 votes to 16. Though they had vehemently opposed him for decades, members of Parliament rose to their feet and cheered wildly for him for never giving up on his noble cause.

The slave trade was now illegal, but Parliament still refused to ban the institution of slavery itself for another twenty-six long years. Wilberforce was again compelled to continue the fight, and finally, in 1833, the House of Commons banned slavery throughout the entire British Empire. Messengers rushed to share the good news with Wilberforce, who was gravely ill. He died three days later.[44]

Initially, William Wilberforce had no power or influence among his fellow legislators to bring about the abolishment of slavery. Yet, after he had worked feverishly for twenty years, his associates saw his sincerity in supporting this noble cause; eventually like the Crescendo sign that extends outward ($<$), his Circle of Influence expanded until it encompassed the whole of Parliament and forever changed history. Striving to live the Crescendo Mentality means you work to support important causes where you see a need, and as you do, your own Circle of Influence naturally enlarges and encompasses many others for good. You may not do it to the extent that Wilberforce achieved, but doing this is part of your unique and *"most important work"* that *"is always ahead of you."*

> *"A small body of determined spirits, fired by an unquenchable faith in their mission, can alter the course of history."*
>
> —Mahatma Gandhi

Find Your Voice and Help Others Find Theirs

Fifteen years after writing *The 7 Habits of Highly Effective People*, I felt compelled to add an 8th Habit: "Find your voice and inspire others to find their voice." You can't effectively help others find their voice until you've figured out your own. Discover what you're good at, and then help other people do the same thing for themselves.

Serving someone who can't repay you, helping another financially when there's a unique opportunity for them to grow and learn, showing people their unique potential when they can't see it in themselves, believing and affirming children throughout their life—all these and so many more contribute to the sum total of who people are and who they can become.

"We drop like pebbles into the ponds of each other's souls, and the orbits of our ripples continue to expand, intersecting with countless others."

—Joan Z. Borysenko

Imagine the impact on the world if everyone worked at doing that at every stage of life; like a domino effect or ripples in a pond—from one to another to another—the impact for good would keep going on and on.

Since 1970, there has been a coveted achievement in football called the NFL Man of the Year Award, which represents professional football's commitment to philanthropy and community service. Each year it honors a singular athlete who exhibits excellence not only on the field but off, volunteering his time in charitable work. Many of the greatest names in football history have won this prestigious award, including Johnny Unitas, Roger Staubach, Dan Marino, and Peyton Manning.[45]

Walter Payton, considered one of the greatest NFL running backs of all time, was given the award in 1977 for work with his foundation that helps abused, neglected, and underprivileged children in the state of Illinois. Payton said:

Children have always brought a tremendous amount of joy to me, and I feel that if you can catch them at a young age, you can really change a life. There are a lot of studies that show that one act of kindness to these children has a 40%

chance of making that child have a completely different outcome in their life. What you hope is that you can get a kid to
believe in something and to believe in themselves.[46]

When Payton died of cancer in 1999, at the age of forty-
five, the NFL renamed the award the Walter Payton NFL Man
of the Year Award, in his honor. In 2015, Anquan Boldin won
the award, becoming the first 49er ever honored. Boldin was
unique in having been nominated four times throughout his
fourteen-year career. His charitable work spread through three
different communities where he lived while playing professional
football.

Years before he won the award, Boldin had established a
foundation dedicated to expanding the educational and life opportunities of underprivileged children, including a summer enrichment program, Thanksgiving food drives, back-to-school
and holiday shopping events, and more. In 2014, Anquan and
his wife, Dionne, donated $1 million dollars to the founda-
tion. Most important are the thirteen four-year scholarships of
$10,000 each Boldin has awarded to deserving students who
need help with higher education.[47]

Boldin spoke of his desire to do more than play football, to
make an impact by giving back:

When I first got into the NFL nobody could tell me anything. I was living life! I had achieved my dream of one day
making it into the NFL, but I soon realized that's not what
life is all about. I realized my purpose in life was not to make
it to the NFL and score touchdowns. God put me on this
earth for something much bigger than that and I realize and
understand what my purpose is now. . . . It's my prayer and

my hope that I can live out the rest of my life honoring God and helping as many people as possible.[48]

What an impact he is making on youth within his ever-expanding Circle of Influence, so that they too have an improved . chance of making the most of their lives.

Ripples in a Pond

Do you know someone who looks up to you as a mentor? Is there someone in need of your support, belief, and inspiration in their life? Take a moment to identify this person. Then spend time with them, get to know them well—their goals, dreams, what's important to them—and just begin to help them find their own voice. Realize as someone who is committed to helping others do this, you do not own their challenges or problems, you simply serve as a source of help, guidance, and inspiration. You'd be surprised what little time and effort it takes to make a significant difference in another's life.

Whatever you give this person—your interest, time, belief, skills—could put them on the right path to discovering their own passion and voice. Doing so will in turn give you a deep sense of joy as you see them progress and succeed.

If you know someone you could help find their voice but aren't yet confident in how to go about it, allow me to lay out a simple process. Begin by asking four basic questions to identify their needs and how you can best help them:

1. Find out how they are doing in life, specifically how they are dealing with challenges.

2. Ask what they are currently learning about what they may want to do.

3. In light of how it's going with them and what they're learning, help them define goals.

4. Simply ask what you can do to help them reach their goals.

The real beginning of influence comes as others sense you are being influenced by them—when they feel understood by you—that you have listened deeply and sincerely, and that you are open. Always remember that what you do has far greater impact than what you say.

William Ernest Henley's father died when he was young, leaving six children for William's mother to care for. As a child, Henley became a student at the Crypt School in Gloucester, England, and for five years he was mentored by a brilliant headmaster named Thomas Edward Brown, a poet and "a man of genius—the first I'd ever seen." Henley and Brown developed a lifelong friendship. Henley later wrote that "he [Brown] was singularly kind to me at a moment when I needed kindness more than I needed encouragement."[49]

When he was only twelve, Henley contracted tuberculosis of the bone, which eventually led to his left leg being amputated below the knee. The disease also affected his right foot, and he endured a three-year hospital stay. But his teacher lit the fire in Henley to explore and write his own poetry. Although Henley eventually died of tuberculosis when he was only fifty-three, his poetry endured and inspired and impacted many.

Years later, Henley's best-known poem, "Invictus," became a great source of inspiration to an imprisoned man in South Africa named Nelson Mandela.[50] And Mandela in turn ultimately influenced South Africa and the lives of millions of people who broke free of apartheid.

One person influencing another—one voice giving rise to others.

Making the World a Better Place

Who knows when we have accomplished our most important work or made our most important contribution? That is why we need to keep learning, trying, and progressing through all ages and stages of life, despite the difficulties that come our way. We must avoid the temptation to keep looking over our shoulder in the rearview mirror at what we have done, and instead look ahead with optimism at what we can still do.

> *"What we do for ourselves dies with us. What we do for others and the world remains and is immortal."*
>
> —Albert Pike

We all know of those who are fortunate enough to have money, fame, talent, and resources and who do an incredible amount of good *after* reaching their Pinnacle of Success. But though "you can't take it with you," many still live like the bumper sticker on an exotic car driven by an older couple that proudly proclaims, "We're spending our children's inheritance!"

Paul Newman epitomized Living Life in Crescendo and consistently lived like his most important work was still ahead of him. Adored by generations of moviegoers, Newman was a film icon, acting in sixty-five movies over a span of more than fifty years. Though he won an Oscar for Best Actor in 1987, when he was sixty-two years old, he ignored retirement and worked well into his seventies, making his last film at seventy-seven, still commanding leading roles. He continued working nearly up to the time of his death from cancer in 2008 at age eighty-three. Despite the stellar acting career he was well known for, his greatest joy and satisfaction came from his charitable work.

Over Christmas of 1980, Paul and his friend A. E. Hotchner decided to concoct some oil-and-vinegar salad dressing to give as gifts. The response was tremendous, and by February neighbors and friends were banging on Newman's door asking for a second bottle. A local grocer suggested the only way it would really sell was to put Paul Newman's "mug on the merchandise."

Never one to promote himself, Newman at first balked at the idea. "If we were to go to the lowest of the low road and plaster my face on a bottle of oil and vinegar dressing just to line our pockets, it would stink!" he told Hotchner. "But to go to the low road to get to the high road—for charity, for the common good—now there's an idea worth the hustle, a reciprocal trade agreement!"[51]

Believing that he had the unique opportunity to make the world a better place through this endeavor, Newman enthusiastically proclaimed, "Let's give it all away to those who need it!" He committed every dime to charity because as he logically explained, "You can only put away so much stuff in your closet!" And so, and with the slogan of "Shameless exploitation in pursuit of the common good," Newman's Own was launched. A great success, the company sold ten thousand bottles of salad dressing within weeks, and by the end of the year sales had topped $3.2 million.

From the beginning, Newman's Own committed to donate 100 percent of its royalties and profits (after taxes) to deserving charities because, as Newman said, "It was the right thing to do." A decade later, more than $50 million had been given away to charity. Newman always claimed he was embarrassed that his salad dressing made a lot more money than his acting career ever did![52]

Live Life in Crescendo

"The need is great and so are the opportunities to make a difference. . . . What could be better than to hold your hand out to those less fortunate than you are?"

—Paul Newman

His personal charity, known as the Hole in the Wall Gang Camps, was closest to his heart (named after the famous band of outlaws in his movie *Butch Cassidy and the Sundance Kid*). He poured $7 million in profits from Newman's Own into his camps, which children with serious illnesses could attend for a full week of fun and adventure without charge. Since 1988, more than 1 million kids have attended a network of thirty camps and programs, helping the organization become the largest global group of family camps in the world. In an effort to restore childhood to children who spend many months of the year severely sick or in a hospital, Hole in the Wall camps provide kids with opportunities to fish, swim, camp, ride horses, make crafts, and just enjoy being kids. Newman's goal was to create a place of hope—a place for kids to discover that despite their illnesses, their lives could be full of possibilities.[53]

Newman observed the power of service with those who were involved. "You think you've created something for kids who are not as lucky as you are," he said. "And you find out that the people who are in service to these kids are getting back more than they're giving."[54] He once told the story of walking to the dining hall at camp one day, when a little girl took his hand and looked up at him and said, "You know, Mr. Newman, all year long, this is the week I live for!" "That's it!" he said. "That's the applause! That's what you really want in life! What could be better than to hold your hand out to people less fortunate than you are?"[55]

Paul Newman was an inspiring example of Living in Crescendo, creating his most important work *after* achieving the

Pinnacle of Success as a first-class actor. Since his passing in 2008, at the age of eighty-three, his family, employees, and supporters still run his foundation, just as he wanted it, giving it all away. Newman's Own helped establish the Committee Encouraging Corporate Philanthropy, and has been in support of the Safe Water Network, the Discovery Center, and other organizations fostering nutrition education and fresh food access and improving the quality of life of military personnel, veterans, and their families, among many, many other worthy causes.[56] Newman's Own produces more than three hundred products, with twenty-two thousand grants given, totaling over an astounding $570 million (and counting) donated to thousands of deserving charities, improving the lives of millions of people around the world.[57]

In January 2018, the foundation challenged people everywhere to be "Newmanitarians," by giving back, including acts of kindness, doing good deeds, and otherwise extending generosity to others. "By asking people to commit acts of kindness, we're hoping to spread the idea that philanthropy isn't just about money. It means that we can all do something to make our world a better place,"[58] explained the president of Newman's Own.[59]

> *"We are such spendthrifts with our lives. . . . I'm not running for sainthood. . . . I just happen to think that in life we need to be a little like the farmer, who puts back into the soil what he takes out."*
>
> —Paul Newman[60]

Many people are familiar with Muhammad Yunus and his microfinance model, which has given hope to millions trying to escape poverty. Yunus was born in 1940, the third of fourteen children in a small village in Bangladesh, on the northeast border of India. His father urged him to seek higher education, but the greatest influence on his life was his mother's example of helping the poor who would often knock on their door. She inspired in him the desire to help eradicate poverty.

In 1974, Bangladesh was in the middle of a terrible famine in which thousands starved to death. At the time, Yunus was a young professor of economics at Chittagong University, and he soon realized the theories he was teaching held no answers for the devastating reality just outside his classroom.

"Nothing in the economic theories I taught reflected the life around me. How could I go on telling my students make-believe stories in the name of economics? I needed to run away from these theories and from my textbooks and discover the real-life economics of a poor person's existence."[61]

He spoke with a woman who needed to borrow only a very small amount of money to buy raw bamboo to make bamboo stools. But because she had no collateral, she was considered high-risk, and banks would not lend to her at a reasonable rate. She was forced to borrow from a middleman at absurdly high rates—often as high as 10 percent a week—leaving her with just a penny of profit. This was barely enough to survive, trapping her in the never-ending cycle of poverty.

Realizing poor entrepreneurs would never be able to pull themselves out of poverty with such high interest rates, Yunus lent the equivalent of $27 from his own pocket to forty-two various women in the village, who then made a profit of .2 cents each on the loan. He discovered it was possible with this tiny amount not only to help them survive, but also to spark the personal initiative and enterprise necessary to pull themselves out of poverty. Yunus believed that credit was a fundamental human right. Giving people the chance to borrow without collateral could teach them sound financial principles, freeing them from poverty. Because of Muhammed Yunus's efforts, microcredit was born in Bangladesh.[62]

He and his colleagues eventually founded the Grameen (which means "village") Bank, offering microcredit to the very poor. This microfinance model has inspired similar efforts in roughly one hundred developing countries, and even in such countries as the United States, Canada, France, the Netherlands, and Norway. As of this writing, the Grameen Bank has provided $4.7 billion dollars to 4.4 million families in rural Bangladesh. It has reversed the conventional banking wisdom by focusing on women borrowers, disregarding requirements for collateral, and extending loans only to the very poorest borrowers. It is a revolutionary system largely based on mutual trust and the enterprise and accountability of millions of women villagers.[63] Amazingly, more than 94 percent of Grameen loans have gone to women, who suffer disproportionately from poverty in Bangladesh, and it was proven that they were more likely than men to devote their earnings to their families.[64]

Yunnus once asked an audience why people climb Mount Everest. They agreed some climb for the challenge, some climb who are blind or crippled, most risk their lives striving for the top—yet there are no piles of money to collect at the summit. Yunnus believes that people are not just motivated by money or profits, but by intentions. This is not your typical MBA rhetoric! He believes that people who want to change their world are genuinely motivated by making not just their own but others' lives better, and the results are more fulfilling than receiving financial rewards.

Yunus partnered with Dannon to provide a nutrient-rich yogurt for pennies a cup; he also teamed with Adidas to provide shoes that cost less than one euro. He started a solar power company that brought electricity to more than 1 million homes in Bangladesh for about the same price as kerosene and discovered a way to provide healthy food and vegetables to help heal children in that country suffering the common affliction of night blindness resulting from vitamin deficiencies. Each company he partnered with sustained itself, and investors not only got their money back, but acquired a sense of that "super happiness" money can't buy.[65]

In 2006, Yunus was awarded the Nobel Peace Prize for giving millions of microcredit loans to the poor.[66] By 2009, more than 128 million of the world's poorest people had received such loans, bringing hope to people who otherwise had none. Today, more than 250 institutions operate microcredit programs based on the Grameen Bank model, while thousands of other microcredit programs have been inspired by its principles.[67]

Many believe that this microcredit program inspired by Yunus is the single most important development in the third world in the last one hundred years!

Just before his seventy-fifth birthday, Muhammad Yunus suggested that "poverty should be in a museum," and spoke of how Americans could end it if they were willing. Although he's reached the Pinnacle of Success, he is still Living Life in Crescendo and not a bit interested in retiring. He actually seems to be gaining energy as he gets older.

Muhammad Yunus challenges audiences to take action when he speaks: *"Just find a way to help five people out of unemployment. If you succeed, do more of it. You might change the world."*[68] His is a legacy that promotes serving others.

A Personal Inventory

Obviously the great majority of us don't have the talent, money, or influence of people like Muhammad Yunus, Bill and Melinda

Gates, or Paul Newman. Their contributions are vast and reach a great number of people—their impact is world-changing. But there are countless inspiring examples of less famous but similarly successful, or even quite ordinary, people who actually do extraordinary things to positively impact the lives of those around them.

Your challenge is not to change *the* world, just *your* world—your own Circle of Influence, which you can directly affect for good.

It is up to you to determine where to place your time, resources, and talents. It could be something small like collecting books for a free lending library, making fleece blankets with your grandkids for a children's hospital, or visiting a lonely elderly neighbor and planting flowers in their yard. You may choose to volunteer to read with kids in an overcrowded elementary school class once a week, organize a group to clean up a blighted area in your community, or collect gently used clothes or winter gear for a local shelter. Even a simple service is helpful such as keeping healthy snacks like fig or protein bars in your car to hand out to people in need. Think of a forgotten friend or family member who could use an encouraging call or visit. During the pandemic, there were people everywhere who took the initiative to organize their own neighborhood or community food drive, often running it out of their garage. Their neighbors and friends eagerly responded to something positive to do during this difficult time, and in support of those among them who had lost their jobs.

One woman, after overcoming breast cancer, visits others who are in the throes of their own treatment, giving them much needed encouragement, a positive attitude, and a desire to fight and hang on. Another actively recruits help for refugees online, collecting supplies and resources so these new families can succeed in their community. A group of seniors who were feeling a little guilty about how much time they were spending playing pickleball every day decided to mix up their fun with some meaningful service. "Pickleball with a Purpose" was born, and now these friends regularly participate in stocking their local food bank, making "to go" healthy snack bags for needy students, tying fleece blankets for a children's hospital, and doing other community service projects.

Look around and you'll see a multitude of opportunities to serve right around you and within your Circle of Influence. It doesn't have to be an extraordinary act to make an extraordinary difference—just choose something that interests you and begin. And keep doing it.

Consider what you have to offer and what you can do to bring about positive change to those around you. Take the Personal Inventory below and discover the possibilities. The Crescendo Mentality suggests that serving others at any stage of your life greatly blesses both the recipient and the giver. As you focus on what's ahead for you to accomplish and stop relying on what you've already done in the past, you can actively demonstrate that "the best is yet to be." And ironically, these contributions could be your greatest in your life so far.

You are a perfect candidate to change your world if you have some or any of these characteristics:

• Time	• Desire	• Influence
• Talents	• Interest	• Money
• Skills	• Vision	• Passion

With your own unique abilities and characteristics in mind, think creatively about the needs you see around you and how you can respond in kind. Record your answers in the space provided in this Personal Inventory. You may be surprised to discover you have more to offer than you initially think.

1. What are you good at? What have you learned from your profession? What talents (or innate character traits) do you have that could help others?

_____

_____

_____

2. What do you feel passionate about—what's important to you? Who could you lend that passion to, or what cause can you help?

_____

_____

_____

3. What needs do you see around you in your neighborhood and community? What specifically could you do to meet those needs, even in a small way?

_____

_____

_____

4. How is your own family doing (immediate and intergenerational)? Do you know of family members—children, grandchildren, great-grandchildren, and other relatives such as siblings, cousins, aunts, or uncles—who are struggling in some way? What can you do to impact those within your own immediate and intergenerational family?

_____

_____

_____

5. List two or three people who look up to you, and determine how you could affirm and support them and become their trusted mentor.

_____

_____

_____

6. What do you want to be known for? What legacy do you want to leave behind?

_____

_____

_____

7. With the Crescendo Mentality in mind and the idea that "life is about contribution"—what will you choose to do?

_____

_____

_____

"Make a difference about something other than yourselves."
—Toni Morrison

PART 3

LIFE-CHANGING SETBACKS

staccato (stac-ca-to) adverb or adjective:
cut short or apart; disconnected, abrupt, disjointed

> *"Hardships often prepare ordinary people for an
> extraordinary destiny."*
> —widely attributed to C. S. Lewis

On August 16, 2008, Christian and Stephanie Nielson went for a day trip in a Cessna 177 Cardinal, never suspecting that the flight would change their lives forever. After refueling in St. Johns, Arizona, the small plane unexpectedly crashed and caught fire. Christian escaped the plane believing Stephanie was also out, but she was engulfed in flames, unable to free herself. She thought she was going to burn to death, but suddenly she sensed her deceased grandmother guiding her hand to unbuckle the seatbelt and leading her to the door. When she escaped from the plane, her body on fire, she heard her grandmother tell her, "Roll!"

Christian Nielson had a broken back and burns on 40 percent of his body, but he was the most fortunate of the three in the plane. Doug Kinneard, Christian's flight instructor and friend, suffered burns on 90 percent of his body. After being airlifted to the Arizona Burn Center in Phoenix, he died of his injuries. Stephanie was burned on 80 percent of her body. To allow their bodies to heal, doctors induced comas in both Christian and Stephanie. Christian woke up about five weeks later, but it was almost three months before Stephanie would regain consciousness.

On November 5, 2008, Stephanie finally awoke and discovered her hands, arms, legs, and face were covered with third- and fourth-degree burns. Her sister Page and her mother were at her side while her other sisters were caring for Stephanie's young children, who were six, five, three, and two.

Soon the Nielsons moved to a burn center closer to their children while they began their long journey of physical and emotional recovery. Stephanie had always been a beautiful young woman, and at first she couldn't bring herself to look in the mirror. When she finally got up the courage to look at her new face, she said she "felt like a monster!" At first, her children couldn't quite handle the physical damage the burns left. Stephanie shared that "my youngest son, Nicholas, who was two, didn't remember me at all. He didn't want anything to do with me! It ripped my heart out. My oldest child, Jane, turned white as a ghost and wouldn't look at me." Claire stayed in the hallway after Jane warned her, "Don't go in there!" Only Oliver, her three-year old, seemed comfortable with his mother, happily playing on her bed.

It took time for her children to adjust to their mother's new face, and Stephanie had to accept her own appearance.

"I still struggle with my scars," she says. "But I remember how grateful I am that I still have a face or a nose. . . . Then I look at my family and friends and think, 'this is all worth it.' I am a wife and a mother. The accident couldn't take that away from me. I'm not as worried about my appearance because I've got this beautiful family around me, and that's what matters most. They don't see me as someone who looks different or can't do the things I used to. My husband sees me as the wife that he married, and my children just see me as Mom. I feel beautiful because I have a beautiful life."[1]

Many thousands of "mommy bloggers" responded to Stephanie's story and raised money through garage sales, balloon launches, benefit concerts, and other fundraisers to help with her enormous medical bills. More than $250,000 came in from all over the world, including China and Australia.[2]

While Stephanie was in a coma, she had felt her deceased grandmother near her, and she remembers being given a choice whether to stay with her children and live with the pain from her injuries, or to return to God and be pain-free. She ultimately made the choice to stay, and she asked her grandmother what she could do to make things better when she returned home. Stephanie remembers her grandmother simply saying: "Share your hope!"

And so she has. Stephanie's response to her tragic accident hasn't stopped her from Living in Crescendo by inspiring others around the world to overcome their challenges with hope, courage, and endurance.

Stephanie received enough letters and cards of love and support to fill an entire room. She was overwhelmed, and five months after the accident wrote in her blog: "Tears gush every time I think about all the support from all of you. I love you all." As of this writing she has an incredible 30 million readers who check out her blog every month for messages of encouragement and inspiration. Almost a hundred thousand follow her on Instagram—motivated by her fighting spirit and the incredibly full life she leads.[3]

Stephanie wrote about her incredible story and journey of hope and triumph in her *New York Times* bestselling book, *Heaven Is Here*.[4] Because of her conscious choice to have a positive outlook and to create a happy life, her message of hope has inspired countless people. She has appeared on *Anderson Cooper 360°*, *Oprah*, *20/20*, and *Today*, has been widely interviewed, and has become a popular motivational speaker. Stephanie realized, "I could become bitter or I could become better." She chose to use her experience to encourage others who have also experienced overwhelming setbacks.

> *"The life you have led doesn't have to be the only one you'll have."*
>
> —Anna Quindlen

Stephanie refers to her life as "before the crash" ("BC") and "after the crash" ("AC") because sometimes it seems like she's had two separate lives. But she has embraced her new life now and has adopted the message of "share your hope!" It has become her mission to help those who have had hard things happen to them or their families.

Though there were difficult losses from the plane crash, the Nielsons also gained valuable insights they wouldn't have had without it. Stephanie has been fundamentally changed, and she wants her many followers and friends to know that life can still be good again. Perhaps surprisingly, in some ways it can be even better.

The Nielsons' marriage has been strengthened in ways that

only they understand, and they have grown much closer as a family. Stephanie writes:

> I want my children to remember that there were miracles that came from our experience. As difficult as it was, I'm grateful, and I feel so proud of where we are. For being so young, our kids have gone through a lot and have come through it wonderfully.[5]

Many have responded to Stephanie's blog or written letters showing that her determination to reclaim a happy life has been worth it, and she has inspired others to face their challenges in the same way. One girl, with tears in her eyes, said to Stephanie: "You help me do hard things."[6]

> *"Only by joy and sorrow does a person know anything about themselves and their destiny."*
> —attributed to Johann Wolfgang von Goethe

So what would *you* do if your perfectly planned life fell apart? How would you react? How would you pick up the pieces and go on? Is this something you've had to face, or has someone close to you had their life turned upside down very quickly? We usually can't control what happens to us. We can, however, choose how to respond to it, and that influences what happens after. Stephanie is still living Life in Crescendo though it's turned out much different than she expected. Like unhappiness, she learned that happiness is a conscious choice and that you can still live a happy life if you don't give yourself over to defeat and despair.

In this section there are several true-life stories of both well-known and unknown people who have had life-changing experiences and yet, in time and with consistent effort, chose to believe they still have more to accomplish and contribute. Though what happened to them may be tragic and even devastating, somehow within themselves they have chosen to Live in Crescendo and make life better for themselves, and then for others.

From people, like the Nielsons, who have reclaimed happiness after tragic setbacks, I have identified some of the "building blocks" for overcoming such experiences:

- Accept your challenge
- Believe that life can be good again—consciously choose happiness
- Look for ways to help others—share your hope

My hope is that you will learn from these courageous examples in the chapters to come, allowing them to lift and inspire you when you face your own challenging setbacks.

Chapter 6

Choose to Live in Crescendo, Not Diminuendo

"We don't even know how strong we are until we are forced to bring that hidden strength forward."
—Isabel Allende

Anthony Ray Hinton was presumed guilty before his trial ever began. In 1985, in a small town in Alabama, "Ray" was racially profiled and framed for two murders he had nothing to do with. Though he had a solid alibi and passed a polygraph test, he was poor and couldn't afford a good defense, which proved critical to getting a fair trial in his racially biased community and local legal system. Despite the prosecution not having credible evidence against him, Ray was quickly convicted and sent to death row at Alabama's Holman Prison.

Knowing he was completely innocent, Ray had fully trusted in the legal system. But after being sentenced, he became so angry and full of despair, he threw his Bible under his prison bed and decided to completely shut down. Normally open and friendly, Ray remained stone silent. Except for his family and friends who visited him, he didn't interact with anyone, no fellow inmates or guards, for three long, miserable years.[7]

Late one night, Ray was awakened by the sobbing and crying of a desperate inmate who was calling out for someone to help him with his pain. In that moment, there awoke within Ray a deep compassion he had consciously suppressed. Though he

131

couldn't do anything about the reality of living in solitary confinement on death row, Ray discovered he had other important choices he could make.

"Despair was a choice," he said. "Hatred was a choice. Anger was a choice. I still had choices, and that knowledge rocked me. . . . I could choose to give up or to hang on. Hope was a choice. Faith was a choice. Compassion was a choice. And more than anything else, love was a choice."[8]

In this revelatory moment, Ray realized, "I had a choice to reach out . . . or to stay in the dark alone. . . . I was born with the same gift from God we are all born with—the impulse to reach out and lessen the suffering of another human being. It was a gift, and we each had a choice whether to use this gift or not."[9]

Through his cell bars, Ray broke his silence of three years and comforted a grieving inmate who confided that his mother had just died. He spent the night listening to a complete stranger tell stories of his mother and giving him the hope to hang on. Ray decided it was time to renew his own hope and faith. He dusted off the Bible still under his bed and committed to remain true to his values and the good person he knew he was, and not give in to deep despair despite the harsh reality of living on death row.

And he made other choices. He became, for the next twenty-seven years, a beacon and a light—transforming not only his own spirit, but extending that transformation to his fellow inmates, fifty-four of whom were executed just thirty feet from his cell. And his influence grew. He created an identity of compassion on death row that caused others to respond the same; he shaped the lives of dozens of inmates around him with kindness and humor, and spread hope that "each person is more than their worst act," as his lawyer Bryan Stevenson believed.[10]

Though it was a daily struggle to stay positive and keep fighting year after year, Ray showed his humanity while living inhumanely—escaping his surroundings by expanding his mind and imagination through devouring books as a way to leave his prison confines. And Ray fiercely held on to the hope that one day the truth would be known about his innocence, and he would be rewarded with true justice and freedom.

After fourteen years in solitary confinement without any progress on his case, Ray finally acquired competent legal assistance from lawyer and justice advocate Bryan Stevenson and the Equal Justice Initiative team. Stevenson immediately recognized the appalling injustice and fought tirelessly in Ray's defense for the next fourteen years in contested litigation, with dozens of motions and appeals.

Finally, in 2015, Mr. Stevenson won a rare unanimous ruling in the United States Supreme Court, and Anthony Ray Hinton was found completely innocent of all charges and released after nearly thirty years in prison, becoming one of the longest-serving condemned prisoners facing execution in America to be proved innocent and released. As he walked out of prison at last, Ray gratefully called out to his family and friends, "The sun does shine!"[11]

Like Mandela, who was imprisoned for twenty-seven years, Ray Hinton also emerged from his long prison sentence with a noticeable lack of bitterness and the ability to forgive. "Bitterness kills the soul," he explained. "What would it profit me to hate?" He consciously chose to forgive those who prosecuted him. "They took my thirties, my forties, my fifties—but what they couldn't take was my joy!"[12]

Though he deeply regrets the wasted decades he was incarcerated—the opportunities Ray missed in a career, and getting married and raising children, something he had always wanted—he has not allowed these negative consequences to consume him and destroy the rest of his life. Ray believes "we have to find ways to recover after bad things happen."[13] He deeply believes he has important work ahead that only he can do—fighting for others also unjustly prosecuted and imprisoned.

Three years after he was released, Ray wrote a troubling but significant memoir that became a *New York Times* bestselling book—*The Sun Does Shine*—about the difficult journey on which he not only learned to survive on death row, but found a way to live.

Ray's story shows that no matter how horrific the circumstances or other challenges we face, we *still* have a choice. We can choose to shut down like Ray initially did and essentially Live in Diminuendo, with the result that our power and influence eventually come to an end, > .

Regardless of the wrongful conviction by the racist legal system he experienced, ultimately no one could take Ray's ability to choose to use his faith, hope, mind, imagination, compassion, humor, and joy. When we too exercise those choices in our lives, as Ray did even on death row, we grow in influence and power and our life begins to expand and enlarge in Crescendo, < .

Now Ray devotes his time to his life's work as an activist and advocate. He has become an extraordinary speaker and powerful community educator, working with Bryan Stevenson and the Equal Justice Initiative team. They strive to bring about criminal justice reform and equality in the legal system, so that other innocent people don't suffer as Ray did. Due to his important mission of fighting injustice, Ray's life and influence have only continued to expand and are a light to those who learn from his courageous story of struggle, choice, and triumph.

"The ability to choose cannot be taken away or even given away—it can only be forgotten."

—Greg McKeown[14]

If you haven't made big mistakes or ever needed a fresh start, then odds are you haven't lived long enough. Setbacks are inevitable. I find it inspiring to learn from those who have made bad choices—or those who have suffered at the hands of others or as a result of cruel fate—and managed to give themselves a break, to forgive themselves or others, to change their lives, and then to help others do the same.

Nelson Mandela summed this up very succinctly: "Do not judge me by my successes; judge me by how many times I fell down and got back up."[15] And South Africa is forever changed because he did.

That's exactly how we can change the world—sometimes it takes just one person to start a domino effect of change. As we shall see, giving yourself or others a break—second chances—is often when miracles happen, leading to lives Lived in Crescendo.

Second Chances

On September 5, 2011, Anna Beninati made a foolish decision that changed her life forever. As a new student at Colorado State University, she got caught up in a dangerous school culture of hopping trains for thrills. After succeeding a few times, she saw a friend being dragged alongside the train after failing to climb aboard. Fortunately, he rolled away in time, but Anna kept running without realizing that another friend behind her was yelling at her not to jump on, because the train was moving too fast.

She never heard him over the noise. Anna got her right foot up on the edge of the train car, but her left leg was dragging along the ground. Realizing she wasn't going to make it, she did the only thing she could do and let go. But instead of rolling away from the train like her friend, her legs went under. She heard her femur snap, and thought she was going to die.

Fortunately, a medical technician and a nurse were both waiting in their car for the train to pass. They got to her quickly, putting pressure on her legs to stop the bleeding. The friend who had tried to warn her happened to be a former army medic and amazingly had a fresh set of tourniquets in his backpack. He applied them and saved her life.

Her left leg was completely severed and only half of her right leg remained. It was a horrific life-changing moment that will stay with her forever.

Before her accident, Anna described herself as a sad, miserable girl who was standoffish, edgy, cynical, and suffering from anorexia. She never liked rules, "which is why I'm here in a wheelchair," she told a group of elementary school students. Today she tells kids about her experience and the lessons she learned, hoping they will benefit from her story about her lack of judgment. The kids are drawn to her because of her spunkiness and sense of humor—traits that helped her survive. She shows a picture of her siblings and says with a wry smile: "I used to be the big sister; now I'm the little sister!" They are clearly riveted by her story as she warns them about making foolish choices especially when you know better.

With the students full attention, she tells them how she reacted to her new reality. "My first week home from the hospital I was really angry and realized I had to make a choice. Either stop where I am and do nothing but wallow in self-pity about why I don't have legs or get on with it. You can give up or get up! My second week home, I decided today is the day I'm going to figure out all the things I can do."

Anna managed to give herself a second chance. After deciding to focus on what she could still do, she was surprised by how long the list was. Anna took up hand cycling, weightlifting, bowling, riding horses, swimming, rock climbing, sit-skiing, and even bungee jumping. She learned to do handstands and wheelies in her chair. Four months after the accident, Anna decided to return to the place where she lost her legs. She had expected to feel anger and fear there, but instead she felt a sense of calm. She also visited the firefighters who had saved her life, and charmed them by dancing in her wheelchair, something she would have never done before.

Though Anna needed more than eleven surgeries to get to where she is today, she has embraced life more fully since the accident, maintaining a busy schedule that is uplifting to those who know her. Her eating disorder disappeared when she decided she had already suffered enough and had worse health problems to deal with. Anna now coaches other disabled people through a sports program and mentors members of a youth symphony once a week, playing the guitar, piano, and bassoon. When she was able to finally hang out with her old friends again, they were shocked to see how she approached her new life with such a positive attitude. "Weirdly enough, I am much happier now than I was with legs," she relates. "I tell people that all the time. The way I am now is how I was supposed to be. This is the real me."[16]

> *"The best way to cheer yourself up is to try to cheer somebody else up."*
>
> —Mark Twain

Anna was eventually interviewed by Ann Curry on the *Today* show and shared her inspiring message: "Life doesn't end with an accident like this," she said. "I chose to get over it and just move on." When Anna was asked to speak to her fellow college students, she expressed gratitude for life and encouraged them to listen to the voice inside when making decisions. "Follow your gut," she advised. "If you get that feeling that something's not right no matter what the situation is . . . you're walking home by yourself at night, you're about to text and drive, or get behind the wheel of a car and you have had alcohol, if it doesn't feel right, don't do it! I will have to pay for my mistake the rest of my life."[17]

Anna's can-do approach shows the power of a positive attitude and believing what happened to her is in the past. She can and does live a full life with a productive future. She isn't focusing on that dark day when she lost her legs. Remarkably, in spite of enormous setbacks, her life is actually expanding instead of diminishing. She has consciously chosen to live a Crescendo Mentality by following a few principles we would all do well to adopt:

- Forgive yourself and move on.
- Maintain a sense of humor.
- Follow your gut—listen to your inner voice.

As you contemplate the stories shared in this "Life-Changing Setbacks" part of the book, and the courageous choices made, remember this important principle: you are not only a product of your circumstances; you are a product of your proactive decisions.

I have always liked this insightful little couplet:

> *Two men looked out the prison bars;*
> *one saw mud, one saw stars.*

What we see in our current circumstance will be greatly influenced by our perspective. Looking down, we may only see mud and bars; whereas looking up, we may see beams of light from the sun, moon, and stars. I know many feel imprisoned by their circumstances and what happens to them, most of which they can't control. Yet the bars that keep them in prison are rarely tangible—there are few, if any, physical barriers or restraints that can't be adjusted or even lifted.

> *"Life is like an old time rail journey . . . delays, sidetracks, smoke, dust, cinders and jolts, interspersed only occasionally by beautiful vistas and thrilling bursts of speed. The trick is to thank the Lord for letting you have the ride."*
>
> —Jenkin Lloyd Jones[18]

When Elizabeth Smart was abducted, she was living every parent's nightmare. For a fourteen-year-old child to totally disappear was horrific to her family and everyone who heard of it. But that's exactly what happened in one of the most followed child abduction cases in history.

On June 5, 2002, Elizabeth Smart disappeared without a trace, taken at knifepoint from her own bedroom in the middle of the night. The horror of her kidnapping and the ensuing rescue efforts brought enormous media attention. But her kidnapper evaded the authorities and kept her captive just three miles from her home.

Nothing could have prepared Elizabeth for what she would have to endure for the next nine months of her life. "It was a sojourn through hell! I went to bed in my 14-year-old perfect world and woke up with a man who might have been the devil himself," she wrote later.[19] She discovered that her kidnappers, Brian David Mitchell and Wanda Barzee, had no intention to ask for ransom in exchange for her release. Instead, she was to be part of their demented lives, as Mitchell's polygamous wife and as Barzee's slave. Constantly threatened with her own death and the death of her family if she attempted to escape, Elizabeth thought the only way she would finally be free was to outlive her captors, many years in the future.

For the next several months, Elizabeth Smart endured thirst and starvation while chained up like an animal in filthy conditions. Constantly subjected to drugs, alcohol, and pornography, she was raped every day of her captivity by an evil man old enough to be her father.[20]

Elizabeth felt completely broken and shattered. She knew it wasn't her fault, but she wondered if anyone would love her after what had happened to her. Then she remembered what her mother told her just a few months earlier when she had felt left out by her friends:

"Elizabeth . . . there are only a few people that matter. God. And your Dad and me. God will always love you. You are His daughter. He will never turn His back on you. The same thing is true for me. It doesn't matter where you go, or what you do, or whatever else might happen, I will always love you. You will always be my daughter. Nothing can change that."

Elizabeth later wrote of that important moment:

The realization that my family would still love me proved to be the turning point. In fact, it proved to be the most important moment throughout my entire nine-month ordeal. It was at this moment that I decided that no matter what happened, I was going to survive . . . I would do whatever it took to live.[21]

For nine months, her family and friends continued to work with police and tried to keep her in the public eye as much as they could. Her younger, nine-year-old sister, who had been awake in the bed next to her during the abduction, finally identified the kidnapper as the homeless man who had done some repair work in their home many months earlier. The profile she described was put on *America's Most Wanted* by John Walsh (whose own child had been kidnapped and murdered years earlier), and on March 12, 2003, someone finally recognized Mitchell from watching TV and called the police.

When the police separated her from the couple, they asked, "Are you Elizabeth Smart?" Elizabeth was still scared to reveal her identity because of her kidnappers' threats. But she later wrote:

> For a moment, my world seemed to absolutely stop. . . . I felt calm. I felt assured. Months of fear and pain seemed to melt before the sun. I felt a sweet assurance. "I am Elizabeth."[22]

But Elizabeth's story didn't just end with her successful rescue. One legacy of her ordeal is that law enforcement agencies across the nation now investigate missing and abducted children differently because of what they learned through her highly profiled case.

Ten years later, Elizabeth wrote *My Story* (with Chris Stewart), an incredible memoir detailing what she experienced:

> I try to encourage other survivors to do what they want in life and to not allow something out of their control to ruin the rest of their lives. . . . It's not their fault. What happened to them doesn't make them less a person or change who they are. . . . It is never too late to start living.[23] . . . I think there are far more

miracles in our lives than we may ever realize. . . . They remind us that God is there and that He cares. . . . In the midst of all the torment, I was able to find a tiny ray of hope.[24]

Elizabeth's courageous choices and remarkable influence continued to expand beyond her abduction, as we will see in the following sections.

Change Yourself First

"One of the things I learned when I was negotiating was that until I changed myself, I could not change others."
—Nelson Mandela[25]

Besides Viktor Frankl, another one of my personal heroes is Nelson Mandela, who I believe was also a supreme example of Living Life in Crescendo. Though imprisoned for twenty-seven years, Mandela went on to become South Africa's first Black president, ending the hateful era of apartheid.

During those long and seemingly wasted years in prison, did he really know or believe that his greatest work was still ahead of him? Doubtful. But though he may not have imagined he would become a great leader in his country, he maintained his values despite his suffering, increased his Circle of Influence, changed his paradigm, and endured with great dignity. While imprisoned, Mandela grew very self-aware, and eventually transformed into a far greater person than the one who had entered those prison gates twenty-seven years earlier. How did he do it?

Mandela had been convicted of sabotage in 1964 and sentenced to life in prison. He was sent to the harsh Robben Island prison near Capetown, where for eighteen of the twenty-seven years he was confined to a small cell with the floor for a bed and a bucket for a toilet—while forced into hard labor in a limestone quarry. For some of the time he was allowed only one visitor a year, for thirty minutes, and a letter every six months. He contracted tuberculosis from the damp conditions and was eventually transferred to two other jails on the mainland where he stayed for nine more years.[26]

While he was in prison, it was forbidden to quote Mandela or publish his picture, yet he and other anti-apartheid leaders were able to smuggle out messages of guidance to the opposition movement. It was in prison where he was impacted by William Ernest Henley's poem "Invictus," which inspires the choosing of one's own destiny regardless of circumstances. He often quoted it to other inmates as a source of inspiration.

> *Out of the night that covers me,*
> *Black as the pit from pole to pole,*
> *I thank whatever gods may be*
> *For my unconquerable soul*
>
> *In the fell clutch of circumstance*
> *I have not winced nor cried aloud.*
> *Under the bludgeonings of chance*
> *My head is bloody, but unbowed.*
> *Beyond this place of wrath and tears*
> *Looms but the Horror of the shade,*
> *And yet the menace of the years*
> *Finds and shall find me unafraid.*
>
> *It matters not how strait the gate,*
> *How charged with punishments the scroll,*
> *I am the master of my fate,*
> *I am the captain of my soul.*[27]

While incarcerated, Mandela realized he had to change himself first if he wanted to lead the people of South Africa. He had gone to Robben Island an angry man who used violence in an effort to obtain freedom; he emerged a man who had learned to listen to his enemies and forgive them. This became the catalyst to his success in reconciling his country.

The main source of personal change is pain. Setbacks lead to pain, which can point down one of two roads: anger or humility.

Mandela's change caused him to do the unthinkable—he befriended his "enemies," the Afrikaner guards. He learned their language, studied their culture, went to church with them, and changed his heart and theirs. And he learned to forgive. The friendships he developed with them were sincere, and ultimately lasted until the end of his life.[28]

On February 11, 1990, South Africa's President Willem de Klerk released Mandela after he had spent a third of his life in prison. Because the government wouldn't release photos while he was in captivity, he was perhaps the world's most famous but least recognizable political prisoner. "As I finally walked through those gates . . . I felt—even at the age of seventy-one—that my life was beginning anew,"[29] he wrote later in his autobiography. "I knew if I didn't leave my bitterness and hatred behind, I'd still be in prison."[30]

Though apartheid was still the law of the land, de Klerk had already begun to bring about sweeping changes to dismantle racial segregation. A new era of hope and equality was beginning to be ushered in. The next year, the hated apartheid laws were repealed.

Four years later, in 1994, South Africa held their first fully representative, multiracial election, and voting lines had never been so long. Surprisingly the elections were peaceful as the country came together in a common cause. Mandela was elected president of South Africa, with de Klerk as his first deputy.

Once the "shoe was on the other foot," the white minority were initially afraid of retaliations by President Mandela, but he immediately and purposefully made many efforts to understand differences and reconcile.[31]

During the World Cup a year after his election, President Mandela strode onto the field in Johannesburg before the final game, wearing a green Springboks jersey in support of South African's national rugby team. There were few symbols that summed up oppression during the apartheid era for Blacks more than the despised jersey and the all-white Afrikaner team. It was an enormous gesture of reconciliation that did not go unnoticed by Blacks and whites alike. After the game, President Mandela took to the field again to congratulate the national team in victory and presented the trophy to South Africa's captain. This sent a strong message that it was time to put enmity aside and unite as a country.[32] The sight of their new black president wearing the jersey and celebrating their nation's victory caused the overwhelmingly white crowd of sixty-three thousand to jump to their feet, chanting "Nelson! Nelson! Nelson!"[33]

Mandela passed away on December 5, 2013, at ninety-five years of age, a global symbol of sacrifice and reconciliation. He had been honored with the Nobel Peace Prize in 1993 along with de Klerk. South Africa celebrated Mandela's life in a way that reflected his sixty-seven years of activism and public work, with a nationwide day of service.[34]

Mandela's life of setbacks and ultimate triumph beautifully exemplifies how to Live Life in Crescendo after suffering a setback:

- Change yourself first (work from the inside out) before attempting to change your situation or others
- Leave bitterness and hatred behind—don't give yourself over to defeat and despair
- Use the power of forgiveness to heal and move forward toward your goals

> *"I am fundamentally an optimist. . . . Part of being optimistic is keeping one's head pointed toward the sun, one's feet moving forward. There were many dark moments when my faith in humanity was sorely tested, but I would not and could not give myself up to despair. That way lays defeat and death."*
>
> —President Nelson Mandela, *Long Walk to Freedom: The Autobiography of Nelson Mandela*[35]

Like Mandela, even at her young age, Elizabeth Smart chose not to let her tragic past define her future. The day she came home, her mother gave her the best advice on how to reclaim her happiness again:

Elizabeth, what this man has done is terrible. There aren't words that are strong enough to describe how wicked and evil he is! He has taken nine months of your life that you will never get back again. But the best punishment you could ever give him is to be happy. . . . To move forward with your life. . . . So be happy, Elizabeth. If you go and feel sorry for yourself, or if you dwell on what has happened, if you hold on to your pain, that is allowing him to steal more of your life away. So don't you do that! . . . You keep every second for yourself . . . God will take care of the rest.[36]

Six years after Elizabeth Smart was rescued, she bravely testified about everything Brian David Mitchell did to her, including the sexual abuse she endured every day. At his sentencing, she told him: "I know that you know what you did was wrong. You did it with full knowledge. But I want you to know I have a wonderful life."[37]

Ultimately, to get better, Elizabeth made the same decision as Ray Hinton, and chose how to respond to her difficult experience:

> I simply made a choice. Life is a journey for us all. We all face trials. We all have ups and downs. All of us are human. But we are also the masters of our fate. We are the ones who decide how we are going to react to life. Yes, I could have decided to allow myself to be handicapped by what happened to me. But I decided very early that I only had one life and that I wasn't going to waste it.[38]

Elizabeth found her pathway toward healing and happiness through her faith and beliefs, through the love and support of her family, friends, and community, and through riding and caring for horses and playing her harp.

She also believes showing gratitude for the good things in her life gave her the courage and strength to forgive her captors. Gratitude and forgiveness: what powerful tools to heal and enjoy life again!

Re-create Your Life

Dave's Killer Bread is a delicious and healthy bread found in many grocery stores today. You may have noticed the picture of a muscular man playing a guitar on the package and read Dave's inspiring story of redemption on the back. But there's much more to his unique story.

Dave's father, Jim Dahl, bought a small bakery in Portland, Oregon, during the 1970s and became somewhat of a pioneer in sprouted wheat bread, baking all sorts of delicious varieties made with whole grains and no animal fat—a rarity in those days. Jim's sons, Glen and Dave, worked with their dad in the bakery, but Dave was restless and rebellious and had no passion for the family business. He also suffered from severe depression. To cope with his condition, Dave turned to drugs, and his life turned to shambles. He was arrested for drug possession, burglary, assault, and armed robbery, and was eventually sentenced to fifteen years in state prison.

Meanwhile, Glen bought the bakery business from his dad and changed the name to NatureBake. Dave eventually completed a rehabilitation program and became eligible for early release in 2004.

Amazingly, Dave's family welcomed him back, and his brother gave him what he really needed most . . . a job. Dave credits Glen with giving him a second chance, for a whole new life. The next year Dave and a nephew went to Portland's Farmers Market to try out a special bread Dave had developed. They quickly sold out of dozens of loaves, and so Dave's Killer Bread (DKB) was born.

By the fall, Dave's Killer Bread products had appeared on the shelves of Portland's stores. The company originally had about thirty-five employees, but it has since grown to more than three hundred. DKB is now available across the United States and Canada, with a loyal following of more than four hundred thousand "BreadHeads."

DKB stands out because of its unique philosophy: "We give people a second chance to create a lasting change in their lives."

Choose to Live in Crescendo, Not Diminuendo

"We believe everyone is capable of greatness. We believe in the power of reinvention and are committed to turning second chances into lasting change. We are on a mission to create change. Too many good employers are reluctant to make a commitment and too many people with potential in the workforce are being passed by—people with drive, commitment, and a will to succeed."

—Dave Dahl[39]

One-third of Dave's Killer Bread employees have felony convictions. The company's director of manufacturing said his biggest concern had been wondering who would give him an opportunity for employment after he was released from prison. He stated that 75 percent of those who get out of prison eventually return within five years if they don't drastically change their lives. Employment is a huge step in this process.

Dave created the Dave's Killer Bread Foundation to foster Second Chance Employment, which he believes can reduce the negative impact of mass incarceration and recidivism. DKB has conducted multiple Second Chance Summits bringing government officials, nonprofit organizers, and businesses together, eliminating stigmas, and helping formerly incarcerated people move forward. The transformative power of giving someone who is ready to change their lives a chance—a second chance—gives them an opportunity not only to make a living, but to make a life.

By his own admission, Dave still struggles but continues to battle setbacks and re-create himself: "You have to be willing to recognize and admit your weaknesses. . . . A lot of suffering has transformed an ex-con into an honest man who is trying to make the world a better place, one loaf at a time."[40]

While it is difficult to re-create your life after a life-changing setback, it is possible, and you can have a positive impact on many other lives, as we will see next with a woman named Ona. No parent feels they should ever outlive their children, but while Ona was in her seventies, she had already buried three of her four children. Her only daughter was killed in a tragic car accident when she was just sixteen, and two of her adult sons died from cancer years later.

Despite her grief, Ona turned her life toward teaching elementary school, with a passion for teaching poetry and writing, subjects that were unusual to teach at their young age. She was creative, caring, and generous, often going the second mile to help students and other teachers who were struggling. Honored by her district as an outstanding teacher of thirty-eight years, Ona has literally blessed the lives of hundreds of children, instilling self-confidence and a love of learning.

After retiring from teaching, Ona re-created her life yet again. Though more than ninety years old, she still maintains a schedule of activities that a younger person would have a hard time matching. She rises early to work in her garden, volunteers for service projects at humanitarian centers and her local church, regularly grinds wheat and takes bread to those who are sick or need a lift, loves to learn anything new, and has been the editor of a quarterly community newsletter for more than ten years. She regularly makes the rounds picking up the "elderly" (though some are younger than her!) to whom she offers rides to activities and cultural events. Though she is experiencing some serious health challenges now, she still wants more time to finish her many projects she's working on simultaneously, including writing her life history, and isn't ready to go anytime soon.

Ona's unique challenges have developed her into an extremely caring, aware, and sensitive person. She often pauses to enjoy a beautiful sunset, or vibrant fall colors, and writes thoughtful handwritten notes of appreciation to those in her life who do even the smallest things for her. She is greatly loved and admired by all who know her, and those who don't know her well would never guess that under her cheerful and positive demeanor, there has been great pain and heartache.[41]

Though she has experienced more than her share of setbacks, like the musical symbol ⟨ , which indicates that volume increases in strength and power, Ona's life is continually expanding and blessing others.

Living in Crescendo during or after a life-changing setback means to:

- Believe in and give second chances
- Never give up on another person
- Intentionally work to recreate your life in your new reality

"I love the man that can smile in trouble, that can gather strength from distress, and grow brave by reflection."

—Thomas Paine

Elizabeth Smart often compares what she went through to having a deep cut on your arm or leg. You can choose to clean it out thoroughly and treat it with medicine to fight infection. It will eventually heal, though it might leave a scar. But even a scar may disappear altogether. Or you can choose to just leave the cut alone. It may heal on its own, but it could also crack open and bleed again, fester and become infected.

It is your choice to treat the cut properly or not, and the same is true of a life-changing event. Ona re-created her life by serving others, and Elizabeth believes every survivor must find their own pathway to recovery. You may choose counseling, medication, or therapy, or you might find a passion in something great you have yet to discover. With support and care, healing will come in time.

Chapter 7

Find Your "Why"

"He who has a why to live for can bear almost any how."
—Fredrich Nietzsche[1]

What do you do if your perfect life falls apart? How do you react? How do you pick up the pieces and move on?

I know of a neglected house in a beautiful neighborhood, an ugly reminder of a ruined marriage. When the couple who owned the house divorced, the angry husband left it unattended for over a decade to spite his ex-wife (and the neighbors who sided with her). The paint is peeling, the roof needs repair, the shutters are hanging broken, and the lawn is yellow and full of weeds. And this bitter man has no intention of selling to another family because he doesn't want to divide the money with his ex-wife.

Instead of finding a new purpose for his life, this man has allowed a broken marriage to define and destroy him. The opposite of Living Your Life in Crescendo, $<$, is to Live in Diminuendo, $>$, which literally means diminishing, decreasing in volume and intensity. I would like to ask this vengeful man: "Why do you allow your ex-wife to ruin your life and still have a significant place in it? Why haven't you moved on past your divorce and begun life again?" Instead of accepting what happened and finding new purpose and happiness, his bitterness and unforgiving heart are diminishing his soul and his future.

By contrast, I've been so inspired by knowing, hearing, and reading about people who have faced great tragedy but didn't let it destroy them. They found a new reason to get up every day. They found purpose in always moving forward, changing the world for the better.

On June 23, 1985, Manjari Sankurathri, her son Srikiran, six, and daughter Sarada, three, boarded Air India flight 182 from their home in Canada for a vacation to London. As the plane approached the coast of Ireland, a bomb placed by Sikh separatists exploded, killing all 329 people on board, the largest mass murder in modern Canadian history. No bodies were ever found.

For three years, Dr. Chandrasekhar Sankurathri (known as "Dr. Chandra") stumbled through his daily routine as a biologist in Ottawa, lost in disbelief that his wife and children were really gone. "I used to think maybe they landed someplace—maybe somebody rescued them." After three years going through the motions and not really living life, Dr. Chandra made a selfless decision to turn his personal pain into an opportunity to bless his native land of India.[42]

"I wanted to do something useful with my life, I needed a purpose. . . . Life is meaningless only if we allow it to be. Each of us has the power to give life meaning, to make our time and our bodies and our words into instruments of love and hope."[43]

At age sixty-four, Dr. Chandra quit his job as a biologist in Ottawa, where he had lived for twenty years, sold his home and belongings, and returned to India. His goal was to improve the quality of life for the needy and destitute in remote areas. He was immediately drawn to two glaring problems: rampant blindness and lack of education.

Approximately 75 percent of the population of India—more than 750 million people—live in villages, and 60 percent of them are destitute. Outside the cities, villagers work under the blazing sun all day long, and the poor diet they consume leaves an estimated 15 million Indians crippled by blindness.

Dr. Chandra also learned that most of these impoverished adults cannot read or write, and their children go to primitive schools where the dropout rate is more than 50 percent. So despite his deep sorrow, Dr. Chandra took his life's savings and created the Sankurathri Foundation (named after his wife), with the mission to improve the health care and education of the poor. He built a school and an eye hospital on a three-acre plot near his wife's birthplace in the small rural village of Kuruthu.

Today the Sankurathri Foundation supports three programs:

The Sarada Vidyalayam School (named after his daughter) is a primary and upper grade school with an amazing zero dropout rate. Sarada provides free books, uniforms, meals, and medical checkups to these rural students, and in return only asks for a willingness to learn and the discipline to study. The Sarada School began with just one grade and has now grown to nine.[44]

As of January 2019, 2,875 students from rural areas have been educated at the school free of charge, along with 661 children from other needy families who have received scholarships to continue their education in various high schools and colleges.

One poor student who had completed his studies at Sarada said: "I owe the credit to Sankurathri Foundation and Dr. Chandrasekhar. Without their help, I would have been a laborer, walking in the footsteps of my father." Because of his education, this young man scored a 96 percent in his high school exams and was admitted to a prestigious engineering school.

The Srikiran Institute of Ophthalmology (named after Dr. Chandra's son) is now a world-class eye care provider in the region. The institute encompasses five buildings and provides eye care services to six different districts in India. The same buses that pick up students for school in the morning are often used later in the day to bring eye care patients from other rural areas to the institute. The government of India has recognized

Srikiran as one of eleven training centers for ophthalmologists in the country, setting high standards for others to follow.

Dr. Chandra says with pride, "Our mission is to provide eye care with compassion, which is equitable, accessible, and affordable to all." Srikiran offers free eye exams, surgeries and medications, accommodations, and food while patients are in the hospital. The inspiration for its work is "Let us light a lamp in the life of the blind."[45]

Since 1993, it has grown substantially and now has fifteen centers. As of 2022, it has served an astounding 3,500,000 patients and performed 34,000 surgeries with more than 1,000 children being treated, 90 percent of which is free to the needy.[46]

Dr. Chandra denies he is doing anything special, and says, "I'm just an ordinary human being trying to do my best to help others. I feel very close to my family. I feel they are here with me," he adds, "and that gives me a lot of strength."[47]

Selflessly putting his pain aside, Dr. Chandra worked to make his corner of the world a healthier and happier place—and this helped him find his "why," and learn how to Live in Crescendo.

"I thank God for my handicaps, for through them, I have found myself, my work, and my God."
—Helen Keller

The Search for Meaning

There are few people I admire more than Viktor Frankl, who survived the German concentration camps and later wrote about his experience in *Man's Search for Meaning*. His book's core message is that humanity's primary motivating force is a search for purpose and meaning in life. Though he suffered greatly, he knew his wounds would eventually heal and truly believed he still had significant work to do.

Rather than fixating entirely on his own misery while imprisoned, Frankl used his imagination and discipline to see himself in his mind's eye—to actually visualize lecturing to university students in the future about the very things he was then experiencing. That gave him motivation and purpose to hope for a better outcome and to endure. He became convinced through his experience and observations that possessing a sense of purpose—a reason or "why"—keeps one alive in the face of adversity.

> *"What we really needed was a fundamental change in our attitude toward life. . . . We had to teach despairing men, that it didn't matter what we expected from life, but rather what life expected from us. We needed to stop asking about the meaning of life, and instead to think of ourselves as those who were being questioned by life—daily and hourly."*
>
> —Viktor Frankl, *Man's Search for Meaning*[48]

Frankl later recorded that initially, all the criteria he had used to evaluate who would survive was wrong. He looked at their intelligence, survival skills, family structure, and their present health—but those factors didn't explain individuals' survival. The only significant variable was the sense that they had a *future*—something significant still to do in life. Frankl learned that trying to restore a man's inner strength in camp first required showing him some future goal. He wrote of two men who seriously considered suicide, believing they had nothing more to expect from life:

> In both cases it was a question of getting them to realize that life was still expecting something from them; some-

thing in the future was expected of them. We found that for the one it was his child whom he adored and who was waiting for him in a foreign country. For the other . . . the man was a scientist and had written a series of books which still needed to be finished. His work could not be done by anyone else, any more than another person could ever take the place of the father in his child's affections. . . . When the impossibility of replacing a person is realized, it allows the responsibility which a man has for his existence and its continuance to appear in all its magnitude. A man who becomes conscious of the responsibility he bears towards a human being who affectionately waits for him, or to an unfinished work, will never be able to throw away his life. He knows the "why" for his existence, and will be able to bear almost any "how."[49]

After Viktor Frankl survived the death camps, his focus, and ultimately his greatest work and contribution, was to understand the importance of finding meaning in one's life. He discovered that not only was it a way to survive, but finding your "why" to live contributed to believing each life had a unique purpose. Ultimately, Dr. Frankl was instrumental in helping others discover this in themselves, and at the time of his death in 1997, *Man's Search for Meaning*, written in 1946, had sold more than 10 million copies in twenty-four languages.

Valuable Lessons When Facing Life's Setbacks

Have you ever been to the desert and seen a cactus flower in full bloom? Cactus flowers have sometimes been called "Mother Nature's fireworks" because their colors are so vibrant. But how could a plain cactus with prickly skin and an unattractive appearance produce such incredibly beautiful flowers? Some cacti, such as the Saguaro, have branches that won't root in certain weather, so they must be grown from seed, and have a forty- to fifty-five-year wait for the first flower![50]

Can you imagine? No blooms at all for half a century, and then finally from a dry plant that never seemed capable of producing anything . . . beautiful flowers. What a great visual analogy for facing life's challenges. Like cactus flowers, if you are patient and persistent, challenges in the end aren't what they were at the start. Challenges and setbacks often seem to have nothing to offer but pain and heartache, but hang on, and after time valuable and useful lessons emerge. Remember, there are significant gains as well as losses in tribulations.

> *"You'll never find a better sparring partner than adversity. Not being beautiful was a true blessing . . . it forced me to develop my inner resources. The pretty girl has a handicap."*
>
> —Golda Meir, former Prime Minister of Israel

When we experience setbacks, troubles, and sorrows, we learn empathy from our own suffering. Further, we learn the noble virtues of faith, courage, long-suffering, endurance, service, charity, gratitude, and forgiveness. Though we may have experienced great loss, there is also incredible *gain* as we discover our true, best selves. As William Shakespeare put it, "Sweet are the uses of adversity."

Overcoming adversity requires us to:

- Find a new fulfilling purpose—discover the why to bear the how

- Work to improve the lives of others—be a catalyst for good
- Be prepared for opportunities suited to our unique abilities and character

If you are prepared and pragmatically seek the Crescendo Mentality, you can look forward to a life rich in purpose.

As her mother advised her, Elizabeth Smart consciously chose to live a happy life after her ordeal. Among other accomplishments, she worked as a feature commentator for ABC News, served a mission in France for her church, graduated from college, married, and now has three children. With the help and support of her parents, she founded the Elizabeth Smart Foundation in 2011 (eight years after her abduction) with the mission of stopping predatory crimes against children. The purpose of the foundation is in answer to a single question the Smarts asked: "What if we could prevent future crimes against children?" This represents their "why." Their goal is to empower children through education and understanding their choices, and to support law enforcement in the rescuing of victims.[51]

Finding your "why" when you are facing life changing setbacks is crucial to adopting the Crescendo Mentality going forward. As the previous inspiring examples of those who have fought through personal setbacks have shown, it leads to rediscovering new meaning and purpose in your life.

Make a Courageous Choice

"It's the ability to choose which makes us human."
—Madeleine L'Engle

How do people like Anthony Ray Hinton or Elizabeth Smart, who faced seemingly insurmountable obstacles, go on to lead productive lives? How do they beat massive setbacks and still succeed and even contribute to make others' lives better? They believe they have a choice.

In 1990, Michael J. Fox's father died unexpectedly and he experienced what he called "the harbinger of the toughest period of my life." In that same year, he was diagnosed with young-onset Parkinson's disease and was told at the age of thirty, and in the midst of a thriving career, that he could probably only work for another ten years. "This was my life skidding horribly sideways," he wrote.

At first, Michael went into denial and sought solace in alcohol. But he soon discovered he was only trying to hide from himself.

"With no escape from the disease, its symptoms, and its challenges, I was forced . . . to resort to acceptance, which simply means acknowledging the reality of a situation. . . . I realized that the only choice not available to me was whether or not I had Parkinson's. Everything else was up to me. By choosing to learn more about the disease, I made better choices about how to treat it. This slowed the progress and made me feel better physically. I was happier and less isolated and could restore my relationships. . . . When things go bad, don't hide! It will take time, but you'll find that even the gravest problems are finite, and your choices are infinite."[52]

Fox has gone on to become the "face" of Parkinson's disease, and—in an effort to win funding for medical research—was even gutsy enough to forgo medication before speaking to a Senate subcommittee, so that his symptoms weren't masked. Since his diagnosis, he has also become an author of several books that are optimistic and inspiring. In *A Funny Thing Happened on the Way to the Future: Twists and Turns and Lessons Learned*, he shares his recipe for success—in essence, "Leave the past behind and live in the moment."

"The scariest person in the world is one with no sense of humor."

—Michael J. Fox

Fox's life with his wife, Tracy Pollan, and their four children is full and happy, though definitely not what he thought it would be. He consciously practices these two principles daily: acceptance and gratitude. "What happened before and what may happen later can't be as important as what's happening now. There's never a better time to celebrate the present. The present belongs to you. Let someone else take the picture . . . just smile."[53]

During the COVID-19 pandemic, Fox was at work painstakingly dictating what he called "a revelatory memoir" to an assistant, since the disease has robbed him of his ability to write or type. *No Time Like the Future: An Optimist Considers Mortality* is a blunt lens on living with an incurable disease for three decades. Giving the same commitment to advocacy and professionalism as he did to his acting career, through the years Fox has now helped raise an incredible $1 billion for research through his namesake foundation.[54]

Even though Fox isn't doing much acting anymore, most people would say he plays a more crucial role now, inspiring others who also suffer from chronic conditions. He made a conscious choice to make the most of what life deals out, Living Life in Crescendo despite a life-altering illness. "I had a high tolerance for difficulty," he acknowledges. "I'd learned to live with Parkinson's and good things came of it." Consistent with his positive outlook that good things are still to come, he believes "the future is the last thing you run out of. The moment until you shut down you've got a future, and then you don't."[55]

The building blocks of his ability to overcome his setback include:

- Understand the gravest problems are finite and your choices are infinite
- Leave the past behind—live in the moment
- Choose optimism and a positive outlook

> *"Gratitude makes optimism sustainable. And if you don't think you have anything to be grateful for, keep looking."*
> —Michael J. Fox

Of course, not everyone has the kind of resources that are available to Michael J. Fox. But even "ordinary people" can make a huge difference by Living in Crescendo after a setback, and choosing to do extraordinary things.

On May 11, 1975, Rick Bradshaw went to Lake Powell in Southern Utah to enjoy a few relaxing days of boating and swimming with friends. One night he dived into the water to retrieve a duffel bag that had fallen in. But even though he was well over a hundred feet offshore, the water wasn't deep enough—he had dived into a sandbar.

The diving accident had caused a spinal cord injury classified as quadriplegia.

At first Rick thought he might, at the age of twenty-two, have to live in an assisted living center with a bunch of old people. He wasn't thrilled with that idea, and that was motivation enough to start looking for options.

"When I was learning how to move my paralyzed body around, making mistakes with position and balance, it would often cause me to fall into unrecoverable positions where I would be stuck until someone helped me up. So I eventually succeeded by first learning how to fall gracefully. As I thought about this, I realized this can apply to all of us in everything we do."

He knew he would never have his previous abilities again, but he came to realize that he could improve at many other skills, if he had the will, and the patience, to practice.

"By knowing I would be horrible at just about everything beforehand gave me the freedom to perform horribly, but I had confidence that I would start making progress. Through this I realized that 'failure' is a sign of engagement and looks more like success than abstinence. Failure leads to success."

In the face of seemingly insurmountable challenges, Rick had to take what he called "thousands of leaps of faith" just to get to the point where he could live and function independently. Enrolling at a university just ten months after his injury, when he could barely write and had no idea how he would perform, required a huge leap of faith.

Rick soon decided to drop government assistance and take a job at the very hospital where he was being treated, even though working meant less money than he would have received on welfare. He also lost the health care benefits he was receiving from Medicaid and had to pay $1,000 a month out of his own pocket. But Rick said, "The easy thing to do would have been to relax and let people take care of me for the rest of my life." According to him, "living off of the government felt like being institutionalized.

"I had to accept that I was paralyzed at a very high level, but I realized I could redefine the pathways to have what I cared about. My true desires were related to getting married and being loved, being with family, having a good career that I enjoyed, learning and traveling. I realized all of those things were still possible."[56]

Rick chose to:

- Challenge preconceived thoughts and perceptions
- Take courageous "leaps of faith"
- Set a good example to those watching

Rick felt he was meant to accomplish something important. He told his family, "If that's my life mission—to set a good example to those watching—then I'm trying my best to do just that."

Rick ended up finding a great new career, marrying a wonderful woman, making money and paying taxes like everyone else, and discovering that success in his career enables other successes. Decades later, he wakes up and likes going to work, and his life is much more than normal. He has recently completed a PhD and a prestigious health leadership training course and is now looking ahead to what is next.[57]

"Great discipline generates enormous strength."
—Robert Schuller

By making a conscious choice to not allow their circumstance to determine their futures, both Michael J. Fox and Rick Bradshaw found the courage to overcome tremendous challenges.

I taught my children to choose to *"be strong in hard moments"* when they are challenged by something new or something out of their comfort zone. Hard moments require tremendous self-discipline and courage to face and overcome. But our strength in these moments will show us just how resilient we really are and influence all the other moments of our lives.

To do this we must consciously *visualize* beforehand exactly what we may face, how we will react, and then decide how to move forward with courage and principle regardless of outside pressure.

These hard moments are usually followed by more tranquil moments if we remain steadfast and endure.

> *"It is not in the still calm of life, or the repose of a pacific station, that great characters are formed. The habits of a vigorous mind are formed in contending with difficulties. Great necessities call out great virtues. When a mind is raised, and animated by scenes that engage the heart, then those qualities which would otherwise lay dormant, wake into life and form the character of the hero."*
>
> —Abigail Adams, Letter to John Quincy Adams,
> January 19, 1780[58]

Adopt a Carpe Diem Attitude— Seize the Day!

> *"Seize the moment! Remember all those women on the* Titanic *who waved off the dessert cart!"*
>
> —Erma Bombeck

In the movie *Dead Poets Society*, Robin Williams plays John Keating, an English teacher at a boys' prep school, and a Transition Person. At one point he calls out to his cautious students in an effort to inspire them: "Carpe Diem—seize the day, boys! Make your lives extraordinary!"

Find Your "Why"

Keating was the only teacher who encouraged his students to push themselves beyond what was required, to break away from learning in the traditional way, and to see things from a different perspective. He wanted these young men to see themselves in a new way—to uncover their true potential, to try new things even if they failed, and to reach for their dreams though they seemed unattainable.[59]

Keating's challenge to "Make your lives extraordinary" means it's within your power to make things happen. It's up to you! Take control and assume the responsibility to live at the edge or even outside of your comfort zone so you can grow and expand.

In our family, we would call out "Carpe Diem!" when one of us had a chance to do or learn something different or try a new and challenging task. Our parents encouraged us to take full advantage of a great opportunity, to "suck the marrow out of life" as Thoreau put it, and to do everything within our power to make it happen!

I think children and older people understand the idea to "seize the day." Neither hurry nor worry about time, but just thoroughly enjoy the moment. Have you ever seen a child walking on the curb, trying to balance while their mother is frantically trying to get into the store? The child is enjoying the moment, reveling in the challenge, totally unaware of the time or schedule their mother believes is so important to keep. And if you ever talk to an older person while they're sitting on their porch, in a store, or at church, they're absolutely in no hurry at all. They want you to linger and talk with them, to listen to their new joke or story—totally unaware that you're in a hurry and need to get going to something supposedly more important. Somehow on both ends of the spectrum, they've got it right, while we get our priorities all mixed up in the middle.

In 2009, Todd Bol, a social entrepreneur in Hudson, Wisconsin, built a small model of a one-room schoolhouse as a tribute to his mother, a teacher who had always loved to read. He put it in front of his house on a post, filled it with some of his favorite books, and invited his neighbors and friends to read and borrow them free of charge. His neighborhood thought it was a great idea and used it extensively, so Todd built several more and gave them away to place in other areas. Rick Brooks of UW-Madison saw Todd's do-it-yourself models and joined him with a goal to share good books and bring communities together.

With a motto of "take a book, return a book," and thereby promoting community connections, these libraries have been called little town squares. As the idea spread throughout Wisconsin, the founders decided to "seize the day" by forming a nonprofit group called Little Free Libraries that would not only impact Wisconsin but spread to other states. Inspired by Andrew Carnegie, the philanthropist who set a goal to fund 2,508 free public libraries across the English-speaking world, Brooks and Bol set their own goal of surpassing that number by the end of 2013. They exceeded their goal a year and a half before their target date.[60]

Their growth has continued steadily every year and the results are astounding. They are now a worldwide book sharing program and social movement with free access to books for all and a goal to promote literacy.[61] Studies have repeatedly shown that books in the hands of children can greatly impact literacy, yet two out of three children living in poverty have no books to call their own. Little Free Library addresses this by placing these little libraries in areas where they are needed most.

Todd's mission of making books more accessible has had a domino effect across the world. As of 2021, Little Free Libraries are found in all fifty states, in more than one hundred countries, and 42 million books are shared annually. Like a domino effect, over one hundred twenty-five thousand little libraries have been placed around the world—from Wisconsin to California, the Netherlands, Brazil, and Japan, to Australia, Ghana, and Pakistan.

The organization is built entirely on volunteers, from the board to sponsors, to neighborhood stewards, to those who take a book and then return one. Run entirely on the honor system, Little Free Libraries keeps going by utilizing a constant stream of people who take the initiative and act in their own neighborhoods.[62]

Todd's vision of a world where neighbors know each other by name and everyone has access to books is being realized. Though sadly Todd passed away from pancreatic cancer in 2018, his legacy of love for books and learning carries on, in Crescendo.

> *"I really believe in a Little Free Library on every block and a book in every hand. I believe people can fix their neighborhoods, develop systems of sharing, learning from each other, and see that they have a better place on this planet to live."*
>
> —Todd Bol[63]

Use Your "R and I" and Make It Happen!

There is an oft-told but powerful tale of two men who came upon a beach covered with hundreds of starfish that had been washed ashore during high tide and left stranded on the sand when the water receded. One man frantically ran back and forth, throwing starfish back into the water in a desperate attempt to save them. The other man stood watching him, mocking his efforts.

"What do you think you're doing?" he asked. "It makes no difference if you throw some back—there are just too many to save!"

Undeterred, the other man picked up one starfish, held it up, and then threw it back into the ocean. "Well, it made a difference to that one!"

If you're a fan of *The Simpsons*, you may remember the episode when Marge came home discouraged because she had narrowly lost a city election. Much to her horror, she discovered that Homer, her own husband, had forgotten to vote! When Marge got mad, Homer got defensive: "But Marge. I'm just one person—how can I make a difference?" To which she angrily replied, "But I only lost by one vote!"

Living Life in Crescendo means that just one person can make a big difference by just using your "R and I"—resourcefulness and initiative. It doesn't matter who you are, or if you have money or influence, if you just work to "make it happen!"

Whenever someone in our family, even one of the younger children, would make an excuse, shirk responsibility, and wait for someone else to provide a solution, we would always tell them, "Use your R and I!" Now, often before we can say it, they answer, "I know—use my R and I!"

What difference can an individual make? Celeste Mergens had been working in Kenya with nonprofit groups to help with the tremendous poverty rampant in the slums there. After praying to learn how she could specifically help children, she woke up at two-thirty in the morning with a burning question that had never occurred to her before: "Have you asked what the girls are doing for feminine hygiene?" She quickly emailed a contact who would know the answer. She was shocked when the reply came back simply, "Nothing! They wait in their rooms!" Her contact said that six out of ten girls lacked access to feminine hygiene products in Kenya.

Celeste learned that most girls were not allowed to go to school during menstruation, and they literally stayed home until their cycle was finished. Missing this much school was devastating to girls' futures, causing them to fall behind in their studies and leading many to simply drop out. If they didn't graduate, they were unable to get decent-paying jobs, making them more likely to be married off by their parents at an early age, totally ending any chance of a better future. Celeste found it hard to believe that a simple lack of feminine hygiene products created a cycle of poverty that was difficult to escape.

So Celeste and a few friends founded Days for Girls, a grassroots nonprofit volunteer organization with the main goal of recovering lost days in school for girls. Their mission is to restore health, dignity, and education around the globe by providing access to a reusable feminine hygiene kit specific to the needs of girls and women who before had nothing to use.

Reusable feminine kits are now made with love by thousands of volunteers all around the world, and also by local women filling the needs in their own communities internationally. All of this adds up to life-changing days for girls who are now able to attend school without embarrassment or shame. The cycle of poverty can be broken. When girls stay in school, it increases confidence, supports healthy communities, and can drastically change their future. Noreen from Kenya wrote, "When we have those kits, we can do something great in the world." Dr. Pedro Sanchez, who has observed this impact, said, "An educated girl can have a profound impact on the development of a community."[64]

With the right care, these precious kits can last up to three years and would be the equivalent of using 360 disposable pads.

Most important, the girls gain back 180 days in school, women can go 36 months without interrupting their jobs, and both groups retain their dignity. After the distribution of kits from Days for Girls, school absence rates dropped incredibly—from 36 to 8 percent in Uganda, and from 25 to 3 percent in Kenya. An incredible 115 million days of missing school have been recovered and replaced with increased education, dignity, health, and opportunity.

Days for Girls now has a global alliance of nearly 1,000 chapters and teams, companies, and government and nongovernment organizations, reaching an astounding number of women and girls—more than 2.5 million in 144 countries as of May 2022. Days for Girls empowers and unites women and boasts seventy thousand volunteers working in chapters all around the world. There are volunteer opportunities for anyone wanting to get involved in large or small ways in local chapters everywhere.[65]

In 2019, Celeste was given the Global Hero award for her proactive efforts as the founder and CEO, helping others find their "why" to serve. Her efforts and achievements all began by asking a question, responding to a need, and working to find a solution.

What other questions we are not asking?

"Lord, let me always desire more than I think I can do."
—attributed to Michelangelo

Become a Transition Person

Major setbacks can often serve as the catalyst for people to free themselves from the "scripting" received from the generation before. Whether we are conscious of them or not, we may be living out destructive or limiting beliefs that have been deeply embedded in our minds and hearts:

- "No one in our family has gone to college; we just don't like formal education."
- "We Murphys all have fiery tempers! It must be the Irish in us."
- "My father lost it when disciplining me, and you parent like you were parented."
- "My brother and I have the same problem keeping jobs—we somehow self-destruct."
- "Most women in our family end up divorced; it's almost like we can't help following the tradition."

Sexual abuse or abandonment or alcoholism may have been passed down through your family line. But even though it may be very difficult, you must be self-aware enough to see and then consciously break free of these negative, destructive scripts.

> *"What is necessary to change a person is to change his awareness of himself."*
>
> —Abraham H. Maslow

The cycle can stop with *you*. You can be the Transition Person in your family for those who follow. Your decision can extend beyond a lifetime, positively benefiting future generations.

In the classic musical *Camelot*, Lancelot tries to justify and excuse his infidelity, telling King Arthur with resignation in his voice, "The fates have not been kind." What he is really saying is "This just happened and there was nothing I could do about it." King Arthur responds with great wisdom when he passionately retorts: "Lance, the fates must not have the last word! We must not let our passions destroy our dreams."[66]

Regardless of what life deals you or what circumstances you face, *you* are the determining force of your own life. Instead of passing those old scripts on to the next generation, you can stop them now by changing yourself through the Crescendo Mentality.

A Transition Person can be a powerful influence in our families and society. Do you know of such a person in your own life? Can you be one to someone else?

In the Bible's Book of Proverbs, there is a wise verse: "Where there is no vision the people perish." Vision is the ability to think ahead and plan the future with imagination and wisdom. It provides the long-range outlook of where you should be and why, and how to get there—how to "Begin with the End in Mind" (the 2nd Habit in *The 7 Habits of Highly Effective People*).

Malala Yousafzai is an incredible example of someone who had the vision and fortitude to become a Transition Person for children and women throughout Pakistan. A young girl when the Taliban banned girls from attending school in her native Swat Valley, Malala gave a speech in Peshawar in September of 2008 with the courageous title "How dare the Taliban take away my basic right to education?" Education was very important in her family. Malala had attended a school founded by her father, an anti-Taliban activist (and a Transition Person in his own right), who had a profound impact on her.

When she was only twelve, Malala wrote a blog under a pseudonym for the BBC concerning her life under Taliban rule and her views on education for girls. Her activism made her one of the best-known teenagers in the world at the time. In 2011, Malala was nominated for the International Children's Peace Prize by Archbishop Desmond Tutu, a notable activist in South

Africa. Though she didn't win, she was awarded Pakistan's first National Youth Peace Prize that same year. In congratulating Malala, Prime Minister Nawaz Sharif said: "She is the pride of Pakistan. . . . Her achievement is unparalleled and unequaled. Girls and boys of the world should take lead from her struggle and commitment."[67]

But giving interviews and speaking out publicly exposed her to danger. Death threats were slipped under her door at home and published in local papers. Though her parents were worried, they didn't think the Taliban would actually harm a child. But Malala knew these threats were real:

> "I had two options. One was to remain silent and wait to be killed. And the second was to speak up and then be killed. I chose the second one. I decided to speak up. . . . I am just a committed and even stubborn person who wants to see every child getting a quality education, who wants to see women having equal rights, and who wants peace in every corner of the world. . . . Education is one of the blessings of life, and one of its necessities."[68]

On October 9, 2012, a gunman sent by the Taliban boarded her school bus, asked for Malala by name, and then pointed a pistol at her head and fired three shots. One bullet struck the left side of her forehead, traveled through the length of her face, and then lodged in her shoulder. The other two shots hit her friends, who were also injured but not as seriously.

The attempt to assassinate a fifteen-year-old girl who dared speak out against the Taliban sparked a national and international outcry and an outpouring of support for Malala. Three days after she was shot, fifty Islamic clerics in Pakistan condemned those who had tried to kill her, but the Taliban boldly reiterated their intent to kill not only Malala but her father as well.

For days after she was shot, Malala was unconscious and in critical condition. But as soon as she was stable enough, she was taken to England, where she underwent multiple surgeries. Miraculously, she suffered no major brain injury. Later she gratefully acknowledged the overwhelming international support and prayers in her behalf. And despite continued threats, Malala returned to school in 2013 and courageously continued as a staunch advocate for the power of education.

Her efforts caused significant movement toward her goal of education for every child. Gordon Brown, the United Nations special envoy for global education and former British prime minister, launched a UN petition in Malala's name that 2 million people signed, demanding that all children worldwide be allowed to attend school by the end of 2015. This led to the passing of Pakistan's first Right to Free and Compulsory Education Bill, a substantial breakthrough for education in that country.[69]

On her sixteenth birthday, July 12, 2013, Malala gave a speech at the United Nations before more than five hundred students at a specially convened youth assembly. The sight of her standing there alive and strong, after being shot, deeply affected her audience and served as a powerful testimony for her message of hope through education. Though she was young, her words electrified all who heard her speak:

> "Dear friends, on the 9th of October the Taliban shot me on the left side of my forehead. They shot my friends too. They thought that the bullets would silence us, but they failed! And out of that silence—weakness, fear, and hopelessness died! Strength, power, and courage was born. . . . I am here

to speak up for the right of education of every child. . . . We must believe in the power and strength of our words. Our words can change the world. . . . So let us wage a glorious struggle against illiteracy, poverty, and terrorism, and let us pick up our books and pens. They are our most powerful weapons. . . . One child, one teacher, one pen, and one book can change the world. Education is the only solution. Education first."[70]

Malala Yousafzai was eventually awarded the Nobel Peace Prize, at seventeen—the youngest person ever to receive this honor. She also received $50,000 for the World's Children's Prize and immediately donated all of the proceeds to rebuild a United Nations school in the Gaza Strip, claiming, "Without education, there will never be peace." As a Transition Person of influence, Malala hopes to lead her country as prime minister one day.[71] Talk about vision.

"You see things; and you say 'Why?' But I dream things that never were; and I say 'Why not?'"
—George Bernard Shaw

The influence of one committed person to a good cause is within the power of all who purposefully choose how to respond to what happens to them. Malala's courage and vision give us building blocks to conquer setbacks:

- Choose to become a Transition Person in your family or community—stop negative and destructive behaviors from continuing
- Believe you have the ability and power to choose how you react to whatever happens to you

- Use the power of one committed person with vision to inspire change

"History has demonstrated that the most notable winners usually encountered heartbreaking obstacles before they triumphed. They won because they refused to become discourage by their defeats."

—B. C. Forbes

Elizabeth Smart also exemplified the power of Life in Crescendo by becoming a Transition Person. After her ordeal was publicized, Congress created a program that has become a crucial tool in finding missing children. In 2003, Elizabeth and her father Ed Smart were invited to be present when President George W. Bush signed the nationwide Amber Alert Protect Act into law for abducted children. (AMBER is an acronym for America's Missing: Broadcast Emergency Response.)

Today this system keeps expanding: beginning in January 2013, AMBER alerts have been automatically sent to millions of cell phones around the country, and as of December 31, 2021, there have been 1,111 children successfully rescued and returned because of them.[72]

Elizabeth has worked with the Department of Justice in creating a survivor's guide entitled "You're Not Alone: The Journey from Abduction to Empowerment." It encourages children who have gone through similar experiences not to give up—to realize that there is life after tragic events.[73]

Through the Elizabeth Smart Foundation, Elizabeth has reassured countless victims with her inspiring example of reclaiming a happy life after suffering abuse. She has continued to tell her story in support of prevention and recovery programs for child victims of abuse, kidnapping, and internet pornography. She is a strong voice of empowerment to victims, survivors, and their families everywhere.[74]

The Smart Foundation has also teamed up with radKIDS— rad is an acronym for Resist Aggression Defensively—a non-profit program created to prevent crimes against children. Their goal is to teach children to recognize dangerous situations and arm them with options, and radKIDS is the national leader in children's safety education, having trained six thousand instructors for three hundred thousand kids through a revolutionary curriculum at schools in forty-six states and Canada.

Of the more than three hundred thousand children who have graduated from the radKIDS program, it has recorded more than one hundred and fifty saves from predatory abduction and tens of thousands of saves from sexual assault and potential human trafficking. These graduates used their new skills and were returned safely to their families. Statistics show that 83 percent of children who fight back, scream, and react are able to escape their attacker; radKIDS empowers children to replace fear and face dangerous situations with confidence, self-esteem, and safety skills. And because of the information and training they received, tens of thousands of sexually assaulted and abused children have spoken up and got the help they needed to stop the abuse. Thousands more have escaped bullying and peer-to-peer violence.[75]

Despite Elizabeth's abduction at a young age, she beautifully exemplifies Living in Crescendo, showing to the world that despite her ordeal, her most important work and contributions were, and still continue to be, most definitely *ahead* of her. And, in keeping with what C. S. Lewis noted, her hardships prepared her for an extraordinary destiny that perhaps only she can fulfill.

"I have learned that my challenges can help me reach out to others with more empathy and understanding than I could ever have had before. When we are faced with a challenge, it is very easy to be mad or upset. But when we have passed our great test, we are then given opportunities to reach out to other people. We are able to effect change in a way that otherwise we wouldn't have been able to. Because of the things I have lived through, I can help other people now. I can reach out to other victims and help them to learn to be happy. . . . If I hadn't had this terrible experience, I'm not sure that I would have cared enough about these issues to become involved. . . . I am grateful for these opportunities that I've had to help other people. They have blessed my life. Gratitude has also helped me to keep a healthy perspective." [76]

—Elizabeth Smart

PART 4

THE SECOND HALF OF LIFE

largo (lar-go) adverb or adjective: slow and with great
dignity; slow, broad, from Latin *largus*: abundant

accelerando (ac-ce-le-ran-do) adverb or adjective:
from Latin, meaning . . . "speed up!"

"There are far, far better things ahead
than any we leave behind."

—C. S. Lewis

Years ago, when I was teaching a large group about what I've
now termed Living Life in Crescendo, I watched a man in the
audience become very animated, trying to engage those around
him. I could hardly wait to talk to him. After my presentation,
he explained that he was a circuit judge turning sixty-five in the
next year who until now had just accepted it was time to retire.
A light had gone on when he realized he still had more to con-

tribute and was in a position to do so. Why quit now? he asked himself. For years his service had made a positive impact on his community, and he still had an intense passion for his work. He realized his city needed him to help with the growing and complicated issues he was very familiar with. As he envisioned his future through the prism of the Crescendo Mentality, he got excited realizing his most important work could still be ahead of him.

"Retirement," or ending all work at a certain period of life, is a relatively new concept. If you look back, you will discover that many great men and women in history never cut back simply because of their age. There were and are many people still productively working into their seventies, eighties, and beyond— making remarkable differences in their fields. Today, CEOs, educators, lawyers, entrepreneurs, coaches, politicians, scientists, farmers, business owners, athletes, retailers, doctors— people from all walks of life—don't buy into society's flawed notion of retirement. They just keep contributing year after year. Only a generation or two ago, our ancestors died exhausted at an age when, thanks to medical breakthroughs, we can now anticipate a full life for many more years.

Much to everyone's surprise, when I was sixty-four, Sandra and I built the "dream home" we had always wanted. We did this after our nine kids were mostly raised, because we wanted a place to create a wonderful family culture where our grandchildren could become best friends with their cousins, and our family could gather to relax, enjoy, and support each other in an inter-generational home.

David, one of my sons, was incredulous that I would undertake such a task toward the "end of my life," as he imagined it. He teased me by standing at the construction site with his arms open wide in awe and bellowing directly at me: "At the sunset of his life—and yet, HE BUILDS!"

Everyone got a good laugh, including me, but I have always believed there was still much more to do, with our family and home being a big part of it. Since completion, our home has become a place of renewal and refuge, laughs and lessons, a gathering place for our growing posterity, to enjoy for many years to come.

I want you to realize how crucial it is to stay open to opportunities to serve and bless others—no matter your age—because your finest and most important work may still await you! I absolutely believe that. So often, the first two-thirds of your life will serve as a preparation for the last third of your life, where you will make your finest contributions.

In 1940, during a time that was referred to as Britain's darkest hour, Winston Churchill said this about becoming prime minister at age sixty-six:

> I felt as if I were walking with destiny, and that all my past life had been but a preparation for this hour and for this trial. . . . I thought I knew a good deal about it all and I was sure I should not fail.[1]

At this time of life, you have more resources, experience, and wisdom than ever before. There are simply too many needs and too much yet to accomplish for you to consider "retiring." You may retire from a career or a job, but you never should retire from making meaningful contributions. What thrilling adventures yet await you!

Chapter 8

Keep Your Momentum Going!

"To me, retirement is death!
I have no idea why people retire."

—Merv Griffin, television host
who created *Jeopardy* and *Wheel of Fortune*

In my book *The 3rd Alternative*, I included a quote from Dr. Hans Selye's *The Stress of Life* that is most insightful concerning retirement and the consequences that follow:

> With advancing years, most people require increasingly more rest, but the process of aging does not progress at the same speed in everybody. Many a valuable person who could still have given several years of useful work to society, has been made physically ill and prematurely senile by the enforced retirement at an age when his requirements and abilities for activity were still high. This psychosomatic illness is so common that it has been given a name: "retirement disease."

In his book, Dr. Selye differentiates between the unpleasant or harmful variety of stress called "distress" (dis = bad) and the useful variety or "eustress" (eu = good). Dr. Selye found that the person who does not stay involved or connected, like they did when they were working, will see their immune system slow and the degenerative forces in the body accelerate. However, if they become engaged in some meaningful work or project where they encounter "eustress" (beneficial stress), they experience fulfillment and purpose.[2]

Dr. Selye believed that people who are looking for a tension-less state actually have a shorter life span because life is sustained by eustress, the tension between where we are now and where we want to be—reaching for some goal that inspires. Life means more when we respond to work that is meaningful to others.

In *50 Simple Ways to Live a Long Life*, Suzanne Bohan and Glenn Thompson discuss *ikigai* (a reason for being), a philosophy widely known and practiced in Japan, which fosters developing a positive purpose in life and a sense of satisfaction. The Ikigai Foundation, promoted by the Japanese government, encourages seniors' independence to relieve the burden on families and social systems. A study of more than one thousand elderly Japanese people found that those who practiced *ikigai* lived significantly longer than those seniors who did not. Another study also reported that "those who had strong motivation for achievement of a purpose were significantly less depressed than those who had no motivation."[3]

Another study of 12,640 middle-aged Hungarians who believed their lives had meaning found they had significantly lower rates of cancer and heart disease than those who didn't feel a sense of purpose. The Blue Zones Project, which studied some of the world's most long-lived people, discovered that having a sense of purpose—or simply having a reason to get out of bed—was a common characteristic found in many of the world's centenarians.

"People who feel their life is part of a larger plan and are guided by their spiritual values have stronger immune systems, lower blood pressure, a lower risk of heart attack and cancer, and heal faster and live longer," writes Harold G. Koenig, MD, who has studied this phenomenon consistently. Deepak Chopra, the bestselling author and cofounder of the Chopra Center for Wellness, is convinced that "purpose gives you fulfillment and joy . . . and that can bring you the experience of happiness."[4]

In his bestselling book *Dare to Be 100*, Walter Bortz, a doctor and respected authority on successful aging, wrote that as we grow older, our responsibility should ironically grow, not decrease. "The older we become, the more responsible we should be, because we have shaped the environment to our usage." Bortz believes we should continue to remain engaged in the affairs of life and use our talents for a higher purpose. However, our society has conditioned us to believe the opposite, so the tendency as we age is to pull away from friends, family, and social circles.

Bortz counsels seniors to strive to experience "flow" in their work, so that they are so immersed in interesting projects and endeavors that time passes quickly and almost unnoticed. He found that "not only does living this fully engaged life allow you to live longer and better, but it allows you to die quicker. You want to go with your foot fully on the accelerator. You don't want to go in idle!"[5]

Fight the tendency to pull away as you age and instead get involved in projects that provide meaning and purpose for you and others. Don't subscribe to the mental and social contagion that spreads the "retirement disease." Look around you and you'll find many examples of outstanding men and women who live happy and productive lives while in this exciting stage of life. Here are several in a variety of occupations. They still have much to contribute in life and believe that the antidote for the retirement disease is *purpose*.

George Burns was one of the few entertainers whose career successfully spanned the generations of vaudeville, radio, television, film, standup comedy, records, books, and movies— a career in show business that lasted literally ninety-three years! At nearly eighty years old, he won an Academy Award for best supporting actor in *The Sunshine Boys*, the oldest actor to win the award. At the time, Burns had been away from a leading role for thirty-five years—joking that his agency didn't want him overexposed! Winning the Oscar launched an amazing second career in Crescendo that kept him busy working in movies and TV specials well into his nineties and beyond.

When in his nineties, the legendary comedian announced with the "straight man" humor he was famous for that he was celebrating his one hundredth birthday at the London Palladium, saying, "I couldn't possibly die now—I'm booked!" He eventually wrote ten books, a couple of them bestsellers and one aptly titled *How to Live to Be 100—or More*. He practiced what he preached, and died at one hundred years of age, working right up until the end. He joked he was going to stay in show business until he was the only one left—and eventually, at one hundred, he was.[6]

There are not many NASCAR drivers older than fifty, let alone in their eighties, but Hershel McGriff has broken the age stereotypes in the racing world and turned some heads doing it. At eighty-one, McGriff became the oldest driver ever to compete in a NASCAR feature race, at the Portland International Raceway, and actually finished thirteenth in a field of twenty-six. He wasn't competing just for the distinction of driving in his eighties—he wanted to make a comeback in the sport that he loved and had competed in for nearly six decades.[7]

When many in their later years are navigating walkers and wheelchairs, Hershel McGriff couldn't bring himself to retire. A twelve-time Most Popular Driver of the Year winner, he was inducted into the Motorsports Hall of Fame of America at age seventy-nine. But his greatest honor came later, when he was one of the five legends to be chosen in the NASCAR Hall of Fame class of 2016—an award few drivers ever receive.[8]

McGriff went on to say, "I've given some thought that when I reach 80, I'd like to try a short track race somewhere, just to see if I can keep up with the young guys!" Of course he did, competing at the Sonoma Raceway at the age of eighty-four.[9]

Research has shown continuing to work into your later years may contribute to longevity. A study that followed 3,500 Shell Oil company employees found that those who retired at fifty-five were twice as likely to die during the next ten years as people the same age who kept working. A European study tracking 16,827 Greek men and women for twelve years discovered that those who retired early had a 50 percent higher mortality rate than those who kept working. "A job is probably the easiest way to help you feel your life has purpose, so consider staying with it as long as you can," says Robert N. Butler, MD, founding director of the National Institute on Aging.[10]

In 2018, Arthur Askin was one of three laser scientists awarded a Nobel Prize for their contributions in physics. At ninety-six years old, he was believed to be the oldest person ever given this honor. This achievement seemed to most to be the highlight and conclusion to a long and successful scientific career, but Askin didn't look at it that way. He "told Nobel officials that he might not be available for interviews about the award because he is very busy working on his next scientific paper." Clearly Arthur Askin still has much more to contribute to the scientific field and didn't want to be held up![11]

However, in October 2019, German-born John B. Goodenough attained the honor of being the oldest Nobel Prize winner. At ninety-seven, Mr. Goodenough won the award in chemistry for his research on lithium-ion batteries used in laptops and smartphones. "I'm extremely happy," he told reporters, "that lithium-ion batteries have helped communications around the world." He is continuing work in his lab and has no plans to retire from the field he loves.[12]

Irma Elder didn't plan on working in the family business, but when her husband had a heart attack and died unexpectedly, this fifty-two-year-old shy, stay-at-home mother of three was suddenly faced with a big decision: she could either sell her husband's troubled Ford dealership in Detroit for hardly anything or make a go of it herself. Irma found she had a knack for turning a troubled car dealership into a success. She learned how to wrangle with the manufacturers, bankers, and credit companies and worked for the next twenty years, opening her ninth and tenth dealerships in her late seventies. She was eventually among the top Jaguar dealers in the world, and her Elder Automotive Group became one of the nation's largest Hispanic-owned businesses.

"If you ask me when I'll retire, I'll tell you it's when I stop having fun!" says the grandmother of three. "It makes me come alive." She is also a pioneering woman in the industry. "I think there's still the perception that women can't run car dealerships," she says. "But what's the big deal? I just accept it, and I know I'll crack that glass ceiling. With age comes patience."[13]

At age sixty-five, Elliott Carter won his second Pulitzer Prize in music for his String Quartet no. 3, and at age eighty-six he received his first Grammy, for a violin concerto. At age ninety, he shocked the music world by trying out a new genre, opera. The *Boston Globe* wrote about his operatic work in a rave review entitled "What's Next?" In his later years, Carter was astonishingly active, publishing more than forty works between the ages of ninety and one hundred. "Talk about a 'late bloomer'! It took me a long time to work out things I had in my mind that I couldn't crystallize clearly," Carter explains. "It's like learning a new language—once you develop the basic vocabulary, it becomes easier and instinctive."

Carter's routine for years was to rise early in the morning to compose when he felt he was at his most creative peak. He published twenty pieces after he turned one hundred, and his last completed work when he was 103, three months before he passed away. He amazed his industry by composing into his eleventh decade, working right up until the end of his life. One of America's most important and enduring composers in contemporary music, his life shows how "good things come to those who wait."[14]

At sixty years old, Clayton Williams decided it was time to end a successful forty-year engineering career as owner and officer of Williams Equipment & Controls Co. But it wasn't to retire and take up golf and relax, or even travel the world, that Clayton was after. Instead, he decided to courageously launch a totally different career in another direction—as an artist. He had always painted as a hobby, and like his mother, he had a keen eye for beauty, and felt the time was right to enter into the art world. Though most would consider engineering and art to be polar opposites, Clayton was not fazed by starting a completely different career later in his life and was anxious to start using the right side of his brain more.

After working full-time on his painting skills, he soon opened Williams Fine Art as an art gallery where he could display and sell his own paintings as well as others'. He displayed and sold paintings from early and current artists, regional Western art, and he loved promoting young artists with talent who hadn't sold yet. Clayton studied and learned from trusted mentors and soon was teaching a variety of art seminars to others. He entered art shows, displayed paintings in his own one-man show, and had others featured in various art books and magazines.

As he entered his eighties and nineties he continued to work full-time in his art gallery, and claimed, "I don't know how not to work. My friends play golf and bridge and while that's fine, it just wouldn't be enough for me. I love always working on a current project with a challenge and a reward—I'm excited for what's cooking every day!"

Clayton painted and sold a few thousand of his own paintings, and also gave many away to his family.

Besides collecting and selling paintings, Clayton has served diligently for decades on multiple art and charitable boards in his community. He also started his own foundation that reaches many in need—providing tutoring for at-risk sixth graders and sponsoring high school scholarships to low-income students, and providing meals for the homeless—in addition to staying involved with other needed projects in his community.

Though Clayton made a good living, money was never a driving force with his art. He easily made the decision to donate a rare drawing by a premier artist of the American West named Maynard Dixon to a local art museum, so that thousands of people could enjoy it through the years, instead of just selling it to one person. He also donated several other valuable paintings to art museums rather than profit from them.

After working for thirty-two years from his art gallery and painting until age eighty, finally, at ninety-four, he now sells paintings from his home, still heavily involved and contributing to the art world. Though he has faced health challenges throughout his life, he surprised younger opponents by playing competitively in singles tennis until he was eighty-five years old.

Now he's anything but idle, heavily involved in various projects and still Living in Crescendo. Every day, he keeps his mind sharp while working on the computer and writing up his mother's life history, sharing ideas on growth for his foundation, serving on an art board, connecting people who bring him art to sell, and working on upcoming art books, and he loves spending time with his large posterity.

Looking back, he says, "My later art years have been my most fulfilling ones because I've been able to contribute to society and give back. I've made so many new friends and it's been such a blessing to feel that I have contributed something of value." And amazingly, he's still looking for the next "challenge and reward" ahead of him.[15]

At age seventy-nine, Barbara Bowman worked for eight years to oversee programs for thirty thousand kids as chief of Chicago's Office of Early Childhood Education. Known as a pioneer in the field of early education, Barbara has advocated for young children throughout her career. An internationally renowned expert in early education, she has worked as a teacher, lecturer, author, and administrator, and was one of three cofounders of the Erikson Institute (for Advanced Study in Child Development), eventually serving as the president. Bowman tirelessly has pursued higher quality and more extensive training for early education, and at eighty-one she served as a consultant to the U.S. secretary of education under President Obama.[16]

A teacher at heart with a love for children, at ninety-one she remains active in educational causes and enjoys inviting anywhere from fifteen to twenty-five people over every Sunday for dinner. "I've done it for 50 years," she explains. "That's what keeps me young."

She believes age gives you a marked advantage, saying: "You can do what you think is right without worrying about your career. . . . And there's a sense of urgency that comes with age—

I don't know how much time I have left, so I don't waste it on things that aren't important."[17]

Now, I'm not sharing such a variety of stories and examples to guilt-trip you, I'm hoping they will *inspire* you to consider what *you* too can do during this crucial time of life. My goal is to inject you with the anecdote to the "retirement disease"—seek a purpose—by believing that this stage of life can be one of opportunity and fulfillment. George Bernard Shaw really summed up what this chapter is all about:

> This is the true joy in life, being used for a purpose recognized by yourself as a mighty one. That being a force of nature, instead of a feverish, selfish little clod of ailments and grievances complaining that the world will not devote itself to making you happy. I am of the opinion that my life belongs to the whole community and as long as I live it is my privilege to do for it what I can. I want to be thoroughly used up when I die, for the harder I work, the more I live. I rejoice in life for its own sake. Life is no brief candle to me. It's a sort of splendid torch which I have got hold of for the moment and I want to make it burn as brightly as possible before handing it on to future generations.[18]

Transitioning from Career to Contribution

But what if you are one who doesn't feel you have much in common with these so-called "overachievers"? Maybe you can't quite subscribe to Shaw's personal mantra that making the world a better place is where true joy is found. Maybe you're asking questions like:

- What if I like the idea of quitting work and playing golf or traveling?

- Why do these [crazy] people want to work this long?
- I'm tired. Where does this kind of energy, commitment, and passion come from?
- Is the desire to continue working and serving and contributing something you're just born with, or is it more of a choice?
- Is everyone capable of such a choice?

First, what I'm proposing is not that everyone should work until they drop! If you don't want to continue working into your seventies, eighties, and nineties, you are definitely not alone. As you grow older, you may choose not to hold to a nine-to-five schedule anymore. Most likely, you may want to do things you haven't had time for while working full-time. This is an ideal and perfect time to take up new hobbies, spend more uninterrupted time with family and friends, travel, and enjoy some downtime. All good things to do at this stage of life.

That said, however, I am hoping to inspire you to squeeze out of you all the contributive juices you have to give. You can retire from a job, but please don't ever retire from making extremely meaningful *contributions* in life. What I'm proposing is that we all look at retirement through a new lens, a different paradigm. A Crescendo paradigm of consciously choosing to move from a life dominated by work and career to a life focused on contribution.

> *"What is my life if I am no longer useful to others?"*
> —Johann Wolfgang von Goethe

Warren Bennis, known as a pioneer in leadership studies, has written more than thirty successful books on leadership. He continued to work and write through his seventies and eighties, writing his memoir, *Still Surprised*, at the age of eighty-five. In an article titled "Retirement Reflections," Bennis suggested two basic ideas concerning how he viewed this later stage of life, both of which I absolutely agree with:

First, successful people are always in transition. "These people never stop. They keep going on. They never think about past accomplishments, or about retirement." Bennis admired people such as Winston Churchill, Clint Eastwood, Colin Powell, Grace Hopper, Bill Bradley, and Kay Graham (among others), saying, "All of these people got off to late starts, but they just keep cresting, never coasting. They didn't talk about retirement or past accomplishments . . . they were always busy redesigning, recomposing, and reinventing their own lives."

Second, people who have been successful in their careers and in life are also successful in their transitions as they continue to age. By studying outstanding leaders, Bennis identified five characteristics of successful transitions. Think of these through the paradigm of contribution and the Crescendo Mentality—for those in the "Second Half of Life" who are looking to transition from working in a career to working to make contributions of significance.

1. They have a strong sense of purpose, a passion, a conviction, a sense of wanting to do something important to make a difference.

2. They are capable of developing and sustaining deep and trusting relationships.

3. They are purveyors of hope.

4. They seem to have a balance in their lives between work, power, and family or outside activities. They don't tie up all of their self-esteem on their position.

5. They lean toward action. They are people who seem not to hesitate in taking risks, who while not reckless, are able to move. They love adventure, risk, and promise.[19]

Most everyone knows people in their seventies, eighties and even nineties who match these characteristics and still work and enjoy activities that their peers stopped doing years ago. If they're fortunate enough to have retained their physical and mental health, they're still capable of accomplishing a lot and are a vital part of family and community life.

Throughout his stellar career, Crawford Gates was a composer and arranger, published and recorded film scores, and also led the Beloit-Janesville, Quincy, and Rockford symphonies in Illinois, where he composed many original symphonies.

At age seventy-eight, and years after what can only loosely be called his "retirement," Gates composed six additional symphonies—one for the National Music Fraternity to celebrate their one hundredth anniversary. He wrote twenty additional pieces since then, as well as an opera. At age ninety, he kept a vigorous schedule, writing music for four hours in the morning (from eight until noon), and then two more hours in the afternoon, five days a week. Before his death in 2018 at the age of ninety-six, Gates was always working on something, and typically always had six or more pieces in the works. "It's as exciting now as it's ever been," he said, "it's an attitude." His wife, Georgia, is a very talented pianist and well into her eighties would volunteer a couple days a week to play the piano for tours at a local conference center. Georgia coined their philosophy with an insightful phrase: *You need to keep your momentum going.*[20]

I love that idea—"Keep your momentum going!" Keep moving ahead even if you're not working in a job or career anymore.

What you've learned can be so useful and valuable to others who haven't had your experience. Can you imagine if everyone who retired from their profession looked around to contribute and willingly shared what had taken a lifetime to acquire? If you consciously choose to Live in Crescendo and believe you have more to learn, to contribute, to do, what a difference you could make in the years ahead. The opposite approach is believing that you've already given your best and there's nothing more to offer in the future; then you would be backsliding and Living in Diminuendo.

> *"Anyone who stops learning is old, whether at twenty or eighty. Anyone who keeps learning stays young."*
>
> —Henry Ford

There is a damaging misconception in our society that as you grow older, there are only two choices—work or retire! It doesn't have to be either/or. The third alternative—*make a contribution*—encompasses them both. This is the paradigm shift I am proposing in this crucial stage. Picture it like this:

MAKE A CONTRIBUTION

KEEP WORKING   **RETIRE**

When I see the word "retire," I only think of looking back, looking down, submission, withdrawing. The Crescendo Mentality suggests the opposite, it's *accelerando*! Meaning *speed up*! When you speed up you naturally don't have time to look back or down, you must look forward, ahead, up—staying laser-focused on making something happen right in front of you.

I'm inspired by two groups of people in this Second Half of Life. There are those who have "retired" or left their day jobs but are still working on significant projects and contributing in other ways; and there are those who have not "retired" at the traditional age, but still keep working in their seventies, eighties, and even nineties. The common factor is that both these groups still want to *contribute*, aiming to accomplish important work still ahead of them. These people may or may not have done great things in their earlier years, but they get up every day now with an attitude of still wanting to make life better for another. What could be more important than that?

> "We make a living by what we get, but we make a life by what we give."
>
> —attributed to Winston Churchill

The Longevity Project

> "We know it's not good to retire and go to the beach. But it's also not good to stay in a stressful boring job. We need to think about negotiating these transitions in a healthy way."
>
> —Dr. Howard Friedman

There is a fascinating eighty-year-old study analyzed in *The Longevity Project,* by psychologists Howard Friedman, PhD, and Leslie Martin, PhD. This project began in 1921 when Lewis

Terman, a Stanford psychologist, asked teachers throughout San Francisco to identify the brightest ten- and eleven-year-old boys and girls so he could track them and perhaps pinpoint early signs of high potential. He eventually selected 1,528 children and began observing them, first as children at play, then as they were growing up. He interviewed them and their parents regularly, and consistently tracked their lives for decades, studying their personality traits, habits, family relationships, influences, genes, academic aptitude, and lifestyle.[21]

In 1956, after thirty-five years of gathering information, Lewis Terman died at the age of eighty, but his team continued his research. In 1990, Dr. Howard Friedman and his graduate assistant Leslie Martin realized the breadth and uniqueness of Dr. Terman's research and determined to carry on where he left off. With decades of data at their disposal, they continued asking the same questions and analyzing why some of the subjects would fall ill and die seemingly before their time, while others enjoyed health and longevity.

Friedman and Martin intended to study Terman's findings and continue the research for a year, but ended up working twenty more years on the project, finally publishing their findings in 2011. A highly valuable and unique, eight-decade study, *The Longevity Project* became one of the most important studies in psychology ever published, as it followed a single set of participants from childhood to death.

Friedman and Martin claim genetic factors offer only part of the explanation for why some people enjoy better health and live longer. Surprisingly some of the results poke holes in many long-held beliefs about health, happiness, and longevity. From a *Reader's Digest* article about *The Longevity Project*, here are a few summarized findings that pertain specifically to the Crescendo Mentality:

1. Happiness is a result, not a cause.

"It's well established that happy people are healthier," Friedman wrote. "People assume that happiness leads them to be healthier, but we didn't find that. Having a job you feel engaged in; a good education; a good, stable relationship; being involved with other people—those things cause health and happiness."

In other words, it appears from their findings that you can create your own happiness and write your own script if you are involved in certain things, and many of those you can control.

- Choosing a job that interests you and is challenging
- Choosing an education to enhance your natural abilities
- Choosing to connect with others in a positive way

These combine to create an atmosphere of happiness in your life and may lead to a healthier lifestyle as well.

2. Stress isn't so bad.

"You're always hearing about the dangers of stress, but the people who were the most involved and dedicated to accomplishing things—they stayed healthiest and lived longest," Friedman wrote. "It's not good if you're overwhelmed by stress, but the people who thrived were the ones who didn't try to relax or retire early but who took on challenges and were persistent."[22]

This finding coincides with what Dr. Seyle says about "eustress"—the good stress—and how important and healthy it is to it experience regularly, especially in your older years. When you have some pressure to produce or expectations to meet, it gets the blood flowing, and you will be motivated to achieve and push yourself in a positive way.

In an interview with the American Psychological Association, Dr. Friedman further explains:

There is a terrible misunderstanding about stress. Chronic physiological disturbance is not at all the same thing as hard work, social challenges or demanding careers. People are being given rotten advice to slow down, take it easy, stop worrying and retire to Florida. The Longevity Project discovered that those who worked the hardest lived the longest. The responsible and successful achievers thrived in every way, especially if they were dedicated to things and people beyond themselves.[23]

If you remember nothing else from this section, remember this: Those who stay highly engaged in meaningful endeavors live longer.

3. Physical exercise is important, if you enjoy it.

Friedman and Martin discovered that pushing ourselves into exercise can backfire. Physical exercise is important, but it's even more important to love what you're doing than simply doing it. It's also never too late to start, even after being sedentary for a long time. Exercise can have a big impact on the rest of your life if you just begin. Friedman explains, "We're really talking here about the difference between people who become sick and die in their 50's and 60's, versus those who thrive into their 70's, 80's, and 90's."[24]

Dick Van Dyke, whose career has spanned almost seven decades, makes a conscientious effort to go to the gym and exercise every day, whether he feels like it or not: "The minute you're out of activities and something to do, you start to get rusty," the actor says. "People accept all the infirmities of age too readily. They claim, 'Well, I can't do that anymore, so that's gone.' But the truth of the matter is, you can! . . . It's never too late. A 90-year-old can get up and start moving a little bit and be amazed at what happens." In 2018, when Dick Van Dyke was ninety-three, he delighted fans by extending his acting career when appearing in *Mary Poppins Returns*, evidence he definitely practices what he preaches.[25]

I have always believed that you need to keep your body moving and eat healthy most of the time to get the maximum results. Keeping your body in shape reflects the "law of the harvest"— you reap what you sow. It's important to take time to "Sharpen the Saw" daily (what I've called the 7th Habit), practicing principles of balanced self-renewal. Through the years, I've found if I maintained my morning routine of riding an exercise bike and reading inspiring literature, besides staying in shape it motivates me to work on improving myself and achieving my personal goals.

4. Flash doesn't last—being conscientious does.

The *Longevity Project* study revealed some surprising secrets. "The key personality predictor of a long life was one that we never expected: *conscientiousness*," Friedman wrote. "Our studies suggest that it is a society with more conscientious and goal-oriented citizens, well-integrated into their communities, that is likely to be important to health and long life. These changes involve slow, step-by-step alterations that unfold across many years."[26]

And it's not just being conscientious in your own life and career but being conscientious in your significant relationships that extends your life. Dr. Friedman further explains:

As a baby boomer, I naturally think ahead to what I should be doing in the next phase of life. Fortunately, careful consideration is a key part of one of the healthy paths we call "the high road." Such an individual is the conscientious sort, with good friends, meaningful work and a happy, responsible marriage. The thoughtful planning and perseverance that such people invest in their careers and their relationships promote long life naturally and automatically, even when challenges arise. Ironically, such prudent, persistent achievers with stable families and social networks are usually the ones most concerned with what they should be doing to stay healthy. But they are already doing it.[27]

5. Stay involved in meaningful work as you get older.

Because life spans have increased and the huge baby boomer generation is now showing its gray, the nation's older people outnumber preschoolers more than two to one. Susan Perlstein, founder of the National Center for Creative Aging, says that seniors need to be continually engaged in activities and communities in order to optimize their emotional and physical health: "When you engage in creative expression, it actually improves health. The number one mental illness for older adults is *depression*. That's because people don't have meaningful and purposeful things to do," says Perlstein.[28]

This significant finding reinforces the main idea of this section: that living the Crescendo Mentality specifically in the Second Half of Life, not only promotes greater purpose and meaning in your life but also has the potential to increase the years and quality of that life.

In 1997, at the age of sixty-two, Julie Andrews had surgery to remove a noncancerous cyst that permanently damaged her vocal cords and left her unable to use her singing voice again. She admitted, "I went into a depression—it felt like I'd lost my identity."[29] Before then she had been a legendary figure in the entertainment industry, known for her beautiful four-octave soprano voice on Broadway and London's West End and in iconic Hollywood films such as *Mary Poppins* and *The Sound of Music*.

She said at first she was in total denial, but then she felt she had to do something. "What I say in *The Sound of Music* is true . . . a door closes and a window opens." This forced her to develop other creative outlets, and she began writing several children's books with her daughter Emma. Eventually they co-authored more than twenty books for children, including a *New York Times* bestselling book and series, *The Very Fairy Princess*. Working with children took Andrews's life in a totally different direction, bringing her to the attention of a new generation of audiences.

Had she not lost her singing voice, "I would never have written this number of books. I would never have discovered that pleasure." It also gave her a new identity, different from before, but still fulfilling.[30] At eighty-four she had written a second memoir, one covering her Hollywood years, and is discovering important work and contributions still ahead of her.[31]

> *"When one door of happiness closes, another opens; but often we look so long at the closed door that we do not see the one which has been opened for us."*
>
> —Helen Keller

6. Maintain a strong social network.

When asked in an interview by the *New York Times* what the single strongest social predictor of long life was, Friedman's answer was clear: a strong social network. Widows outlive widowers. Friedman claims, "Women tend to have stronger social networks. Genes constitute about one-third of the factors leading to long life. The other two-thirds have to do with lifestyle and chance."[32]

I have found that those who are still active and contributing in their seventies, eighties, and nineties recognize the importance of keeping friendships alive and growing. I heard about a group of older women who have been friends since elementary school and formed a "Friendship Club" in high school. Since then, they have met every Wednesday night to keep up on one another's life, share a meal, make a craft, or complete a service project together. This club has been their lifeline, as many have dealt with the normal ups and downs of life, from health issues to the loss of spouses. The weekly connection has not only preserved their friendship, but provided a reason to keep going.

In the journal, *PLoS* (Public Library of Science) *Medicine*, professors Julianne Holt-Lunstad and Timothy Smith have studied the influence and power of relationships in people's lives, and the findings are astonishing. Their research showed that healthy relationships improve survival odds by 50 percent. For seven and a half years, these researchers measured frequency of human interaction, tracked health outcomes, and analyzed data from 148 previously published longitudinal studies. They found that *not* having vibrant connections has roughly the same impact on longevity as smoking fifteen cigarettes a day, equivalent to being an alcoholic, more harmful than not exercising, and twice as harmful as obesity.

"And this effect is not just isolated to older adults," Smith said. "Relationships provide a level of protection across all ages. We take relationships for granted as humans. . . . Constant interaction is not only beneficial psychologically, but directly affects our physical health."[33]

Friedman summarized his findings in this way:

"The respondents to the study who fared best in the longevity sweepstakes tended to have:

- A fairly high level of physical activity,
- A habit of giving back to the community,

- A thriving and long-running career, and
- A healthy marriage and family life."

If people were involved, worked hard, succeeded, were responsible—no matter what field they were in—they were more likely to live longer.

Those who lived the longest:

- Stayed active and productive through all ages and stages of life and as they grew older
- Found ways to stay socially connected and involved in meaningful work[34]

In other words, these people with longevity had greatly enlarged their Circle of Influence to not only include others, but also positively affect themselves. More evidence can be found in a study, "Work in Retirement: Myths and Motivations" (by Merrill Lynch and research firm Age Wave), which examined how older Americans are shifting the demographics of the labor force. "Retirement" used to mean the end of work, but this study finds that a majority of people will now continue working after they retire—often in new and different ways.

Nearly half (47 percent) of today's retirees say they either have worked or plan to work during their retirement. But an even greater percentage (72 percent) of pre-retirees age fifty plus say they want to keep working after they retire. The Bureau of Labor Statistics reported that 32.7 million people over the age of fifty-five were employed in September 2014, and that's up from 21.7 million who worked over the same age just ten years ago.

The reasons for this shift to more people working later in life are varied. Perception of older age has changed, resulting in what the study refers to as a "re-visioning of later life." Increasing life expectancy, along with better overall health during those later years, has also made working longer a more viable option.

This landmark study—based on a survey of 1,856 working retirees and nearly 5,000 pre-retirees and non-working retirees—dispels four important misconceptions concerning retirement.

Myth 1: *Retirement means the end of work.*

Reality: Over 7 in 10 pre-retirees say they want to work in retirement. If I had my way, in the future it would be more unusual for older people not to work than to retire.

Myth 2: *Retirement is a time of decline.*

Reality: A new generation of working retirees is pioneering a more engaged and active retirement—the New Retirement Workscape—comprised of four different phases: (1) Pre-Retirement, (2) Career Intermission, (3) Reengagement, and (4) Leisure.

Myth 3: *People primarily work in retirement because they need the money.*

Reality: This study finds four types of working retirees: Driven Achievers, Caring Contributors, Life Balancers, and Earnest Earners. While some work primarily for money, many more are motivated by important nonfinancial reasons:
- 65 percent to stay mentally active
- 46 percent to stay physically active
- 42 percent for social connections
- 36 percent for a sense of identity/self-worth

- 31 percent to have new challenges
- 31 percent for the money

Myth 4: *New career ambitions are for young people.*

Reality: Nearly three out of five retirees launch into a new line of work, and working retirees are three times more likely than pre-retirees to be entrepreneurs.

Many found that the accumulated experience from their professional years was just too valuable to put on the shelf and not use just because they turned sixty-five.[35]

The opportunity to work past the typical retirement age is there, but it's important to plan for it. Those who are healthy enough and have the desire to work into their seventies, eighties, and even nineties have many advantages and so much to offer with their experience and expertise earned over a lifetime— something *The Longevity Project* documents and the Merrill Lynch/Age Wave study supports.

No Retirement from Service

Even when you do retire from a job or career, you should never retire from serving. You should never retire from making contributions in your family, neighborhood, and community, from serving in your church, local school, a worthy charity, or supporting some great cause that needs volunteers. You should never retire from perceptively responding to the many needs of those you see in your Circle of Influence. Don't think you have to travel somewhere far away to do this either. To put it simply, look around you, see the need, and respond!

At seventy-seven years old, Hesther Rippy moved from Texas

to Lehi, Utah, with a goal to spoil her grandkids who lived nearby. She did do that, but also found a great cause to improve literacy she could help with, right in her new neighborhood. Instead of being overwhelmed with the task and wondering what someone her age could really accomplish, she focused on what she could do to help children reach their potential.

Hesther was shocked to discover that nearly 30 percent of the elementary students in her area were reading below their grade level. She talked the mayor into giving her a chair, a desk and computer, and she ended up in a good-size storage room in the city's Art Center. She organized a fundraiser to buy books, enlisted a few volunteers, and started teaching children (and adults) to read for free. With Hester's persistence, she soon got school buses to bring children to the center and used high school students and other volunteers to tutor them.

Hesther worked hard and was extremely persistent in trying to get what she envisioned for the literacy program, to the point where city council members joked that they would hide from her when she came to the meetings. "She never takes no for an answer," they complained good-naturedly.

Years later, through her efforts and with support from the city, she was given the west wing of the city library, where the Hesther Rippy Literary Center was officially established. From 1997 to 2014, Hesther worked to organize a center to help children and adults with reading free of charge, and also to increase their math, computer, and language skills. Passionate about literacy, Hesther prompted the inspiring idea that "Readers make Leaders" and told her volunteers that the more you get into helping children learn, the more you want to help.[36]

Among other service awards, Hesther Rippy earned the Presidential Volunteer Service Award for more than four thousand hours of service, and the L'Oréal Paris Women of Worth award. In 2003, she was honored by President George W. Bush as a "Point of Light." Her literacy center has been a model for other cities and elementary schools in states like Alabama, where they have tried to duplicate what she did in her community.[37]

By 2015, the Hesther Rippy Literacy Center had organized 180 volunteer tutors (ranging in age from eight to eighty), to tutor five hundred kids who came in twice a week. The center has more than seven hundred students in the summer tutoring program every year, all at no cost to the students. It also sponsors an early reading intervention program, teaching preschoolers to read so they will be more prepared when they start school.

After Hesther's passing at the age of eighty-seven, the center has continued honoring her legacy by serving approximately four hundred students at any given time, taught by seventy-five to one hundred volunteer tutors year-round. As of this writing, the Rippy Literacy Center has helped more than three hundred thousand people learn to read.[38] What a beautiful example of being actively engaged in meaningful work and transitioning through contribution.

Hesther always claimed her real payoff was when a light would come on and her students understood what reading was all about. This passion has translated into helping tens of thousands break the cycle of generational illiteracy and reach their academic potential. Her important work continues even after she is no longer around to do it herself, a testament to her legacy.

"What is coming is better than what is gone."
—Arabic proverb

Of course there is nothing wrong with enjoying some much anticipated downtime, especially when you're not working full-time anymore. This stage of life is the perfect time to do all the things you always wanted to do but never had time for. As I said, I have always been a big believer in "Sharpening the Saw"—taking time to renew your body and mind through relaxing activities. It's vital to not only work hard but play hard. Our family loves to go up to a cabin each year where we can unwind and enjoy unstructured time together in a beautiful setting without the pressures of work and a demanding schedule. This tradition enriches our family relationships and regenerates us.

However, you can make time for things you haven't had time for *and* still find time for meaningful projects that contribute to others and bring you joy. You definitely have to work for that balance. However, there is a significant difference between a person whose focus in life is to contribute and someone who wants to retire solely to live a life of leisure. Contrast the stories you've read of those who have the Contribution (Crescendo) Mentality to those with the Retirement Mentality. The message to seniors promoted by the travel industry and many of the norms in our society seems to be one of passivity and doesn't ask or expect much from them. The resorts proudly tempt and advertise: "Retirement! You've worked for it. You deserve it. And at last you can kick back—and do nothing!"

We've all heard the well-used phrase "Been there—done that!" You may in fact have "done that" very well in your career, but isn't there something meaningful and important for you to do now? Obviously, no one will criticize you for leaving full-time work to enjoy some travel, relaxing activities, and more uninterrupted time with family and friends. But if this new lifestyle becomes all-consuming and your top priority, do not be surprised if you sense that your life lacks purpose. There's nothing wrong with golf—but there's so much more to do! Especially when you have more time, experience, skills, and wisdom to offer than ever before. So go ahead and play some golf . . . but be involved in something meaningful as well.

In contrast to the typical retirement mentality, the Crescendo Mentality requires a "paradigm shift" in your thinking. This mind-set needs to be cultivated early in your career. Whatever stage of life you are in now, if you can visualize your life after sixty-five with this new paradigm, you can then prepare for and anticipate an active time of significant contribution and fulfillment, and not just a self-serving, coasting period. Remember, you will be modeling behavior for your children and grandchildren to follow.

Getting started—adopt the Crescendo Mentality by utilizing the following criteria for ideas:

1. *Need/Conscience*: Identify a need around you, like Hesther Rippy did. Ask yourself: Where can I make a difference? What is life asking of me? Then listen deep inside to your conscience, and you will be inspired to choose a particular project or cause and help certain people that only *you* can reach. There are so many needs and problems in communities everywhere, and you can help in an important way if you choose to get involved. Look around and assess where you are needed and respond—to read at an overburdened elementary school, to collect for a community food or clothing drive, to work as a volunteer during an election, to help beautify a neglected neighborhood, or is there a refugee family you could help orient and assist so they can succeed in your community? Or how about giving hands-on support to your daughter going through a difficult divorce and be there for your grandchildren? You will find so many needs and opportunities all around you as you become more sensitive and aware. You may already sense or know what you should be involved with. It may be helpful to develop a personal mission statement that will guide you for this period of life.

2. *Vision/Passion*: Your vision and passion are greatly needed because your life experiences are unique. What have you learned by raising a family, running a business, or working in a partic- ular profession? Dealing with all sorts of people and problems, finding solutions, and managing relationships throughout your lifetime have given you vision and insight. You are needed to share those with people who lack confidence or direction or who need a mentor or a good example in their lives. Discover where your passion truly lies—what you care deeply about—and apply your passion where it can make a difference. Sharing what you know and feel strongly about can accomplish a lot of good.

3. *Resources/Talents*: Use the valuable resources at your disposal—your time, talents, opportunity, skills, experience, wisdom, information, money, desire—to make a difference. What a great chance to do something that will really matter and give your life meaning. Why not jump at the opportunity to serve with no reward for you other than the joy of seeing posi- tive results in another? How rewarding would that be? After a lifetime of working and learning, you have more to share than you realize if you simply volunteer your resources, time, and unique abilities. What a difference you could make to those who need you.

4. *Resourcefulness/Initiative*: Your resourcefulness and initiative will go far as you serve in this stage of life if you are smart, aware, and act. Start to become involved by asking questions, probing for needs, and then becoming a resource in working for smart solutions that involve not only you, but also others around you. Think creatively and you will find endless opportunities to serve. You could take a meal to a shut-in, donate books to an elementary school, make a quilt for a children's hospital, give money anonymously to someone in need, do yard work in an older person's yard, visit a forgotten friend, volunteer your professional services at a homeless support event, write a letter of encouragement to a family member struggling with addictions, visit someone going through a health crisis, welcome and orient a new family into your neighborhood. The possibilities to bless and serve are endless and exciting! Just go to work and make it happen! You'll be amazed what you can do with a little "R and I."

> *"Use me, God! Show me how to take who I am, who I want to be, and what I can do, and use it for a purpose greater than myself."*
>
> —Oprah Winfrey

Living in Crescendo by shifting your focus from pursuing a career to focusing on contribution is a life-changing mentality that can be adopted at any stage of life—from your thirties to your sixties—so you are prepared to live it from your sixties to your nineties and beyond. The fulfillment and happiness you will experience as you make positive contributions to the lives of others will greatly bless your Second Half of Life.

> *"It is not often that man can make opportunity for himself. But he can put himself in such shape that when or if the opportunity comes, he is ready."*
>
> —Theodore Roosevelt

Pamela Atkinson's poverty-stricken childhood in England helped her develop a special empathy for those less fortunate. Her father raced greyhounds and gambled and eventually deserted his family after losing all their money, leaving her mother to raise five children on her own in an awful, mouse-infested house without indoor plumbing. Her mother didn't have much education and had to work long, hard hours in a low-paying job to support the family. Pamela remembers having to cut up newspaper squares for toilet paper and put cardboard in her shoes to cover the holes.

When Pamela was around fourteen, she realized that school was the gateway to escape poverty, and she was determined to get a good education so she could have a higher-paying job and more options than her mother. It wasn't easy, but she worked hard and earned a nursing diploma in England, and immediately put her new skills to work in Australia, working with aborigines for two years. Pamela then came to the United States to obtain an undergraduate nursing degree at the University of California and a master's degree in education and business at the University of Washington.

Pamela eventually put her skills to work in hospital administration and then as a vice president of mission services at Intermountain Healthcare, specializing in assisting low-income and uninsured people. This was where she found her mission of helping the poor.

After Pamela retired from Intermountain Health Care, she volunteered as a full-time advocate for the poor and homeless. She has served them tirelessly for more than twenty-five years. Even today, her car is filled with sleeping bags, hygiene kits, warm clothes, and food for anyone she meets who needs them. She has served on nineteen community boards, and during most legislative sessions she can be found at the state capitol talking to legislators about ways to help underserved people, becoming a valued advisor to three governors. The money she receives for her work on boards is her "God-wants-me-to-help-others" fund, buying medicine, bus tickets, winter clothes, socks, underwear, paying utility bills—whatever is needed.[39]

Pamela knows that even small acts of service help change lives. One man spent a year camping out with several other homeless people. Pamela visited him every week for months, but eventually lost touch with him when his camp broke up. A year later, a clean-cut man in a sports jacket approached her at a residential alcohol treatment center. He had put his life back together and was working there helping others to overcome their addiction.

"Do you remember that cold winter day when none of us had any gloves," he asked her, "and you went to a store and bought six pairs of gloves for us?" He said his self-esteem was very low at the time, but at the back of his mind he thought, "You must be worth something. Someone bought you a new pair of gloves!" That single act of kindness motivated him to eventually change his life, and he kept the gloves as a reminder that people really do care. "You never know what action on your part may affect somebody's life," Pamela says. "We should never underestimate the power of even a small amount of caring."[40]

Through the years she has learned a lot about how to best advocate for people who sometimes are invisible to the public. Now in her seventies, during her so called "retirement years," Pamela shows no signs of slowing down. In an article in *Forbes* magazine by Devin Thorpe, Pamela shares some of the most important things she has learned that we too could use within our own Circle of Influence:

1. *Small things make a difference.* Over the years of working with the poor, Pamela has learned, service doesn't always have to be huge to make a difference. Once she stopped in on a low-income family and found they were discouraged because their water was turned off, and they had no soap, shampoo, or toiletries. She had a hygiene kit in her car that had been donated by those in her church, and she got the gas turned back

on so the family could have hot water to bathe. Their gratitude showed Pamela that the small things are often the big things.

2. *There is power in a touch and a smile.* Years ago, when Pamela served dinner at the Salvation Army, she was told by the mayor to greet people with a "warm smile and a hearty handshake." He told her that some homeless people wouldn't have been touched by another person that entire week. She has never forgotten the lesson and makes sure she gives those she serves a friendly greeting, a genuine smile, and an appropriate touch. "I don't think we should ever underestimate the power of caring," she said. "I've seen how a little thing like a hug or a smile can turn someone's life around."

3. *Volunteers make a difference.* The first time Pamela volunteered to serve dinner to the homeless on Christmas Day in Seattle, she was surprised to see how grateful the people were. She learned how crucial volunteers are to run so many programs, and their skills and desire to help are just what is needed. Her influence is inspiring, and her vision of volunteerism is contagious. At a fundraiser for the Boys and Girls Club she said, "We all have the power within us to make a difference in other people's lives."

4. *Use your faith as a positive influence and resource.* Pamela often feels guided and directed by a divine hand and believes her faith is a big influence and strength in her work. "The Lord had a plan for me," she confides. "I have a strong conviction to do something that would make a difference; that is what I was meant to do."

5. *Collaboration is the key.* Pamela names three "C's" important for service: coordinate, cooperate, and collaborate. Drawing on the first experience that ignited her volunteerism years ago, Pamela still organizes a full dinner for the homeless on Christmas Day, serving as many as a thousand people. One year, when she served as an elder in the First Presbyterian Church, the dinner was held at the St. Vincent de Paul Center (Catholic Community Services), and the Church of Jesus Christ of Latter-day Saints donated eight hundred steaks and two hundred hot dogs for the occasion. True collaboration!

6. *Everyone can do something.* Pamela once spoke to a group promising them that they could make a real difference in the lives of others if they just did what they could. An older woman told her she was wrong, saying, "I'm eighty years old, rarely get out of the house, and have a limited income—so how can I make any difference?" Pamela asked if she could contribute just one can of soup a week to the food bank. She told her to close her eyes and envision a single mother in poverty, feeding her children the soup she had donated, and picture the kids going to bed without being hungry. She asked if she thought that contribution would make a difference in their lives. This elderly woman began donating one can of soup every week, and after several years she ultimately provided hundreds of meals for people who would have gone hungry had she not helped.[41]

As a young girl lying in a crowded bed in England with her two sisters, Pamela remembers promising herself she would marry a rich man and never have anything to do with poor people again. She became a true Transition Person, ending the cycle of poverty with her family, instead of passing it on to the next generation. Yet now, decades later, it is her love of the poor and the homeless that has made Pamela Atkinson's life "rich." She has come full circle.

"We are all connected in this life, and we should look for opportunities to make a difference in other people's lives—which in turn, makes a difference in our own."

—Pamela Atkinson

Primary Greatness

In my book *The 8th Habit*, I explain a characteristic that I call Primary Greatness. In contrast to Secondary Greatness, which is popularity, title, position, fame, and honors, Primary Greatness is who you really are—your character, your integrity, your deepest motives and desires. And while primary greatness may often escape the headlines, it has everything to do with the character and contributions of the Pamela Atkinsons of the world.

Primary Greatness is a way of living, not a onetime event. It says more about who a person is than what a person has. It is revealed more by the goodness that radiates from a face than the title on a business card. It speaks more about people's motives than about their talents, more about small and simple deeds than about grandiose accomplishments.

You don't have to be the next Gandhi, Abraham Lincoln, or Mother Teresa to exhibit Primary Greatness. Theodore Roosevelt put it as succinctly as I've ever heard:

"Do what you can with what you have where you are."

—Theodore Roosevelt

I love the simplicity of that idea. In other words, whatever you have right now to offer to those around you is exactly what's needed. Just do what you can—it is enough. You already have the tools if you will just look around, see a need, and respond. Here are a few everyday examples of simple, ordinary people who apply the Crescendo Mentality in this stage of life, using skills and talents they naturally had, and who received as much joy as those they served. I'm hoping these will spark some creative ideas of what *you* can do within your own Circle of Influence.

Orphan Slippers: Mimi was never one to sit without doing something. Even at eighty-five, she constantly knitted slippers and gave them away to her family and friends. When her grand-niece, Shannon, volunteered to work in an orphanage in Romania for the summer, Mimi got to work and made over one hundred slippers and some colorful wall hangings for her to take with her. When Shannon arrived, she found the orphanage dull and shabby, so the colorful wall hangings instantly brightened up the room and gave the children something interesting to look at besides the stark, blank walls. Shannon had a fun time giving the slippers away to orphans who had very little to call their own. She gave one pair to a little ten-year-old girl whose eyes lit up as she held them close, and who said, "I just had a birthday and didn't get anything; this can be my present!"[42]

The Bike Man: When family members arrived at the funeral of Reed Palmer, they were surprised to see so many kids' bikes lined up against the side of the church. The bicycles themselves spoke volumes of this caring man whom the entire community came out to honor. To the neighborhood kids, Reed Palmer was known simply as "the bike man." Reed believed every child should have a bike of their own, so he would regularly fix up an older bike or use his resources to get a new one for whoever was in need. Reed served one child with one bike at a time, and he enjoyed it as much as they did. "And if the truth were known," his friend and neighbor Earl Miller said, "there would be thousands of bikes lined up there."[43]

"No act of kindness, however small, is ever wasted."

—Aesop

The Life-Saving Room: For several years, a group of mostly women ages seventy-five to ninety plus at the Seville Retirement Center have been working every morning and often into the afternoon, enriching the lives of thousands of children across the world. Their motto, *"I have no hands but yours"* (from Mother Teresa), hangs on the bulletin board next to the items that have been made that month. Norma Wilcox, eighty-seven, who exudes personality and initiative, is the founder of this group of "do-gooders" that began in 2006. They work every day but Sunday sewing baby quilts (they average thirty-five quilts a month), blankets, stuffed animals, dolls, dresses, pants, slippers, and toy balls. They also put together newborn kits and take on whatever assignments their local Humanitarian Center gives them. In one year alone the group managed to make 7,812 items sent to places around the globe, from Cuba to Armenia, South Africa, Mongolia, and Zimbabwe. All for children they'll never meet.

"It makes me mad that people said we're too old to help do anything!" Norma explained. "We just want to serve until we die, and I can't tell you how many have died on me in the middle of our projects . . . and I don't like it! In the meantime, we want to have as much fun as we can."

"Fun" to this group means sewing furiously and chatting away with friends in their center's activity room that they've converted into a charitable production line. At first they used their own money for material, but soon word got out about their projects and people began donating fabric. Somehow, they never run out—when they are low, someone always shows up with more leftover material that was forgotten in their basement. Norma is a dogged recruiter who goes after anyone at Seville by simply asking, "Wouldn't you like to get involved?" Ella McBride, eighty-six, though blind, was recruited to stuff toy balls that will be sent to children in Africa, in an area where they don't have toys to play with.

Norma estimates that well over a hundred people, mostly women (but some men), have helped with their grandiose projects over the years. "Norma is the genius behind this, and involves people who can't sew because of arthritis; so they cut, and those who can't cut, stuff toy balls," says her friend Dora Fitch, who has been working alongside her for ten years. "The joy is in thinking who we're working for and what a new toy, blanket, or dress means to a child."

True to their motto, there's a strong feeling among them that they're God's hands for needy children. "When I make these newborn kits," says one woman in her late eighties, "I ask God to lessen my pain, and He always helps me finish my work." The group changes from week to week when someone has surgery or passes away, but without fail there is always someone new who can fill in.[44]

Linda Nelson is their activity director and is astonished with what they accomplish. "I've never worked with such active seniors. Those who aren't involved in these projects are not as responsive and just exist. But with this group they live every day with a purpose. They could sit in their rooms and just feel their pain and age, but most of their body parts still work so they want to contribute. I call their activity room the 'life-saving room.' It's all in their attitude; they want to make life better for others and it makes me humble just to watch what they accomplish."

Living Life in Crescendo from a so-called retirement home? For these ladies it is anything but retirement—they know they have important work ahead of them to accomplish, and it gives them joy and purpose. "I want to work until I drop," says Norma with a smile. "And if you can be busy, what can be better than that? This is God's program; He'll make it work."[45]

The latest research is now suggesting that older people who volunteer have better physical and mental health and a lower mortality risk. Stephanie Brown, a psychologist at the University of Michigan, reported that the risk of premature death among "giver" study participants during a five-year period declined by more than half compared with "non-givers." The "givers" in the study were people sixty-five years and older who regularly volunteered to help others with various tasks. Scientists strongly suggest that the very act of giving and serving someone else releases endorphins, creating a "helper's high." Other positive benefits are satisfaction and enjoyment and feelings of pride, which counteract the stress and depression which many feel as they age.[46]

So if you are "retired"—in your seventies, eighties, or even nineties—now is a great time to keep contributing. Like many of these inspiring people in their Second Half of Life, it seems that life begins at retirement. Remember that primary greatness is achieved by those who have a mission, a purpose to serve that is higher than themselves, a lasting contribution to make.

Give Anonymous Service

"It's amazing what you can accomplish if you do not care who gets the credit."

—Harry Truman

One of my father's favorite movies was an inspiring old classic called *Magnificent Obsession*. Rock Hudson plays Bob Merrick, a rich playboy who is always pushing the limits and then buying his way out of trouble. One day he crashes his speedboat and the only available resuscitator is taken from the local doctor, Dr. Phillips, to successfully revive Bob. But Dr. Phillips dies from a heart attack without the resuscitator, and his widow, Helen (played by Jane Wyman), bitterly blames Bob for her husband's death.

When Bob tries to apologize, Helen runs away from him and is hit by a car, leaving her blind. Bob, who had sincerely been humbled and changed by Dr. Phillips's death, now feels even worse after the accident.

Searching for meaning in his life, he seeks the advice of a trusted friend of Dr. Phillips's, who tells Bob about the doctor's secret life of anonymous service for others. After Dr. Phillips died, many people came forward and told how he had helped them when they most needed it, though he always had two conditions in his giving:

- They couldn't tell anyone
- They could never pay him back

This man further warned Bob about giving this type of service: "Once you find the way, you'll be bound. It will obsess you! But believe me—it will be a magnificent obsession!"

Bob seeks Helen out and they begin to fall in love, though because of her blindness she doesn't realize that he's who he is. In record time (since this is less than a two-hour movie), Bob becomes a skilled doctor and begins the "magnificent obsession" of anonymous service, helping others without any recognition or payback. He also researches a cure to restore Helen's sight.

Helen travels to Europe seeking medical care but is terribly disappointed when doctors tell her that her blindness is permanent. Bob shows up unexpectedly to console her and reveals who he really is (though she already knows and forgives him) and asks her to marry him. Though she loves him too, she doesn't want to be pitied and a burden, and without warning she disappears, leaving Bob heartbroken.

Bob desperately searches for her but eventually returns to his medical career and continues his new obsession with anonymous service. After years, Helen is finally found, and Bob successfully restores her sight. Bob is the first face she sees when she wakes up.[47]

Though the plot is pretty dramatic, the film's message is inspiring and was motivated by a passage in the Bible: "Take heed that ye do not your alms before men, to be seen of them."[48] My father explained the power of anonymous service in this way:

> To serve without regard for accolades is to truly bless others. And with anonymous service—no one knows and no one necessarily ever will. Influence, not recognition, then becomes the motive. Whenever we do good anonymously, without hope of reward of recognition, our sense of intrinsic worth and self-respect increases. A wonderful by-product of this kind of service is that it repays in ways only the giver can see and feel. And you will find that such rewards often come in the "extra mile" of our service—after we have done more than was expected.

—*Cynthia Covey Haller*

Chapter 9

Create Meaningful Memories

"Grow old along with me!
The best is yet to be."

—Robert Browning

When my parents married in 1956, they determined to make faith and family their top priority. That decision governed how they spent their time, where they put their resources, and what priorities we valued as a family. They believed, as many do, that the most meaningful relationships as you look back over your life will be within your own family, immediate and intergenerational.

In his many years as a business/leadership consultant, my dad traveled around the globe and interacted with various world leaders, CEOs, and business executives, and often some of their families. He observed that their greatest and most lasting joy—more than anything they achieved professionally—came from their relationships with their families. Conversely, the lack of close family relationships caused them the most pain and regret, despite the "success" they appeared to have. In the end, most people are generally the same throughout the world—fame, career, wealth, and worldly success ultimately pale in comparison to love, acceptance, and association with the ones you love the most.

Someone once told me that "memories are more precious than wealth." Of course money is absolutely necessary and essential for the basic necessities of life, but beyond sustaining life, money should be there to enrich lives and create experiences and memories that will ultimately become a part of who you are.

When you think about your own family, your childhood, or the childhood you created for your own children, what stands out? What do you remember? For me it's the years of family traditions that began at my great-grandparents' cabin and have continued through my grandparents, parents, and now my generation, our children, and grandchildren. Our vision has been to enjoy family time together, deepen relationships, appreciate nature, build faith and character, renew, and create wonderful memories together through the years.

I realize not every family has the opportunity to have a cabin or special place, and some may not have had a childhood with good memories or a healthy family culture. However, the Crescendo Mentality teaches that you are not a victim of your past, and you can start new and create your own beautiful family culture. It doesn't really matter what you do or where you go, as long as you do it together and create your own family traditions with those you love. Camping, hiking, working on a project or a hobby, traveling, serving others, enjoying nature, playing sports—any activities enjoyed together as a family can be renewing, bonding, and create wonderful, joyful memories.

These family traditions can build stability, confidence, self-esteem, gratitude, loyalty, love, character, and a family culture that can help you endure challenges together. Creating meaningful memories for those you love will bind you to them, strengthen your relationships, and serve as a foundation in your lives—as well as enjoying fun and unforgettable times together you will always treasure.

"God gave us memory so we might have roses in December."

—J. M. Barrie

Create Meaningful Memories

Since my parents have both passed away now, memories of them being together brings our family great joy and serves as an inspiring example. I'm not claiming they had a perfect marriage, but we knew their relationship was a top priority, and they invested time, effort, and love into it. And as they aged, it increased in Crescendo. They truly loved and supported one another and enjoyed each other's unique personality.

Years ago, Dad discovered Shakespeare's beautiful Sonnet 29, which best described the value he placed on his relationship with my mother and her impact on his life. He committed it to memory and would recite it often, even in his business presentations. Our family never tired of hearing it, as it inspired us to seek the same in our own most important relationships.

> When in disgrace with fortune and men's eyes,
> I all alone beweep my outcast state,
> And trouble deaf heaven with my bootless cries,
> And look upon myself and curse my fate,
> Wishing me like to one more rich in hope,
> Featured like him, like him with friends possessed,
> Desiring this man's art, and that man's scope,
> With what I most enjoy contented least;
> Yet in these thoughts myself almost despising,
> Haply I think on thee, and then my state,
> Like to the lark at break of day arising
> From sullen earth, sings hymns at heaven's gate;
> For thy sweet love remembered such wealth brings
> That then I scorn to change my state with kings. [49]

—William Shakespeare

—*Cynthia Covey Haller*

Autumn—the Richest Season of All

"The prime of life has moved. . . . We should be reveling in this stage of life and not resenting it. . . . The prime of life should be defined as the time when we have the most free-dom, the most options, when we know the most, and can do the most—and that prime is now! 65 is the new 45!"
—Linda and Richard Eyre[50]

Linda and Richard Eyre, my good friends and *New York Times* bestselling authors, have written extensively about balancing what is truly important in life. They give some sage advice concerning ignoring old clichés about aging and enjoying the journey, even appreciating the advantages of growing older. Their upbeat, positive attitude and their way of looking at aging is refreshing! Here is part of an article by the Eyres titled "Ignore Those Old Clichés About Aging," about enjoying the Second Half of Life.

There are a lot of bad clichés and metaphors in this world, but one of the worst of all is the phrase "over the hill," used in the negative connotation of people in their autumn years. The fact is, Fall is the best season, and just over the hill is the best place to be.

Anyone who hikes or bikes or runs knows that cresting the hill and starting down the other side is what we work for and what we love. It's exciting, it's fast and it's beautiful. And it's easier. Coasting a little is fantastic! It allows you to pay more attention, to be more aware, to see where you are. Once you crest the hill, life becomes more aesthetic, more present, more in perspective. The crest, just over the summit, is the best place to be.

We've discovered that almost all of the common metaphors about this phase of life are negative—and wrong. Some examples are:

Empty nest: An empty nest is foul (excuse the pun); it stinks. But our empty nest has never smelled better—no kids around to stink it up! We miss them, of course, but we can go see them or have them come see us, and we can have them go home!

Slowing down: We don't think so! It's over the hill where you pick up speed and efficiency. Things are easier because you know how to get things done and you know what matters.

Put out to pasture: If you've done most of the work and paid your dues in life, what's better than a pasture?

Fading fast: Most of us do fade a bit as we get a little older—physically, at least—but usually it is anything but fast. Most of us actually change less between 60 and 80 than during any other 20-year span of life. Autumn can be a long, fairly flat plateau where, if we take care of ourselves, change happens very slowly.

Young at heart: Usually a patronizing phrase used by juniors to suggest that seniors are irrelevant and trying to imagine that they are younger. The fact is, as Jonathan Swift said, "No [truly] wise man ever wished to be younger."

So if you are in autumn—or Indian summer—like we are, don't listen to the clichés. Or if you do, redefine them. Because this is the best part of life! And we haven't even mentioned the best part—grandchildren![51]

The Eyres have written a book on this subject titled *Life in Full: Maximizing Your Longevity and Your Legacy.* Now in their seventies, they are busier than ever, with more than twenty-five

Live Life in Crescendo

titles in print, many of them written after raising a large, successful family, and book sales in the millions. They have been popular guests on *Oprah*, *Today*, *The Early Show*, *60 Minutes*, *Good Morning America*, and many other programs, talking about families, life balance, values, parenting, and aging.[52]

On one family vacation, after all our kids were raised, my son David described Sandra and me during this stage of life in a way that I thought was pretty accurate, as well as entertaining:

> After all of the kids in our family were married and we had children of our own, I noticed that my mom and dad had a new way of enjoying our family vacation time at the lake. I called them "the swooping birds," which fit their stage of life perfectly. I observed how they would swoop in and out whenever they wanted to, without feeling any responsibility whatsoever. . . . I realized they had thoroughly enjoyed raising their nine kids and all the busyness that went with it, but now they were free to choose what activities they wanted to attend. They would often take the grandkids out on the boat for a few hours, go on a Honda ride to "talk it over," swoop in and eat dinner that they didn't help make, hang out with the family and then swoop out without doing any dishes, and go into town to a movie! I have to admit, they earned this time of life after years of responsible parenting—and this new stage sure looked fun to me.

> *"Age is just a matter of mind. If you don't mind, it doesn't matter!"*
>
> —Mark Twain

Through the years, Sandra and I always felt a strong tie to our many grandchildren and great-grandchildren. We've tried

232

to attend as many activities, celebrations, and special occasions as we could to support the rising generation. We also wanted to be an example to our posterity by own service to community, charitable, and church activities. We felt a keen stewardship to be role models and mentors, showing interest in and spending quality time with our kids and grandkids, giving them support and encouragement, and continually trying to model good values and character. This was important to us because parenthood is one of the only roles we will never be released from, no matter how old we get.

Maximize your autumn years—focus on the advantages of getting older and not on the disadvantages. As the Eyres advise, don't buy into the old age clichés and label or limit yourself. Think of what you can do instead of what you can't do. During the grandparent stage, too many tend to check out, not feeling like they can or should be involved or even give advice. But *now* is when you can enjoy your intergenerational family without all of the day-to-day responsibilities, and make a positive difference in their lives. Keep your heart open and spend time with them. That creates natural opportunities to connect. In this Second Half of Life you have more wisdom and experience to offer than you've ever had before. Look for appropriate opportunities to be a resource and help to those who matter most, in their own journey through life.

Children need the encouragement and wisdom of grandparents. Parents need the help and backup that grandparents can give in raising kids. And grandparents need the energy and enthusiasm that comes from spending more time with grandchildren. . . . Maybe we are not being proactive enough in our grandparenting. Maybe we are not taking enough initiative. . . . We need to remember

that our most profound influence with our grandchildren
comes not as much when we have them together in groups,
as it does when we communicate individually with them
and do things with them one on one.

—Linda and Richard Eyre[53]

I know of an outstanding couple who did exactly this and because of their efforts saved their grandson's life. When Joanne and Ron's daughter, Laurie, got into drugs, they tried to do whatever they could to help her shake her addiction. Laurie's drug addiction became all-consuming, and it became apparent she couldn't care for herself, let alone her two-year-old son, James. Joanne and Ron feared what would become of this little boy with an unstable mother and a father who was in and out of prison.

Joanne had thoroughly enjoyed being a full-time mom, having raised four children of their own with Ron. But she had also anticipated the time when she would finally have the freedom to do things she had put aside, such as play competitive tennis at the club with her friends. Yet, after considering Laurie's instability, Joanne and Ron made the life-changing decision to drastically readjust their lives and raise their toddler grandson while in their mid-fifties.

What a paradigm shift these grandparents had to undergo! Unselfishly, Joanne and Ron made personal sacrifices, and though it was very hard starting all over again, they knew their little grandson was worth it and they felt they were doing the right thing. James thrived under their love and care. While Joanne's friends played tennis at the club and enjoyed a leisurely lunch after, Joanne, at fifty-four, took her turn helping in James's co-op preschool. Over the next several years, these caring grandparents signed James up for baseball, soccer, and football, organized playgroups, helped him practice the piano, took him to church and taught him good values, and did all the things as grandparents that parents usually do. Simultaneously, they were heartsick about Laurie's safety, sometimes not hearing from her for a year at a time, and not knowing if she was dead or alive.

After several years, Laurie finally hit rock bottom and returned home ready to change her life for good. With the help of her loving parents, and after a lot of hard work, she was able to overcome her drug problem. She found that James had blossomed under his grandparents' care and had become a happy, well-adjusted child during her long absences. How fortunate Laurie was to have such unselfish parents who were willing to put aside their personal lives for several years to raise their grandson. When Laurie disappeared, Joanne and Ron had become the stable influence during James's formative years. Because of their decision, Joanne and Ron literally saved James's life, while giving their daughter a second chance at parenthood.

James has since graduated from high school and become a good young man. He is talented at many sports as well as piano, has succeeded in school, and his life will be a tribute to the efforts of his devoted grandparents. In the long run, raising James proved to be far more rewarding than being a regular at the tennis club.[54]

This situation could have turned out so differently if Joanne and Ron had not responded as they did and decided to raise a vulnerable grandchild during their Second Half of Life. Though they didn't know it at the time, after they had raised their kids and as the Crescendo Mentality promotes, they still had an enormous contribution to make to their family. Looking back, though those weren't always easy years raising a grandson when they were older, they know they were meant to be there for him.

His grandparents' satisfaction at seeing the fruits of their labors was evident to anyone who watched as James accompanied a choral group of his friends on the piano. What a blessing that they responded when he was young and at risk. Now it's up to James to create a bright future for himself with the second chance at life he was given.

> *"One hundred years from now . . . it will not matter what my bank account was, the sort of house I lived in, or the kind of car I drove. But . . . the world may be different because I was important in the life of a child."*
>
> —Forest Witcraft, professional Boy Scout of America trainer[55]

I know there are many conscientious grandparents who have had to assume the role of parents because their children were unable or incapable of caring for their own. In some cases because of financial strain, families live in an intergenerational home with the grandparents acting as parents because both parents are working full-time. I salute those who have been willing and able to parent in their older years, especially when it hasn't been easy or convenient.

Parenting opportunities show up in different ways for conscientious grandparents who go the extra mile. For example, some grandparents pick their grandkids up from school (saving them from being "latchkey kids"), take them to lessons or activities, provide an afternoon snack, help with homework, or provide a safe and loving place until their parents get off work. Other caring grandparents give their kids a break by having a "grandparents' night" over at their house, playing games or just being together, benefiting both the parents and the grandkids. Some grandparents help with bills when there isn't enough money to go around when raising a family. Others may assist with college or fund a special opportunity such as a semester abroad or an internship, which could be a game-changing experience in the life of a grandchild.

If you are involved in any way in helping your children raise their children, realize these efforts are invaluable and will bless their lives more than you may realize. Remember that whatever you give, whether requested or voluntary, comes back to bless your own life. You will never regret the time or efforts spent on their behalf. You may not realize it now, but you are affecting generations to come by your involvement, and your influence for good will be felt through different stages of their lives. Stepping up and providing guidance can allow your own posterity to have stability, love, and direction in their lives, and ultimately, a bright future.

At the end of life, I can't imagine anyone in their so-called "golden years" wishing they'd spent more leisure time sleeping, golfing, playing cards, tennis, or even seeing the world, instead of making a difference in the lives of their own posterity. Blessing your own family through this kind of unselfish service is the epitome of Living Life in Crescendo.

> *"Perhaps the greatest social service that can be rendered by anybody to the country and to mankind is to bring up a family."*
>
> —George Bernard Shaw[56]

When it comes to developing character, strength, inner security, and unique personal and interpersonal talents and skills in a child, no institution can or ever will compare with, or effectively substitute for, the positive influence of home and family. Again, I affirm that some of the most meaningful experiences of life will be with your own family. Every family is different and yours may not be traditional or look the same as others, but family is family, and typically your own loved ones can bring you your greatest joy.

My brother John and his family have developed a family mission statement together that communicates what they value. It is simply "No empty chairs." This phrase essentially means that there's a place for everyone in their family, and each one is precious and important. It's a beautiful statement and summarizes the value of a watchful, caring, conscientious grandparent, aunt, uncle, brother, or sister who sees a need in their family and unselfishly helps where they can. I commend the idea to you of developing your own personal or family mission statement. Then unify around it and work to achieve it. You will find no greater joy.

Chapter 10

Detect Your Purpose

*"Our souls are not hungry for fame, comfort, wealth,
or power. Our souls are hungry for meaning, for the
sense that we have figured out how to live so that our
lives matter, so that the world will be at least a little bit
different for our having passed through it."*

—Rabbi Harold Kushner[57]

At Charlie and Dorothy Hale's home in Rochester, New York, every day might look like Christmas—with so many packages being delivered. But these packages actually contain a variety of musical instruments in some sort of disrepair. A few years ago, Dorothy took a class in instrument repair, and ever since the couple got hooked on buying and repairing broken instruments. Both in their mid-eighties, Dorothy, a retired chemist, and Charlie, a retired doctor, are passionate about breathing new life into musical instruments so they can give them away free to someone who will create music. And they haven't repaired just a few—as of December 2019, they've donated nearly one thousand working musical instruments to the Rochester School District through the Rochester Education Foundation.

"It's unbelievable for two humans to care so much about other people's children," said Alison Schmitt, who is the lead teacher for the Rochester Arts Department. She believes the impact of the Hales giving the repaired musical instruments to their community has been huge, as studies show that music education has a lasting impact on helping students do better in school overall.[58] And for this outstanding couple who work hard to benefit students they don't even know, their actions go a long way to show there are people who truly care. As they restore each instrument with their recipient in mind, the Hales have found a purpose that not only brings others joy but enriches their lives as well.

Richard Leider, preeminent life coach and author of *The Power of Purpose*, explains the vital importance of purpose: "Purpose is fundamental. It's not a luxury. It's essential for our health, our happiness, our healing and our longevity. Every human being wants to make a dent in one way or another. Our generation is living longer than any generation before. We're retiring differently than our parents did. . . . Every day that we wake up is a new opportunity to create the good life."[59]

The insightful principle attributed to Pablo Picasso at the beginning of this book extends, as we have seen, through all four pivotal periods of Living Life in Crescendo: "The meaning of life is to find your gift. The purpose of life is to give it away." Looking through this unique paradigm, it is essential to discover our gifts and talents, develop and expand them, and then apply them so they benefit others.

Each of us has a unique mission that is needed in this world, and if it involves serving other people, it is the most meaningful. I have always believed that we don't *invent* our missions, we *detect* them. Just as we can listen to our conscience to know what to do and whom to help, we can also detect or discover what our own unique mission in life is meant to be. This is ultimately the purpose of this book: to inspire and encourage you to actively seek out your personal purpose and mission—at whatever phase of life you happen to be. I agree with Oprah that the greatest gift you can give is to honor your own unique calling.

If we are self-aware, we can discover our mission, even if we have to remake ourselves in the process. Viktor Frankl, who suffered in the Nazi death camps, taught that rather than asking ourselves "What is it I want from life?" we should instead ask "What does life want from me?" That's a very different question. Once we have reflected on it, we can make goals and plans accordingly.

> *"Everyone has his own specific vocation or mission in life to carry out a concrete assignment which demands fulfillment. Therefore he cannot be replaced, nor can his life be repeated. Thus everyone's task is as unique as is his specific opportunity to implement it. . . . Ultimately, man should not ask what the meaning of his life is, but rather he must recognize that it is he who is asked. . . . To life he can only respond by being responsible."*
>
> —Viktor Frankl[60]

Ryland Robert Thompson, who studied Dr. Frankl, concluded that he taught that we discover our purpose by:

1. creating a work or doing a deed;
2. experiencing something or encountering someone; and
3. Taking a positive attitude toward unavoidable suffering.

Only when we discover our mission in life will we experience the peace that comes from fulfilling our purpose—the fruits of true happiness.[61]

One of the most important things we can do then is bring our mission to the forefront and carry it out. Oliver Wendell Holmes said, "Every calling is great when greatly pursued." It is up to you to take the initiative to greatly pursue your unique mission so that it can bless and benefit others.

"Do what you can to show you care about other people, and you will make our world a better place."
—Rosalynn Carter

When President Jimmy Carter and First Lady Rosalynn Carter left the White House in 1980, they didn't see it as the end of their contributions or even the end of their most important work. After serving as President of the United States and reaching what some would certainly call the Pinnacle of Success, most might find a hammock, a good book, and be done. Most ex-Presidents go on the speaking circuit and build a library in their name.

But the Carters have always been involved helping in humanitarian causes. They still wanted to contribute and use their status and influence to address the urgent needs they saw around them. Just one year after leaving the White House, they established the Carter Center, with a goal of promoting human rights, advancing peace, and alleviating suffering worldwide.

The Carter Center currently helps people in more than seventy countries by resolving conflicts; advancing democracy, human rights, and economic opportunity; preventing diseases; improving mental health care; and teaching farmers to increase crop production. In addition, the Carters volunteer with Habitat for Humanity, a nonprofit organization that helps needy people in the United States and other countries renovate and build homes. In 2002, Jimmy Carter was awarded the Nobel Peace Prize in Oslo by the Norwegian Nobel Committee "for his decades of untiring effort to find peaceful solutions to international conflicts, to advance democracy and human rights, and to promote economic and social development."

Upon acceptance of this award, Carter's words mirrored his life mission and gave a call to action for future generations:

> The bond of our common humanity is stronger than the divisiveness of our fears and prejudices. . . . God gives us the capacity for choice. We can choose to alleviate suffering. We can choose to work together for peace. We can make these changes—and we must.[62]

Ever the "champion of the neglected," Rosalynn Carter has continued to be an advocate for neglected mental health issues just as she did as the First Lady in Georgia, where she worked to overhaul the state's mental health system. Besides working alongside the former president for human rights and conflict resolution, Rosalynn has advocated for early childhood immunizations, addressed the needs of returning U.S. soldiers, and authored numerous books on mental health and caregiving, as well as an autobiography. Rosalynn had the rare honor of being inducted into the National Women's Hall of Fame and also received the Presidential Medal of Freedom along with her husband for their tireless humanitarian work, including their decades of continuing dedication to Habitat for Humanity.[63]

Rosalynn and Jimmy Carter have donated their time and leadership to Habitat for Humanity for thirty-five years and have become the face of this organization. Along with more than one hundred thousand other volunteers, they have personally helped to build, renovate, and repair 4,390 homes in fourteen different countries around the world, working even after President Carter was treated for a rare form of cancer. Still active into their nineties, in October of 2019, the Carters announced that Habitat for Humanity was now entering the Dominican Republic, their fifteenth country, where they helped to build and repair homes during 2020.[64]

In an inspiring book, which echoes their Crescendo Mentality, titled *Everything to Gain: Making the Most of the Rest of Your Life*, the Carters talk about the value of seeing the needs around them, being involved in meaningful projects, and finding joy in the value of service. Former President Carter has written an astonishing number of books—more than forty—and all but one after his presidency. In 1998, he wrote *The Virtues of Aging*. When someone glibly asked "What's good about aging?" he humorously responded "Well, it's better than the alternative!"

Though he was elected President of the United States, many believe President Jimmy Carter's greatest legacy will be his important humanitarian and social activist work *after* leaving the White House, and as the most productive former president in our nation's history.

President Carter writes about this unique opportunity of retiring from a profession, but clearly not retiring from life:

There is great satisfaction in being able to "make a difference" for someone who needs help. There is something that all of us can do, even the busiest of the younger people, but we in the "second half" of our lives often have more time for getting involved. And especially with our life span lengthening and the chances of good health so great, there is an additional stage of life after work when we can devote more of our time to voluntary service. The talents, wisdom, and energy of our retirees are badly needed by our communities. . . . And retirees who are active and involved have a new sense of self-worth, a source of daily enrichment . . . and the aging process is slowed.

Helping others can be surprisingly easy, since there is so much that needs to be done. The hard part comes in choosing what to do and getting started, making the first effort at something different. Once the initiative is taken we often find that we can do things we never thought we could. . . . Involvement in promoting good for others has made a tremendous difference in our lives in recent years. There are serious needs everywhere for volunteers who want to help those who are hungry, homeless, blind, crippled, addicted to drugs or alcohol, illiterate, mentally ill, elderly, imprisoned, or just friendless and lonely. There is clearly much left to be done, and whatever else we are going to do, we had better get on with it.[65]

Even if you've already experienced the Pinnacle of Success in some aspect of your life, and are now in the exciting Second Half of Life, this is your chance to start again and create something new and different from your life before. Even if you're not a past president or first lady, there is so much you can offer and contribute if you just "get on with it," as President Carter challenged.

The tiredness that comes from any physical activity that is worthwhile makes the spirit soar. Working with Habitat for Humanity has been that kind of experience for us. Of all the activities we have undertaken since leaving the White House, it is certainly one of the most inspiring. To help build a home for people who have never lived in a decent place and never dreamed of owning a home of their own, can bring both a lot of joy and an emotional response.[66]

At this stage of life, you truly have the opportunity to make a difference in your own way, perhaps more than at any other time in your life. But what if you're not at this age and stage now? Rather than wait until you're there and then decide, it's crucial that you anticipate this time when you're younger. You can be much more effective in the Second Half of Life if you plan ahead and start Living in Crescendo during your first half.

> *"Preparation for old age should begin not later than one's teens. A life which is empty of purpose until 65 will not suddenly become filled on retirement."*
>
> —Dwight L. Moody[67]

Wherever you are now, prepare and plan for the Second Half of Life and you will be more productive and the transition will be easier and feel more natural. One survey showed two-thirds of retired baby boomers report having challenges adapting to the later years. Among other adjustments, they are searching for ways to give meaning and purpose to their days. With that in mind, what if a purpose, mission, and meaning aren't readily apparent? How do you find your purpose then?

In *Shifting Gears to Your Life and Work After Retirement*, coauthor Marie Langworthy recommends asking yourself:

- What is my temperament?
- What are my skills?
- What are my values?
- What are my interests?
- If I could do anything in the world, what would it be?[68]

To assist you in focusing in on your mission and purpose, let's take a look at some common excuses, myths, and then truths, as they relate to Living Life in Crescendo.

Excuses and Myths of Living the Crescendo Mentality in the Second Half of Life

- I'm too old, tired, burnt-out, and outdated to make a difference.
- I have no special skills or talents to offer.
- I have already accomplished a lot in life—"been there, done that!"
- I am concerned about the time and effort it will take and I don't want to be tied down.
- I don't really believe what I do will make a significant difference to others because I'm not particularly skilled, talented, or unique.
- I wonder why I should care or volunteer if it doesn't affect me or my family.
- I don't know what to do, how to help, or how to start—it seems out of my comfort zone.
- Getting involved in the community seems overwhelming because there are so many needs.
- I'm too hesitant or scared to try something new that I don't know anything about.
- It's not my problem or responsibility.
- I want to rest, relax, and wait out my days—I don't want to add any more stress to my life.
- I've worked hard my whole life—I don't want to do anything but enjoy my "retirement" in leisure.

The Truth About Living the Crescendo Mentality in the Second Half of Life

- Great adventures and exciting opportunities await you!
- No unusual or special skills or knowledge are needed—what you have is sufficient.
- Your involvement serving others will keep you younger, more vital, and alive longer.
- Your ability and capacity will increase with your involvement in meaningful projects.
- You can find more meaning and purpose in your life that will bring happiness and fulfillment.
- You will feel more gratitude for your blessings as you look outward and serve others.
- You have more time available to you than ever before.
- You have a lifetime of valuable skills, talents, knowledge, and abilities to offer, much more than you may realize.
- You have a lifetime of acquired experience with people, professions, and systems.
- You have a lifetime of friends, colleagues, and resources to network with and enlist.
- You have a lifetime of wisdom gleaned through the years in many areas of life.
- You could be a valuable mentor to someone who needs a role model to follow.
- You have a golden opportunity to serve and bless others—the choice to positively impact your family, friends, neighborhood, community, and even the world for good.

- You can make an incredible difference in the lives of many people, including your own loved ones, if you take the challenge to Live Life in Crescendo.

- Your most important work and contributions are still ahead of you—despite what has happened in the past—if you desire them and seek them.

Don't wait. Time will pass anyway—why not spend it in worthy pursuits and for important causes that you feel passionate about, or can grow to feel passionate about? As has been shown by the variety of examples, you already have what it takes to do some good with all your experience and learning. You don't have to be extraordinary to do extraordinary things, as Dr. Salerno discovered.

Though retired from clinical practice, Dr. Judith Salerno is the president of the New York Academy of Medicine. When the COVID-19 pandemic hit, then New York governor Andrew Cuomo issued a plea for retired nurses and physicians to help with on-call work. Without hesitation, instead of going into isolation due to her age, Dr. Salerno didn't hesitate to go back to work. She said, "When the call first went out, I signed up immediately."[69]

"I'm in the wrong demographic, in my 60's," she explained, "but I have a set of skills that are needed, that are important, and that are going to be in very short supply in a very short period of time. . . .[70] As I look to what's ahead for New York City, where I live, I'm thinking that if I can use my skills in some way that will be helpful, I will step up."[71]

As a physician executive Dr. Salerno is one of the nation's preeminent leaders in health care and is now among the eighty thousand health care professionals who have volunteered their services during the pandemic. "I have what I could consider 'rusty' clinical skills, but pretty good clinical judgment," said Dr. Salerno. "I thought in this situation that I could resurrect and hone those skills, even if it was just taking care of routine patients and working on a team, there was a lot of good I can do."[72]

So what will you choose—to retire or renew? Live in Crescendo or Diminuendo? If you *renew*, you can deny old stereotypes and capitalize on the benefits and advantages in this great time of opportunity in your life when you have so many more options. Plan ahead so that you can make this stage productive, a time of contribution, excitement, change, and transition, as well as a time of enjoyment. You've experienced so much of life already, but now keep being curious and see what you can accomplish.

I have always felt a sacred stewardship to contribute and not just to retire to leisure. I believe the most important legacy I can leave, is to be an example of someone who is consistently making a difference in the world.

Believe that *you* can make a difference and dare yourself to bring it about. It's in your hands—it's up to you to make it happen! What will you be remembered for? What legacy will you leave behind? Begin now to adopt the Crescendo Mentality. Consciously work to make this period of your life a time of contribution and move from success to significance. Do so and this stage will prove to be sweet and rewarding.

PART 5

CONCLUSION

Our Family's Journey
of Living in Crescendo

by Cynthia Covey Haller

"The nearer I approach the end, the plainer I hear around me the immortal symphonies of the world which invites me. It is marvelous, yet simple. For half a century, I have been writing my thought in prose and in verse, history, philosophy, drama, romance, tradition, satire, ode and song; I have tried all. But I feel I have not said a thousandth part of what is in me. When I go down to the grave, I can say like many others, 'I have finished my day's work.' But I cannot say, 'I have finished my life's work.' My day's work will begin again the next morning."

—Victor Hugo[1]

A Final Tribute to My Parents

The Crescendo Mentality was really Dad's last big idea—his "Last Lecture," so to speak, which he was excited about. As the oldest of Stephen and Sandra Covey's nine children I have been privileged to shepherd this book—a book that my dad and I began many years ago. He believed Living Life in Crescendo was a powerful idea that could change and enrich the lives of those who would embrace it. He deeply believed *"your most important work is always ahead of you"* in whatever stage of life you are in, and he tried to live this mentality himself.

253

Live Life in Crescendo

As a family, we have chosen to share some things about our dad that haven't been generally known, with the purpose of giving hope and encouragement to those who are also facing difficult challenges. Though it is very personal to us, we know so many have similar and even greater trials, so we share our family's story in the spirit of love and empathy.

In 2007, my mother had back surgery, and titanium rods were placed down her entire back. The rods proved effective in stabilizing her back, but she developed a serious infection, causing nerve damage to her legs and feet. She was hospitalized for four months and had to undergo many surgeries, and her life was threatened numerous times. During this period, we didn't know if she would ever be well enough to leave the hospital and have a normal life again, or if she would even recover.

To our family's great disappointment, the nerve damage in her spinal cord left her confined nearly full-time to a wheelchair. For our mother, who had never had any previous back problems and "had never been sick a day in her life" (as she often reminded us), this was horrific! She went from being a person who never missed anything—to someone we hardly recognized. She was left completely unable to walk and needed round-the-clock, full-time care. Our wonderful mother and grandmother's life changed overnight, with complicated health issues now consuming every waking moment. In a very short period of time, she went from independence to complete dependence. It was a very traumatic time, and as a family we relied on our faith and each other, and continually prayed that things would improve.

Before Mom's back surgeries, every day Dad was in town, they had a ritual of riding a Honda 90 motorcycle around the neighborhood, "talking it over," as they called it. It was their favorite part of the day and it kept their relationship vibrant and renewed them. Later, as adults with children of our own, we loved seeing them riding and talking together, and admired the closeness they shared.

Our parents had a wonderful partnership, and though sometimes they approached things differently, they balanced each other and had the most important things in common. They had raised nine kids together, served in many leadership positions at church and in their community, and had both accomplished much. Our father often traveled for his consulting, writing, and speaking, and after the kids were raised, Mom often traveled with him, giving crucial feedback, sometimes speaking in his presentations, and often singing—since this was a wonderful talent of hers. Their marriage was a great example to us of love and commitment.

During Mom's various surgeries and hospitalization, we looked to Dad for leadership and comfort. But around this same time, we began to notice Dad wasn't acting like himself. He showed little initiative when meeting with Mom's doctors, and often when visiting the hospital, he immediately went to sleep instead of helping deal with the complicated medical decisions. Worst of all, our father, who had always been very empathetic and family oriented, began to seem distant and even a little apathetic.

It was obvious to us he was having a difficult time dealing with Mom's condition. We chalked it up to his dislike of hospitals, because when he was a young boy he had a traumatic operation on his hips that confined him to crutches for three years. Since then, he always paled a little in hospitals due to bad memories.

After four long and painful months, our family was thrilled when Mom was well enough to leave the hospital, though confined to a wheelchair and totally dependent on others for everything. Dad, who had always adored her and treated her like a queen, showed his love by providing twenty-four-hour medical care to make her life easier. He bought a van to accommodate her wheelchair, adapted their home for wheelchair accessibility, and tried to make her life as easy as possible. He hoped she would soon walk again, and that they could resume a normal life together.

Though Mom's health issues were hard on all of us, they seemed to affect Dad the most, and he continued to withdraw. Dad was a private person, but now nurses were there every minute, often two at a time as they had to bathe and dress Mom. Dad became more removed and agitated and seemed disinterested in life.

When it became obvious that something was definitely wrong with him, he got tested and was diagnosed with frontotemporal dementia. We were stunned that he would have this terrible disease, since he was always so mentally and physically active. He adamantly refused to accept the diagnosis, scoffing at the doctor's analysis. But it was clear that he had it. We increasingly witnessed a dramatic personality change. He started becoming socially inappropriate, exhibiting a lack of judgment and a loss of inhibition, repeating stories he had just told, and saying and doing things that were totally out of character for him.

It was at this time that we had to insist he stop traveling, speaking, and writing and basically put a stop to his professional career, against his will. It was a very sad and hard time for all of us, and the end of an era of incredible contributions he'd made for so long.

We finally realized he had been struggling with the beginning stages of this disease for a while. All of these symptoms were devastating as we watched our "bigger than life" dad and family patriarch decline in front of our eyes, powerless to stop it. We watched as his fun, unique, and outgoing personality changed into someone we hardly recognized. At times, we could see genuine fear in his eyes as he knew something was happening to him that he couldn't control. But we also felt such great love for him and wanted to support and care for him through this difficult time.

As a family, we were saddened and overwhelmed with a mother who was in a wheelchair and dealing with a variety of complicated health issues, and at the same time a father who had dementia and was rapidly deteriorating. We felt like we didn't fully have *either* of our parents anymore. It was a most challenging and difficult time for the Covey family.

And so, we did the best we could—together. We relied on each other, rotating time to be with Mom and Dad, trying to make their lives happy and giving back all the love and care we had received from them our whole lives. Everyone got involved— siblings and spouses, grandchildren, aunts and uncles, extended family members, and lifetime friends.

Along the way we also saw many blessings we had never experienced in easier times. We became much closer as siblings and spouses than ever before, sharing our grief and relying on each other for support. Our relationships became richer, we freely forgave each other for little things that now seemed unimportant, and we became less judgmental. We experienced true joy in serving our parents. We were more tender with our own children and grateful for the faith that was our anchor, giving us the strength and courage to go on. We savored the days that were good and the times when we made our parents happy, and we loved reminiscing over memories of better days.

And instead of crying all the time, as we did at first, we drew from our parents' optimistic personalities and began to laugh again! We loved to sing a classic song from one of our favorite productions, *Joseph and the Amazing Technicolor Dreamcoat*, that described how we felt: "Those Canaan days, we used to know, where have they gone, where diiiiiiidddddddd they go!"[2]

For us, "those Canaan days" represented our life before

surgery, before dementia, before all the drastic changes in our parents—how grateful we felt for our wonderful memories of better days.

Our family has always loved movies, and we remembered a line from one of our old favorites, *The Three Amigos*, that was very applicable to our situation. In an effort to encourage his friends to forge ahead during hard times, Lucky Day (Steve Martin) says: "In a way, all of us has an El Guapo to face. [El Guapo was the bad guy.] . . . For us, El Guapo is a big, dangerous guy who wants to kill us!"[3] We realized this trial was our family's personal El Guapo, and our go-to phrase to "have a laugh" often saved us during this dark time.

Besides growing closer, we discovered we had developed more charity and understanding for others' hardships and sorrows. We knew firsthand what it was like to suffer and experience loss, and to helplessly watch our parents struggle and decline. We became much more aware of what other people were going through during their hardships, and we had more empathy as a result. To make it through, we put into practice one of Dad's favorite sayings: "Be strong in hard moments." And we slowly realized how hard he had fought this disease and tried his very hardest, to Live Life in Crescendo until he just couldn't do it any longer.

We soon discovered how many people really loved our parents and just how much they had given and contributed to so many throughout their lives. Longtime friends and extended family regularly came to sit with Dad or take him out to lunch. They also showed great love and support to Mom, who often needed a friend or a listening ear, a shoulder to cry on, and encouragement to go on. Dad's brother, John, who had always been his best friend, was a lifeline to us, and he came regularly to be with his brother and supported us like the father we didn't have anymore. His wife, Jane, also visited regularly and was a true friend to our mother, which she really needed and appreciated. We realized just how blessed we truly were that we weren't in it alone; we had friends and family who cared, and we believed God was still watching over us.

In time, Mom adapted beautifully to her new life in a remarkable and courageous way, and once again she became involved in our lives. Her health improved gradually over time, and soon we couldn't keep her down. She hosted many family events, became involved with her friends and activities again, and enjoyed as happy and rich a life as possible, despite the wheelchair. Like the many inspiring people highlighted in this book, she did not allow herself to be defined by her challenges and setbacks but faced them with faith and courage and continued to look forward to what was yet to be.

Most of Mom's time, however, was spent trying to make life wonderful for Dad. His mental and physical abilities began to be more affected, and soon he became very dependent on her and others for all his care. Every day Mom planned fun things for them to do together, an outing or a meaningful activity, spending time with old friends and our family, and filling his days with things he enjoyed. Mom recounted wonderful memories with the family, places they'd traveled and times they had enjoyed together. Dad spoke less and less but listened intently to what she said and wanted to be with her all the time. Mom did all she could to keep him safe and taken care of, though this was the saddest and loneliest time of her life.

In April of 2012, Dad was taking a ride on his electric bike near their house, a favorite activity of his that he could still enjoy. Though he was with an aide, somehow he lost control going down the hill, hit the curb of the sidewalk, and flew off his bike, landing on his head. Although he was wearing a helmet, he experienced internal bleeding. He was hospitalized for some time, and we wondered if this was when we would lose him. However, after several weeks, he seemed to recover somewhat and was able to go home again, and though his abilities were more limited now, he was still with us.

That summer, we visited our family cabin in Montana and enjoyed what we didn't know then would be our last days with Dad. We had a wonderful barbecue on the 4th of July, talking and singing together around the fire, roasting marshmallows and making s'mores, enjoying cousins of all ages laughing and playing together, making up crazy dances to the music, singing patriotic songs, and shooting off fireworks—capping off the perfect summer night. Dad seemed to respond and enjoy himself more than he had in a long time. Years earlier, he had envisioned such a night when he built our cabin, which he appropriately named "Legacy." He had carefully planned out every area of the yard for his family to enjoy together in beautiful "Big Sky Country," our favorite place of all. This beautiful cabin and area were truly the legacy he gave us, and we look back on that magical night now with great fondness, as just a few weeks later, our dad would be gone.

On July 15, the bleeding in his head began again unexpectedly, and he was taken by ambulance to the hospital. After hearing Dad was in such a serious condition, all nine children and spouses drove from wherever we were to be at Dad's side. Miraculously, we all arrived in time to say goodbye and were part of a spiritual experience as our father passed away peacefully, early on Monday, July 16, surrounded by his wife and family just as he would have wanted. There was an overwhelming feeling of love as he passed, and we experienced a deep peace that we will always remember and cherish. He died just a few months shy of his eightieth birthday—years earlier than we'd ever thought he would go. As a family we strongly believe we will be with him again.

We all missed our wonderful father so much in the weeks that followed, but because of the physical and mental constraints the disease imposed on him, we were grateful he was free from his pain and suffering. In the end, he could hardly speak, one of the symptoms of his type of dementia. We thought it ironic that his great gift that blessed so many—speaking and inspiring others through words and ideas—was ultimately what was taken from him. He had come full circle.

"Don't cry because it's over; smile because it happened."
—Unknown

In this book, you have been *challenged* and hopefully *inspired* to Live in Crescendo. But we haven't discussed the possibility that mental or physical health challenges, or other circumstances beyond your control, may keep you from doing that for as long as you'd like. In reality, you can only do the best you can do.

We believe our father set an example of trying to live the Crescendo Mentality until he just couldn't do it anymore. Before he began to show signs of dementia, Dad was literally working on several different writing projects, including this book, and was involved in many other significant ventures that were thrilling to him. He was fully engaged as a father and grandfather and had many activities and trips planned to help gather and strengthen our family. He always shared his experiences, key learnings, and new ideas that he was writing and teaching about at family gatherings, or during personal calls which each of us siblings regularly received. Yes, he was fully and enthusiastically engaged, and deeply believed that his greatest work was still ahead of him, until the time he began experiencing his mental decline.

Not long before this book was finished, our mother, Sandra Merrill Covey, passed away unexpectedly but peacefully—also a powerful example of Living in Crescendo. Despite being in a wheelchair the last twelve years of her life, she exemplified this mentality daily, and fully enjoyed life as the matriarch of the Covey family. She amazed and inspired us all right up to the end.

At her funeral, each of her nine children gave a short tribute of some admirable characteristics she exhibited throughout her life. I told one of my favorite stories about her feisty personality and her proactive ("Carpe Diem") attitude toward purposeful living. Years ago, while in France, after a day of sightseeing, Mom was desperately searching for a restroom. When she entered a restaurant, the owner waved her off, pointing to the closed sign. But my mother persisted.

"Please—I really need to use your restroom," she told the owner.

But the woman was insistent. "Madam, it is *finished*!"

To which my mother pushed by her, called over her shoulder, "It is *not finished*!"—and hurried down the stairs.

Mad that she had gone without permission, the woman purposely turned the lights off on her, so that she had to stumble around to find the restroom in an unfamiliar basement, and feel her way back up the stairway in the dark. After some time, she finally reached the top, met the woman's glare, raised her arm in triumph, and loudly called out "VIVE LA FRANCE!" and went out the door!

Her statement "It is *not finished*!" is indicative of how she lived her life. In Crescendo! After her surgeries and recovery, she was *not finished* living, and despite the odds, she fought hard to get her life back and return to her many activities, even with her continuing health challenges. She didn't look back and pity herself when she was confined in a wheelchair, but always looked forward to what was ahead—the next family gathering, the next great event, the next era of life—excited at what was to come and always wanting to do more.

Our Family's Journey of Living in Crescendo

Though navigating life every day in a wheelchair, our mother was *not finished* enjoying social clubs, leading the discussion in her book club, participating in church and service opportunities, serving on the President's Council at the local university, cheering on her team at football and basketball games, supporting her grandkids in their activities, and enjoying outings with her many friends. She celebrated each holiday in a big way and with as many people as possible.

On St. Patrick's Day she would deliver shamrock cookies to her neighbors, and would laugh her head off when she pranked anyone she could on April Fools' Day. She tried to include a variety of people socially, often inviting random neighbors and their families to have a fun s'mores night around her firepit. She loved discussing politics, and during elections she would invite a wide variety of friends to participate in an open discussion about current topics in her home, naïvely identifying them as either a conservative or liberal friend and asking them to share their perspective in a friendly environment.

Just three weeks before she passed away, she asked her daughter Colleen to buy and wrap sixty presents for Christmas gifts. She rode in the van and directed her youngest child Joshua and his kids to personally deliver each gift to the door of sixty of her closest friends and neighbors. She exemplified a Carpe Diem attitude throughout all seasons of the year.

Though experiencing health issues years earlier, she was *not finished* contributing to her community and fulfilled a lifetime dream of building an arts center in her town of Provo, Utah. She had spent several years working as the chairman of a committee dedicated to this project, getting city officials and citizens on board, finding a building to remodel, and constantly fundraising to bring it to fruition. Now, the Covey Center for the Arts (named in her honor), is in full use more than three hundred days a year, hosting opera, ballet, plays, performances, and other cultural and entertainment events.

But more than anything else, our mother was *not finished* being the matriarch to her large and ever-growing family. She rebounded multiple times in the hospital when her body was literally shutting down and experienced what we considered "miracles" that extended her life, again and again.

She never missed an opportunity to gather her posterity for many special occasions throughout the year. She was involved in celebrating births, baby blessings, baptisms, graduations, weddings, birthdays, holidays, grandkids' games and performances—any important occasion. Right up to the end, she sent individual birthdays cards to every single person in the family—and with nine kids and spouses, fifty-five grandkids, and forty-three great-grandkids—it was practically a full-time job! Every family member felt loved and connected to her and visited her regularly. She had a special relationship with her grandchildren and great-grandchildren, who affectionately called her "Mere Mere!" To use our dad's description, she was "magnificent!"

At her funeral, all of her grandchildren and great-grandchildren stood and paid tribute to her legacy, singing "Fill the World With Love" as she had requested with words that reflected her life's mission.

We are happy to say our beloved mother did fill our world with love. She purposely *chose* to Live in Crescendo despite the challenges she faced, and was " strong and brave and true" to the end. She has been an inspiration to us and everyone who knows and loves her. And so as a family, we proudly proclaim, "VIVE LA SANDRA!!"

I share these personal insights with the hope that no matter *your* circumstances in life, it is still possible to live the Crescendo

Mentality—whatever that might look like for you, and for as long as you can. Although our parents are temporarily gone from our sight, their *legacy* lives on—through their posterity and through those who are also inspired to Live Life in Crescendo.

> *"To live in the hearts of those we leave behind is not to die."*
> —Thomas Campbell

Bridle Up Hope:
The Rachel Covey Foundation

"Once you choose hope, anything's possible."
—Christopher Reeve

Two months after Dad died, my beautiful niece, Rachel Covey, passed at the age of twenty-one, due to the effects of depression. It was especially hard for her loving parents, my brother Sean and his wife, Rebecca, and even more difficult after just losing Dad. Rachel was the oldest daughter of eight children, niece and cousin to many on both sides of her family, and we all loved her and were deeply affected by her passing.

Rachel exhibited Primary Greatness and possessed many remarkable gifts that truly mattered: she was kind, caring, sensitive, fun, loving, creative, unselfish, adventuresome, and generous. She had an infectious laugh, was adored by children, and had an unusual passion and love for horses. We were comforted by our faith in God and believed it wasn't by chance that her grandfather had passed right before her.

Sean and Rebecca courageously chose to include her battle with depression in Rachel's obituary so that it would help others struggling with it. It was a generous thing to do in their sorrow, and it blessed others who were suffering similarly. Many came to them and tearfully shared their own experience, or that of a family member, opening up healing paths. The Covey family rallied again and embraced Sean and Rebecca and their children, as did extended family and friends.

With good intent, a neighbor told my brother Sean that he would always have a hole in his heart for the rest of his life from Rachel's passing. Sean was really disturbed by this statement, and as he thought about it he decided that instead of always having a hole he would develop a new muscle in his heart. With this mindset, both Sean and Rebecca inspire and amaze us all in their journey of recovery. Though it has been incredibly difficult, they have chosen to move forward with faith and courage, and their family is strong and functioning extremely well.

Rachel had loved competing in twenty-five-mile horse endurance races, and after completing her first one, she'd enthusiastically told her parents, "I've found my voice." After her passing, some of Rachel's friends came to Sean and Rebecca and related how she had helped them during hard times by teaching them how to ride. Though still grieving, Sean and Rebecca felt inspired to honor and celebrate their daughter's life by starting a foundation that would help other young women experience the same joy.

When they began their foundation, Rebecca recounted: "One side of me said, 'I don't even want to be doing a foundation, I just want Rachel back! . . . I want her back on her horse, I want to see that smile on her face.' But then another side of me said, 'Okay, but she's not here. So we're going to go find girls who are struggling, and bring them to the barn, and teach them to ride a horse, so they can feel good about themselves and overcome their struggles.'"

So in the midst of their grief, Bridle Up Hope: The Rachel Covey Foundation was born, with the mission of inspiring hope, confidence, and resilience in young women through equestrian training. It offers a unique fourteen-week program for girls, ages twelve to twenty-five, who struggle with low self-worth, anxiety, or depression, have experienced trauma or abuse, or have simply lost hope. At the Bridle Up Hope ranch, girls learn how to ride and bond with horses, develop life skills, and find perspective through service. In a world where too many girls feel they never measure up and can't succeed, Bridle Up Hope helps them recognize their inherent worth and potential, build confidence, and overcome personal struggles.

Sean is the author of the international bestseller *The 7 Habits of Highly Effective Teens*—based on the same principles as our father's *7 Habits*, but specifically geared toward teens. These same habits are taught in the Bridle Up Hope course, where learning and applying them are an essential part of the program. Besides gaining confidence in how to handle and ride a horse, the life lessons the girls learn spill over into succeeding in school, handling peer pressure, making good choices and decisions, avoiding addictive substances, finding perspective and gratitude through service, and other valuable lessons that can help them navigate the ups and downs teens inevitably encounter. Sean and Rebecca believe if you save one girl you save generations!

One graduate of the program recently shared her story:

Before I experienced this program, I had been to over a year of counseling and was still struggling to get my feet back under me. I was trying as hard as I knew how, to cope with the trauma and subsequent problems I was facing, but it felt like my life was ruined. I truly wondered whether I could ever be happy or successful again. Hope is what was missing from my life for years, and hope is exactly what I found at Bridle Up Hope. I learned, through the horses, amazing instructors, and 7 Habits, how to harness the power of hope in my life and to finally begin moving forward.

The most impactful thing I learned was the concept of personal responsibility. It was a tricky balance to avoid feeling guilty for things that weren't my fault, while still accepting responsibility for my healing and current life. Through working with the horses, I learned how to establish and maintain boundaries and communicate them clearly to others. Over time, I felt like my own personal power to create the life I wanted was given back to me. Learning how to put the 7 Habits skills into practice and believing that I could achieve the life I had hoped for before the trauma, was the biggest blessing in my life during a seemingly hopeless time.

Bridle Up Hope has now transformed the lives of well over a thousand girls and has expanded into multiple states and countries. Their vision is that the foundation's symbol—the pink horseshoe—will one day be recognized as a global symbol for building hope in young women, just as the pink ribbon is a global symbol for breast cancer awareness. They plan to establish Bridle Up Hope chapters in as many as a thousand locations around the globe, ultimately impacting tens of thousands of girls.[5]

Anxiety and depression in teens, especially teenage girls, has become a global pandemic. Girls struggle to feel good enough, smart enough, pretty enough, or skinny enough, and social media isn't helping. They feel they need to live up to this impossibly perfect standard and it is taking a toll on their mental well-being. As a consequence, the demand for the program has been so great that it is outpacing how fast the foundation is able to raise funds. So to help raise money and provide scholarships for girls, Sean and Rebecca opened an online store called the Bridle Up Hope Shop. The shop sells hoodies, sweatshirts, T-shirts with affirmation statements, jewelry, and other items, all with an equestrian twist. Similar to Newman's Own line of products, a full 100 percent of the profits go to supporting the Bridle Up Hope Foundation.[6]

A little more than three years after Rachel passed away, Sean spoke at a grieving conference where all in attendance had recently lost someone close to them. It was a hard assignment for him since he had never publicly spoken of Rachel's passing. He began by saying,

"I am here to grieve with you, not try to fix you. As you've probably experienced, well-meaning people will say the most insensitive things in their attempts to help you heal. There are no shortcuts to grieving. You have to go through it. I want you to know I feel your loss—I understand."

Sean then courageously told his own story of grieving and recovery over the previous three years. After Rachel's passing, he discovered: "You basically have three choices when faced with a tragedy or life-changing situation. First, it can destroy you. Second, it can define you. Third, it can strengthen you."

Though it was the hardest thing he'd ever done, he made the conscious decision to embrace the third choice. Though Sean acknowledged there is no magical timetable for healing, he shared a few ideas that helped to strengthen him and his family so they could keep moving forward.

• *Write down what you want to remember.* In a special journal, Sean and Rebecca recorded experiences, feelings, and memories they didn't want to forget, some they'd received from their family and others. They wrote of the many small miracles that occurred after Rachel's passing, and what others had said about her influence in their lives. They read this often as a family when they want to feel close to her and as a way to honor her.

• *Celebrate meaningful days.* Sean and Rebecca didn't want to focus on the day she died, so they still celebrate Rachel's birthday with their children and often their extended family. They tell stories about Rachel, laugh at her hilarious one-liners, relive memories, and make her amazing banana bread and homemade salsa. And they always serve watermelon—Rachel's all-time favorite. It's a meaningful time they look forward to spending together, and it makes her birthday bearable by celebrating her life.

• *Find your voice and make something good of what's happened.* This is the reason Sean and Rebecca founded Bridle Up Hope. Through the work of this foundation, they are seeing lives change every day, and they are honoring Rachel by helping others who struggle in similar ways. In Sean's words, "Bridle Up Hope is Rachel—spread everywhere."

When you *"find your voice and help others to find theirs,"* it helps you deal with your own loss. You will heal and find happiness again as you bless others.

Sean ended by acknowledging that there is not a set timetable for grieving. It is different for everyone. His final message was one of hope: "God cares, life goes on, and someday you can feel whole and happy again, just as I have. I promise."[7]

Author's Note

I hope you've enjoyed reading this book as much as I've enjoyed writing it (with my father), and that it has helped you shift your paradigm and ignite your passion. By now I also hope you realize that at whatever age and stage you're in, you can always live your Life in Crescendo.

For me it has been a sacred stewardship, given to me by my father many years ago when we began working on it together. It's been a long and difficult journey finishing it, but I've learned so much and have been truly inspired by the multitude of uplifting examples I've found around the world.

No matter what your age or position in life, you are never finished contributing. You should always be seeking something higher and better from life. You may get satisfaction from past accomplishments, but the next great contribution is always on the horizon. You have relationships to build, a community to serve, a family to strengthen, problems to solve, knowledge to gain, and great works to create. Whether you are in a midlife struggle, have experienced the Pinnacle of Success, are facing a life-changing setback, or are in the Second Half of Life, please know that despite the challenges, *your greatest and most important work can truly be ahead of you*, if you so choose.

As you read in the Conclusion, our family's journey of learning to Live in Crescendo took on new meaning as we went through our own personal challenges. The dozens of inspiring stories I have shared in this book are evidence that the Crescendo Mentality can be successfully integrated at any stage and will greatly enrich your life.

Think of all the talents you can share, the good you can accomplish, the lives you will bless, and the joy that will flow into your heart as you do so. So get started, and create your own wonderful legacy of contribution! Don't doubt yourself. It's within your power and ability, and your capacity will expand. I am confident that as you do this, you will light up your own life, your family, your community, and even the world with your gifts and talents and life-changing contributions.

—*Cynthia Covey Haller*

Appendix

Ideas for where to find volunteer opportunities and places to serve around you.

volunteermatch.org. Volunteer Match is one of the largest data bases for connecting nonprofits and volunteers globally.

justserve.org. JustServe is an international service to help link community needs with volunteers; volunteers can easily search to meet local needs within their own communities.

createthegood.org. This nonprofit, sponsored by AARP, offers a database of volunteer opportunities and connects charities with volunteers to match your interests and skills.

bbbs.org. Big Brothers and Big Sisters of America. This nonprofit has a mission to "create and support one-to-one mentoring relationships that ignite the power and promise of youth."

encore.org. This organization encourages people older than fifty to find a new purpose in meaningful causes. It involves older adults who help mentor and inspire younger volunteers in their own area.

unitedway.org. United Way is one of the oldest and most esteemed volunteer organizations; you can browse opportunities and find a service or job that suits you and meets needs.

doinggoodtogether.org. With a mission to raise children who care and contribute, Doing Good Together enlists parents and children to work together in the spirit of selfless service.

pointsoflightengage.org. This is the world's largest digital volunteer network, and it connects people to local volunteer opportunities; you can also start a new service project where there's a need.

catchafire.org. This is a network of volunteers, nonprofits, and funders working together to solve urgent problems and lift up communities.

globalvolunteers.org. This organization offers volunteering opportunities worldwide for students, families, individuals, professionals, and retirees, involving them in the culture/people they support.

americorps.gov. AmeriCorps members and AmeriCorps seniors volunteers serve directly with nonprofit organizations to tackle our nation's most pressing challenges.

nvoad.org. National Voluntary Organizations Active in Disaster is a coalition of more than seventy national organizations that alleviate the impact of disasters and deliver services to affected areas.

habitat.org. Habitat for Humanity is a global nonprofit housing organization working in local communities across the U.S. and in approximately seventy countries, striving for better housing.

redcross.org. The American Red Cross prevents and alleviates human suffering in the face of emergencies by mobilizing the power of volunteers and the generosity of donors.

Volunteer locally. Food banks, homeless shelters, animal shelters, hospitals, park cleanups, Meals on Wheels, assisted living centers, reading and after-school tutoring, coaching, and so on.

Acknowledgments

With deep appreciation, I wish to thank the many individuals who have made the writing and publication of this book possible. *Live Life in Crescendo* has been more than a decade-long project, and I am so appreciative of the tremendous support that many caring people have provided along the way.

I will be forever grateful to my best friend and husband of forty-two years, Kameron Haller, for his constant love and unwavering support of me and *Crescendo*. Kameron has bolstered my confidence and believed in my ability to complete this book in the best way possible. His insightful ideas, wisdom, and judgment have always been on the mark and have sustained me through times of discouragement and setbacks. I so appreciate his influence in my life.

Additionally, I'd like to acknowledge my six wonderful children and their spouses who stood by me: Lauren and Shane, Shannon and Justin, Kameron and Haley, Mitchell and Sara, Michael and Emilie, Connor and Hannah. Not only have they offered encouraging words of support, but they have also submitted helpful feedback, shown patience when I was busy writing, and cheered me on. As my youngest son, Connor, good-naturedly reminded me: "Finish it already! You've been writing this book for half of my life!" My twenty-five adorable grandchildren also provide me a constant opportunity to "live in Crescendo!"

A special thank you to my brother Sean who believed in me and *Live Life in Crescendo* from the start and guided me throughout the entire process from writing to publication, including valuable editorial assistance, contractual expertise, and marketing guidance. I appreciate my eight siblings who read early drafts of the book and offered encouragement: Maria provided additional editorial assistance, while Stephen promoted *Crescendo* wherever he could.

Acknowledgments

Thanks to my Uncle John, whose calls of encouragement were timely, and to my extended family members and friends for their interest and support, particularly Carol Knight for her important contributions early on, and Greg Link who read multiple drafts and provided invaluable advice for many years.

My gratitude extends to the team at FranklinCovey, especially Debra Lund for her extra-mile efforts in gathering endorsements; and for the welcome aid of Annie Oswald, Laney Hawes, and Zac Chaney.

I'm indebted to my agent, Jan Miller, and her associate, Shannon Miser-Marven, who believed in the concept of "living in crescendo" from its inception. How grateful I am to have had such excellent editors, namely Dave Pliler and Robert Asahina, whose professional skills elevated both the content and presentation. Jan Miller and Robert Asahina were also my father's agent and editor of *The 7 Habits of Highly Effective People*. While preparing this manuscript for publication, I was fortunate to have worked closely with my team at Simon & Schuster, including my competent editor, Stephanie Frerich, along with Emily Simonson and Maria Mendez, who led me, a first-time author, through the entire process.

Live Life in Crescendo was my father's "last lecture," so to speak, and I feel his approval as I have kept my word to finish the book he envisioned and that we began together, back in 2008. Throughout the writing process, I have felt his influence abundantly, and I pay tribute to him as a magnificent father and inspirational leader who "lived, loved, and left a legacy." My mother, Sandra Covey, was Dad's equal in every way. She also believed in and affirmed me and my siblings throughout our entire lives. What a gift to have been so powerfully shaped by such noble parents!

Lastly, I would be ungrateful if I did not acknowledge God for His goodness and influence in my life. With all my heart, I express my profound gratitude for His guidance and inspiration, for instilling me with the courage and confidence to undertake such an enormous endeavor, and for the ability to see it to completion.

Notes

PART 1: THE MID-LIFE STRUGGLE

1 Quote attributed to George Bernard Shaw, https://www.goodreads .com/quotes/1368655-two-things-define-you-your-patience-when -you-have-nothing.
2 Cynthia Haller, personal interview, August 2017.
3 Frances Goodrich, Albert Hackett, and Frank Capra, *It's a Wonderful Life* (Liberty Films, 1946).
4 Phil Vassar, "Don't Miss Your Life," RodeoWave Entertainment, lyrics mode.com, 2012. Reprinted with permission.
5 Clayton Christensen, hbr.org/2010/how-will-you-measure-your-life.
6 Cynthia Haller, personal interview, May 2018.
7 Cynthia Haller, personal interview, October 2019.
8 goodreads.com/quotes/273511.
9 Kenneth Miller, "Don't Say No," readersdigest.com, 2008.
10 Middle School Principal Drops Weight and Inspires Students," ksl .com, March 18, 2008.
11 Tiffany Erickson, "Glendale's Big Losers: Principal Drops 173 Pounds; Staff Also Slims Down," deseretnews.com, January 2, 2007.
12 Cynthia Haller, personal interview, May 2018.
13 John Kralik, John *A Simple Act of Gratitude: How Learning to Say Thank You Changed My Life* (Hyperion, 2010).
14 Carol Kelly-Gangi, editor, *Mother Teresa: Her Essential Wisdom* (Fall River Press, 2006), p. 21.
15 As told to Cynthia Haller, July 2015.
16 burritoprojectslc.webs.com.
17 Heather Lawrence, "Engineer Returns to Thank Engaging Churchill Science Teacher," *Holladay Journal*, November 2020.
18 As told to Cynthia Haller, April 2010.
19 Lawrence, "Engineer Returns."
20 As told to Cynthia Haller by Mindy Rice, May 20, 2018.
21 As told to Cynthia Haller by Robyn Ivins, 2020.
22 As told to Cynthia Haller, 2020.
23 As told to Cynthia Haller, 2016.

Notes

24 brainyquote.com/quotes/marian_wright_edelman.

25 goodreads.com/quotes/15762.

26 Cynthia Haller, personal interview, October 2019.

27 Tennessean.com/story/entertainment/music/2019/11/20/garth
-brooks-exploded-like-no-country-star-before-him-cma-entertainer
-year-4226820002/.

28 dailymail.com.uk/tvshowbix-3030642/Garth-Brooks-chose-family
-fame-walked-away-music-14-years-article-3030642/.

29 tennessean.com/story/entertainment/music/2019/11/22/garth
-brooks-bled-reclaim-top-spot-country-music/4261813002.

30 usatoday.com/story/entertainment/music/2020/03/29/coronavirus
-garth-brooks-trisha-yearwood-announce-cbs-live-show-2935608001/.

31 Netflix. "*The Road I'm On*," 2019.

PART 2: PINNACLE OF SUCCESS

1 Brian Williams, interview with Peter Jackson, rockcenter.nbd.news
.com, December 6, 2012.

2 Kent Atkinson, "Peter Jackson Gives $500,000 for Stem Cell Re-
search," Nzherald.co.nz, July 15, 2006.

3 Susan Strongman, "Sir Peter Jackson Rescues Beloved Church,"
nzherald.co.nz, August 12, 2015.

4 As told to Cynthia Haller by Chip Smith, July 23, 2012.

5 Aleksandr Solzhenitsyn, in *At Century's End: Great Minds Reflect on
Our Times* (Alti Publishing, 1997).

6 Carol Kelly-Gangi, editor, *Mother Teresa: Her Essential Wisdom* (Fall
River Press, 2006), p. 101.

7 Henry Samuel, "Millionaire Gives Away Fortune Which Made Him
Miserable," telegraph.co.uk, February 2010.

8 E. Jane Dickson, "Nothing But Joy," *Readers Digest*, October 2010,
pp 142–146.

9 From *The Quiltmaker's Gift* by Jeff Brumbeau. Text copyright © 2000
by Jeff Brumbeau. Reprinted with permission of Scholastic Inc.

10 Alena Hall, "How Giving Back Can Lead to Greater Personal Success," *Huffington Post*, June 2014.

11 Neal Tweedie, Bill Gates interview: "I Have No Use for Money; This
Is God's Work," telegraph.co.uk, January 18, 2013.

12 David Rensin, "The Rotarian Conversation: Bill Gates," *Rotarian*,
May 2009, pp. 45–53.

13 gatesfoundation.org/Who-We-Are/General-Information/Letter-from
-Bill-and=Melinda-Gates, Annual Report, 2018.

Notes

14 Bill and Melinda Gates, "We Didn't See This Coming," gatesnotes .com/2019-Annual-Letter.

15 Melinda Gates, *The Moment of Lift: How Empowering Women Changes the World* (Flatiron Books, 2019), pp. 14, 15, 38.

16 Ibid, p. 11.

17 cnbc.com/2017/10/24/bill-gates-humanity?-will-see-its-last-case-of -polio-this-year.

18 Sarah Berger, "Bill Gates Is Paying Off This Country's $76 Million Debt," cnbc.com.

19 Rensin, "The Rotarian Conversation."

20 Gates, *The Moment of Lift*, pp. 19, 118–121.

21 Ibid, pp 50–53.

22 givingpledge.org.

23 Ibid.

24 Laura Lorenzetti, "17 More Billionaires Join Buffett and Gates' Giving Pledge This Year," fortune.com, June 1, 2016.

25 Buffet, Warren. "My Philanthropic Pledge." givingpledge.org.

26 Brendan Coffey, "Pledge Aside, Dead Don't Have to Give Away Half Their Fortune," bloomberg.com, August 6, 2015.

27 As told to Cynthia Haller, June 2018.

28 cnbc.com/2017/02/07/ruth-bader-ginsburg-says-this-is-the-secret -to-living-a-meaningful-life.html.

29 Cynthia Haller, personal interview of John Nuness, July 2012.

30 Kenneth H. Blanchard and Spencer Johnson, *The One Minute Manager* (William Morrow & Co, 1982).

31 Kim Lacupria, "Single Mom at Pizza Hut Amazed When Stranger Pays Tab," Inquisitr.com, October 28, 2013.

32 Ibid.

33 Stephen R. Covey, "Affirming Others," *Personal Excellence*, August 1996, p. 1.

34 Viktor Frankl, *Man's Search for Meaning* (Simon & Schuster, 1984), p. 116.

35 Will Allen Dromgoole, "The Bridge Builder," *Father: An Anthology of Verse* (EP Dutton & Company, 1931).

36 As told to Cynthia Haller, October 2018.

37 As told to Cynthia Haller, April 2020.

38 coachwooden.com/the-journey.

39 John Wooden and Don Yaeger, *A Game Plan for Life: The Power of Mentoring* (Bloomsbury USA, 2009), pp. 3–4.

40 Ibid, p. 13.

41 coachwooden.com/favorite-maxims.

Notes

42 Don Yaegar, success.com/article/mentors-never-die, August 27, 2010.

43 John Wooden and Don Yeager, *A Game Plan for Life*, p. 4.

44 The Abolition Project, "John Newton (1725–1807): The Former Slaver & Preacher," abolition, britannica.com/biography/William-Wilberforce.

45 nfl.com/manoftheyear.

46 teamsweetness.com/wcpf.html.

47 Andie Hagermann, "Anquan Boldin: Named 2016 Payton Man of the Year," nfl.com, February 2016.

48 Ibid.

49 John Connell, *W.E. Henley* (Constable, 1949), p. 31.

50 Ibid.

51 "The Good Guy," *People* Tribute Commemorative Issue—Paul Newman, 1925–2008, pp. 82, 88, 89.

52 newmansownfoundation.org (about-us, history, and mission).

53 https://www.holeinthewallgang.org/about/.

54 "The Good Guy," p. 80.

55 Natasha Stoynoff and Michelle Tauber, "Paul Newman 1925–2008: American Idol," *People*, October 13, 2008, p. 63.

56 newmansownfoundation.org/about-us/timeline.

57 newmansownfoundation.org/about-us/total-giving.

58 newmanitarian.org.

59 If you go to newmansownfoundation.org, you will be inspired by stories of philanthropy, fun camp experiences, and video testimonials. An opportunity to volunteer your time, skills, or money in whatever interests you can be easily found right in your own hometown or state.

60 *People* Tribute Commemorative Issue, p. 96.

61 "Meet the New Heroes," PBS, New York, July 1, 2005.

62 "Muhammad Yunus—Biographical," nobelprize.org, 2006.

63 "Meet the New Heroes."

64 "World in Focus: Interview with Professor Muhammad Yunus," *Foreign Correspondent*, March 25, 1997.

65 Jay Evensen, "Muhammed Yunus Still Saving People One at a Time," *Deseret News*, March 13, 2013.

66 "Muhammad Yunus—Facts," nobelprize.org, 2006.

67 "Meet the New Heroes."

68 Evensen, "Muhammed Yunus Still Saving People."

Notes

PART 3: LIFE-CHANGING SETBACKS

1   Jane Lawson, "Stephenie Nielson of NieNie Dialogues: Sharing Her Hope." ldsliving.com, July/August, 2012.
2   Shana Druckman and Alice Gomstyn, "Stephanie Nielson's Story After Tragic Crash, Mom of Four Nearly Lost All," abcnews.go.com, May 12, 2011.
3   nieniedialogues.com.
4   Stephanie Nielson, *Heaven Is Here* (Hyperion, 2012), p. 308.
5   Lawson, "Stephanie Nielson of NieNie Dialogues."
6   Ibid.
7   eji.org/cases/anthony-ray-hinton/.
8   Anthony Ray Hinton with Lara Love Hardin, *The Sun Does Shine: How I Found Life, Freedom, and Justice* (St. Martin's Press, 2018), pp. 104,145.
9   Ibid., p. 147.
10 Ibid., p xvi.
11 Ibid., pp 291–294.
12 abcnews.go.com/nightline/video/30-year-death-row-inmate-celebrates-days-freedom-30548291.
13 Ibid.
14 Greg, McKeown, *Essentialism: The Disciplined Pursuit of Less* (Currency, 2014), p. 36.
15 goodreads.com
16 Doug Robinson, "The Comeback Kid: After a Devastating Accident, Anna Beninati Finds Happiness," *Deseret News*, October 2012.
17 "Teen in Tragic Train Accident: 'I Remember Thinking I Was Going to Die'" *today.com*, January 27, 2012.
18 goodreads.com.
19 elizabethsmartfoundation.org.
20 Elizabeth Smart with Chris Stewart, *My Story* (St. Martin's Press, 2013), pp. 25–50.
21 Ibid., pp. 60, 61.
22 Ibid., p. 275.
23 Elizabeth Smart, keynote speaker, Crimes Against Children conference, 2011, elizabethsmartfoundation.org.
24 Smart, *My Story*, p. 53.
25 goodread.com/quotes/80824-one-of-the-things-i-learned-when-i-was-negotiating.
26 "Biography of Nelson Mandela," nelsonmandela.org.
27 William Ernest Henley, "Invictus," Poetry Foundation.

Notes

28 Johann Lochner, "The Power of Forgiveness: Apartheid-era Cop's Memories of Nelson Mandela," cnn.com, December 12, 2013.

29 Marcus Eliason and Christopher Torchia, "South Africa's First Black President Known for Role as Peacemaker," *Deseret News*, December 6, 2013.

30 "Top 10 Nelson Mandela Quotes," movemequotes.com.

31 Eliason and Torchia, "South Africa's First Black President."

32 Dominic Gover, "Four Acts of Forgiveness That Sowed South Africa Path Away from Apartheid," https://www.ibtimes.co.uk/nelson-mandela-forgiveness-south-africa-apartheid-5281531.

33 Eliason and Torchia, "South Africa's First Black President."

34 "Nelson Mandela Dead: Former South Africa President Dies at 95," *Huffington Post*, January 23, 2014.

35 Nelson Mandela, *Long Walk to Freedom* (Back Bay Books, 1995).

36 Smart, *My Story*, pp. 285–286.

37 "Elizabeth Smart Relieves Kidnapping Ordeal at Mitchell Hearing," ksl.com (full court testimony).

38 Smart, *My Story*, p. 302.

39 daveskillerbread.com.

40 daveskillerbread.com/about-us.

41 Cynthia Haller, personal interview, October 2019.

42 "His Tragic Loss Helps Others Gain Sight," cnn.com, cnn heroes, August 15, 2008.

43 "Dr. Chandrasekhar Sankurathri: A Real Hero," global1.youth_leader.org.

44 "His Tragic Loss Helps Others Gain Sight."

45 srikiran.org/our-model.

46 srikiran.org.

47 "Dr. Chandrasekhar Sankurathri: A Real Hero."

48 Frankl, *Man's Search for Meaning*, pp. 84, 85, 88.

49 Ibid.

50 "Does Every Cactus Bloom?," homeguides.sfgate.com/cactus-bloom-62730.html.

51 elizabethsmartfoundation.org.

52 Michael J. Fox, *A Funny Thing Happened on the Way to the Future* (Hyperion, 2010).

53 Amy Wallace, "Michael J. Fox's Recipe for Happiness," readersdigest.com, May 2010, p. 83.

54 Chris Powell, "The Incurable Optimist," *Costco Connection*, November 2020, pp. 48–49.

55 Ibid.

56 Cynthia Haller, personal interview, June 2016.

57 Ibid.

Notes

58 goodreads.com/quotes/14830-these-are-the-times-in-which-a-genius
    -would-wish.

59 *Dead Poets Society* (Touchstone Pictures, 1989).

60 littlefreelibrary.org/about/history/.

61 Smith, Russell C, Foster, Michaell. "How the Little Free Library is
    Re-inventing the Library." huffpost.com/entry/little-free-library_b
    _1610026, June 21, 2012.

62 littlefreelibrary.org/about/.

63 littlefreelibrary.org/about/history/.

64 daysforgirls/history.org.

65 daysforgirls/ourimpact.org.

66 *Camelot* (Warner Bros., 1967).

67 Danica Kirka, "Malala's Moment: Teenage Nobel Laureate Gives
    Primer in Courage and Peace," startribune.com., December 10,
    2014.

68 biography.com/activist/malala-yousafzai.

69 Baela Raza Jamil, ElenaBaela Raza, Matsui, Elena, and Rebecca Win-
    throp, Rebecca. "Quiet Progress for Education in Pakistan," brook-
    ings.edu, April 8, 2013.

70 "Malala Yousafzai's Speech at the Youth Takeover of the United Na-
    tions," theirworld.org, July 12, 2013.

71 nytimes.com/2014/10/31/world/middleeast/malala-yousafzai-nobel
    -gaza-school.html.

72 amberalert.ojp.gov/statistics.

73 Elizabeth Smart with Chris Stewart, *"My Story."* St. Martin's Press,
    2013, Epilogue.

74 elizabethsmartfoundation.org.

75 radKIDS.org/2018/07/2018-radKIDS-at-a-glance.

76 Elizabeth Smart with Chris Steward, *My Story*, p. 303.

PART 4: THE SECOND HALF OF LIFE

1 Winston Churchill, *The Second World War* (Houghton Miflin, 1951).

2 Hans Selye, *The Stress of Life* (McGraw Hill, 1978), pp. 74, 413.

3 Suzanne Bohan and Glenn Thompson, *50 Simple Ways to Live a Longer Life* (Sourcebooks, Inc., 2005), p. 188.

4 Dan Buettner, "Find Purpose, Live Longer," *AARP The Magazine*,
   November/December 2008.

5 Bohan and Thompson, *50 Simple Ways*.

6 Albin Krebs, "George Burns, Straight Man and Ageless Wit, Dies at
   100," *New York Times*, March 1996.

Notes

7 Shav Glick, "Hershel McGriff Finishes 13th at Portland," Espn.go .com, July 2009.

8 "Nominees Announced for Hall of Fame Class," nascarhall.com /media/press/nascar-announces-nominees-for-nascar-hall-of-fame -class-of-2023-landmark-award/.

9 Glick, "Hershel McGriff Finishes 13th."

10 Buettner, "Find Purpose, Live Longer."

11 Robert Lee Hotz and Joanna Sugden, "Nobel Physics Prize Awarded to Trio for Laser Inventions," *Wall Street Journal*, October 2018.

12 Allen Kim, "John B. Goodenough Just Became the Oldest Person, at 97, to Win a Nobel Prize," cnn.com, October 2019.

13 Bill Gray, "Making Deals, Irma Elder: The Businessperson," *AARP The Magazine*, November/December 2007.

14 Bill Gray "They Got Game," *AARP The Magazine*, November/ December 2007, p. 58.

15 Cynthia Haller, Cynthia, personal interview, May 2021.

16 Cindy Kuzman, "Barbara Bowman's Tips for Living to 90," chicago-mag.com, January 28, 2019.

17 Ibid.

18 goodreads.com/quotes/649680-this-is-the-true-joy-in-life-being-used-for.

19 Warren Bennis, "Retirement Reflections," *Personal Excellence*, July 1996.

20 Cynthia Haller, personal interview with Crawford and Georgia Gates, 2015.

21 Laura Landro, "How to Keep Going and Going," *Book Review*, March 2011.

22 Beth Dreher, "For a Long Life, Watch Your Attitude," *Health Digest*, summary by readersdigest.com, March 2011.

23 Amy Norotney, "The Real Secrets to a Longer Life," *Monitor. American Psychological Association*, December 2011.

24 "Secrets to Longevity: It's Not All About Broccoli," author interviews, NPR Books, npr.org, March 24, 2011.

25 Elbert, Sarah. "Step in Time." Renew, November 2016.

26 Dreher, "For a Long Life."

27 Norotney, "The Real Secrets."

28 Marjorie Cortez, "Activities, Art Aid Senior's Health," dn.com., November 2007.

29 Julie Andrews, "I Went into a Depression—It Felt Like I'd Lost My Identity," *AARP: The Magazine*, October/November 2019.

30 Alynda Wheat, "Julie Andrews: 'Losing My Voice Was Devastating,'" people.com, March 20, 2015.

31 Andrews, "I Went into a Depression."

Notes

32 Katherine Bouton, "80 Years, a Longevity Study Still Has Ground to Cover," *New York Times*, April 18, 2011.

33 National Science Foundation, "Staying Alive: That's What Friends Are For," usnews.com, July 29, 2010.

34 Bouton, "80 Years."

35 "Work and Retirement: Myths and Motivations—Career Innovations and the New Retirement Workscape," https://agewave.com/what-we-do/landmark-research-and-consulting/research-studies/work-and-retirement-myths-and-motivations/.

36 Cathy Allredd, "Lady of Legacy: Lehi-Rippy Family Literacy Center Founder Dies," heraldextra.com, February 15, 2014.

37 "Hesther Rippy," Pointoflight.org, December 17, 2003.

38 lehi-ut.gov/recreation/literacy/about-us/.

39 Lois Collins, "Pamela Atkinson Is Welcomed Among Kings and Paupers," *Deseret News*, October 2, 2010.

40 Kim Burgess, "Pamela Atkinson," *Community Magazine*, 2010.

41 Devin Thorpe, "13 Lessons from a Great Social Entrepreneur," forbes.com, September 20, 2012.

42 Cynthia Haller, personal interview with Romana May, 2014.

43 Tonya Papanikolas, "A Show of Love," dn.com, February 6, 2007.

44 Andrew Marshall, "Group Sews Humanitarian Items for Kids," *Deseret News*, 2010.

45 Cynthia Haller, personal interview, October 2010.

46 Suzanne Bohan and Glen Thompson, *50 Simple Ways to Live a Longer Life* (Sourcebooks, Inc., 2005), pp. 43–44.

47 *Magnificient Obsession.* Universal International Technicolor, 1954.

48 Matthew 6:1, King James Version.

49 William Shakespeare, Sonnet 29, *The Complete Works of William Shakespeare* (Avenel Books), p. 1196.

50 Linda and Richard Eyre, *Life in Full: Maximizing Your Longevity and Your Legacy* (Famillus, LLC, 2015).

51 Linda and Richard Eyre, "Ignore Those Old Clichés About Aging," *Deseret News*, October 21, 2015.

52 theeyres.com.

53 Linda and Richard Eyre, "Ignore Those Old Clichés About Aging."

54 Cynthia Haller, personal interview, October 2019.

55 passion.com/inspirational-quotes/4244-a-hundred-years-from-now-it-will-not-matter.

56 brainyquote.com/quotes/george_bernard_shaw_103422.

57 Harold Kushner, *When All You've Ever Wanted Isn't Enough: The Search for a Life that Matters* (Fireside, 1986), p. 18.

Notes

58 Steve Hartman, "Couple Who Restores Musical Instruments Has Given Away Hundreds to Rochester Students," cbsnews.com, December 13, 2019.

59 "Why Keep Going?" Question and Answer, Renew by UnitedHealthcare, 2015.

60 Frankl, *Man's Search for Meaning*, p. 113.

61 Robert Ryland Thompson, "In Search of a Logo," *Personal Excellence*, November 1996, p. 2.

62 biography.com/us-president/jimmy-carter.

63 biography.com/us-first-lady/rosalynn-carter.

64 "Rosalynn and Jimmy Carter Center: 2020 Habitat for Humanity Work Project to Take Place in Dominican Republic," habitat.org, October 11, 2019.

65 Jimmy and Rosalyn Carter, *Everything to Gain: Making the Most of the Rest of Your Life* (Thorndike Press, 1988).

66 Ibid.

67 azquotes.com/quote/203937.

68 Nanci Hellmich, "How to Make a Smooth Transition to a New Life," *USA Today*, May 19, 2015.

69 nyam.org/news/article/nyam-president-dr-judith-salerno-discusses-covid-19-response-inside-edition/.

70 nyam.org/news/article/dr-judith-salerno-discusses-covid-19-response-goo-morning-america/.

71 Salena Simmons-Duffin, "States Get Creative to Find and Deploy More Health Workers in COVID-19 Fight," npr.org, March 25, 2020.

72 Simmons-Duffin, "States Get Creative."

PART 5: CONCLUSION

1 quotefancy.com/quote/926564/Victor-Hugo-The-nearer-I-approach-the-end-the-plainer-I-hear-around-me-the-immortal.

2 genius.com/Andrew-lloyd-webber-those-canaan-days-lyrics.

3 quotecatalog.com/quotes/movies/three-amigos/.

4 bridleuphope.org.

5 bridleuphope.org/shop.

6 Cynthia Haller, personal interview with Sean Covey, November 2015.

About the Author

Recognized as one of *Time* magazine's twenty-five most influential Americans, Stephen R. Covey (1932–2012) was an internationally respected leadership authority, family expert, teacher, organizational consultant, business leader, and author. His books have sold more than 40 million copies (print, digital, and audio) in more than fifty languages throughout the world, and *The 7 Habits of Highly Effective People* was named the #1 Most Influential Business Book of the 20th Century. After receiving an MBA from Harvard University and a doctorate from Brigham Young University, he became the cofounder and vice chairman of FranklinCovey, the most trusted leadership company in the world.

Cynthia Covey Haller is an author, teacher, speaker, and an active participant in her community. She has contributed to the writing of several books and articles, notably *The 3rd Alternative* by Stephen R. Covey, *The 7 Habits of Highly Effective Teens*, and *The 6 Most Important Decisions You'll Ever Make,* both by Sean Covey. Cynthia has held multiple leadership positions in women's organizations, served as a PTSA president, as an organizer for refugee aid and a food pantry volunteer, and she is currently working with her husband, Kameron, as a service volunteer helping with employment needs. She graduated from Brigham Young University and lives with her family in Salt Lake City, Utah.

FranklinCovey
Education

For nearly three decades, FranklinCovey Education, a division of FranklinCovey, has been one of the world's most prominent and trusted providers of educational leadership programs and transformational processes. Our mission is to enable greatness in students, teachers, and schools everywhere. The FranklinCovey Education team is primarily composed of outstanding former teachers and administrators from various educational levels and entities.

FranklinCovey is a global, public company specializing in performance improvement. We help organizations and individuals achieve results that require a change in human behavior. Our expertise is in seven areas: Leadership, Execution, Productivity, Trust, Sales Performance, Customer Loyalty, and Education.

For more information about *Leader in Me* or other FranklinCovey Education offerings, contact us at:

educate@franklincovey.com
800-236-5291
LeaderinMe.org

Developing Life-Ready Leaders®

Thousands of *Leader in Me* schools and districts across the globe are using the 7 Habits and 4DX to

- Provide a powerful framework for highly effective life skills.
- Give students the skills they need to succeed in our ever-changing world.

Learn how to bring *Leader in Me* to your school and help students develop key college and career readiness skills like collaboration, self-discipline, managing stress, and developing resilience.

LeaderinMe.org
1-800-236-5291

LeaderinMe

FIND YOUR VOICE

© Franklin Covey Co. All Rights Reserved.

Teach Leadership to Your Children

The 7 Habits of Happy Kids books bring the 7 Habits to life for children using age-appropriate language and fun, engaging stories and characters.

Available wherever books are sold. Find out more about the 7 Habits at leaderinme.org!